The Competency Casebook

Twelve Studies in Competency-Based Performance Improvement

Edited by
DAVID D. DUBOIS, PH.D.

HRD PRESS
&
International Society for Performance Improvement

Published by: HRD Press, Inc.   ISPI
                 22 Amherst Road   1300 L Street NW
                 Amherst, MA 01002   Suite 1250
                 (800) 822-2801   Washington, DC 20005
                 (413) 253-3488   (202) 408-7969
                 (413) 253-3490 (Fax)   (202) 408-7972 (Fax)
                 http://www.hrdpress.com

First Edition, First Printing

Copyright © 1998 by *HRD Press, Inc.*

ISBN 0-87425-425-6

Typesetting by Michele Anctil
Cover design by Eileen Klockars
Editorial work by Mary George

PRINTED IN CANADA

TABLE OF CONTENTS

Preface
David D. Dubois, Editor

THE TWELVE CASE STUDIES

PREFACE

Competencies, and human competence itself, are rapidly receiving well-deserved recognition as an essential, required element of business and societal success. Competencies are those characteristics—knowledge, skills, mindsets, thought patterns, and the like—that, when used either singularly or in various combinations, result in successful performance. "Successful performance" in this context refers to the performance of both one's work (or job) and life roles. Without worker competence and supportive organizational practices, the strategic outcomes desired of organizations cannot be achieved.

Consequently, it is not difficult to understand why competencies are quickly becoming a unifying theme for many organizations' human resource management practices. The traditional, highly defined job of the recent past is giving way to the definition of job roles and outputs as a way of designing and assigning work to individuals in organizations. In the new configuration, job outputs that must be produced by workers are linked with human competencies (rather than the tasks that workers performed in the past) as an approach for assigning work and producing work outputs.

In order to support these human resource practices, competency-based recruitment and selection, placement, training and education, life-career planning and development, performance management, and rewards and compensation are rapidly finding their way among contemporary approaches that organizations are taking to have the talent needed, when and where it is needed, for immediate success. Concurrently they are finding it necessary to install organizational strategies and practices that ensure nurturing human competence in consistent ways.

The purpose of this book is to make available to readers information about twelve comprehensive case studies of competency-based performance enhancement practices in organization settings. The case studies provide a comprehensive snapshot of how a variety of organization practitioners have embarked upon the journey destined to help their organizations achieve strategic objectives through enhanced human competence. The organizations represented in the cases represent profit and not-for-profit organizations from the services and product development sectors.

The case description found in Chapter 1, by Michael Brousseau, describes the analysis, design, development, and implementation of a large-scale technical skills training program in a petrochemical company employing approximately 500 people. This competency-based training program was created to close gaps in supervisors' competencies when the organization moved from a traditional supervisory environment to one that included self-regulating teams who share responsibility for a particular unit of production. The ultimate strategic purpose of the competency development investment was to transform the company into a learning organization; their specific purpose was to create the best environment possible to foster continuous learning and to allow people to reach their full potential.

Jeremie Hill Grey, Ph.D., et al. describe in Chapter 2 a major technician training project at the Motorola Semiconductor Products Sector. The parameters and methods of this project are particularly interesting because they became a model for creating other competency-based curricula within Motorola. The chapter includes a highly comprehensive, in-depth presentation of the strategies and methods used during each stage of the program's creation.

Chapter 3 provides details of a case that describes how the National Imagery and Mapping Agency (formerly the Defense Mapping Agency) of the U.S. Defense Department addressed the need to facilitate change by taking a competency-based approach to human resource practices. Dierdorff, et al. describe the steps taken to implement strategic, technological change within a traditional technical mapping environment. A major contribution of the contents of this chapter is the discussion of how the agency created, tested, and gained acceptance of a competency-based job certification system that was consistent with the constraints of federal human resources policies and procedures, including employment equity issues.

In Chapter 4, Bina and Newkirk provide readers with detailed information on how a competency-based, integrated human resources system was conceived and implemented for Prudential HealthCare Group—Western Operations (PHG). The project's purpose was to create a human resources system that would complement PHG's desire to produce a major cultural change and be able to support management decision-making in compensation, performance planning and appraisal, training and development, selection processes, and human resources strategic planning. The authors share the lessons that they, and their organization learned throughout the project development and implementation stages.

Debra McDaniel, SPHR and Senior Human Resources Associate with Eli Lilly and Company shares, in Chapter 5, the details of how a competency model for the human resources function was developed. One important contribution of this case, among others, is the description of how behavioral event interviews were used in the competency modeling development process. Further, organizations will oftentimes embark upon the development and implementation of competency projects without first having a clear understanding of the foundation terms that must be used in consistent ways by the users. At Eli Lilly, a glossary of terms was created and implemented in order to ensure having a consistent understanding of the competency-based processes, procedures, and materials that were developed for the Human Resources Account Manager position. Their glossary is found as an appendix to the chapter.

In Chapter 6, Marcia Sanderson and her coauthors present information on a competency-based intervention for supervisors employed by the Texas Child Protective Services (CPS) program. CPS staff members investigate child abuse and neglect, and provide in-home services to families, foster care and adoption services, and programs for runaway children. Consequently, CPS is a training-intensive business since it requires comprehensive, effective, detailed knowledge of policy and law, and a high level of professional judgment and skill. In particular, supervisors—who are a critical link in casework quality and liability issues—received limited specialty training prior to the time the present training was created. A strategic planning model was developed, and it is included in the chapter, that provided direction for the development of competency-based supervisor training intended to close the specialty gaps. The chapter contents rigorously portray how the strategic model was applied and the outcomes from each step. The evaluation plan, and the evaluation results that were achieved are included and should be of particular interest to those who evaluate competency-based programs.

Next we return to Jeremie Hill Grey and the Motorola Semiconductor Products Sector (Chapter 7) where we learn about the development and implementation of a competency model and its use for creating an integrated human resources system for first-line leaders. First, this case includes an explanation of how competencies were used to help Motorola supervisors, who held extensive employment longevity with Motorola and held traditional views of supervision, make the transition to leadership in a team-based environment. Second, the case illustrates how these leaders were helped to close their own technical and business competency gaps that their many years of experience on the factory floor could not otherwise close. This chapter also includes the details of how Motorola successfully dealt with compensation and implementation issues that were made an integral part of the change process.

In Chapter 8, American Express' experiences in creating a competency-based approach for managing the training delivery function is explained. The transition to this approach was grounded in their concerns that any training they provided have increased business impact while achieving best-in-class economics. They were successful in their efforts by improving their course design process in ways that would eliminate unnecessary duplication of course content and by including line management as active partners in the learning process. Further, to ensure additional quality, a competency-based trainer certification program was implemented, vendor management was improved, and training measurement was implemented. The case author, Carmen Hegge-Kleiser, provides detailed information on all major aspects of program development.

Mindy Hall, in Chapter 9, describes how Rhone-Poulenc-Rorer, a global pharmaceutical corporation, used a competency-based approach to build a development culture across the North America zone of responsibility. Hall tracks for us how competencies were used throughout a five-stage change process. The change process included the following steps: creating a vision; generating energy and enthusiasm for the vision; building support for the change with key individuals; providing a common purpose, direction, and language; and, aligning key human resources systems (including recruitment, performance measurement, rewards, and so forth) to support and reinforce the desired culture.

In Chapter 10 American Express's Carmen Hegge-Kleiser returns to explain how competency-based selection and training practices were applied to select and train internal process consultants at American Express. These internal process consultants helped American Express with its reengineering efforts. Hegge-Kleiser includes for her readers extensive information about the development and implementation work that was completed, such as the details of competency modeling procedures, scoring sheets that were used, and so forth. The training for the process consultants is also reviewed.

Making the transition from the traditional learning environment to a performance- and competency-based learning environment can be a serious challenge for all parties, and especially for the learners, to the learning situation. By contrast, in a traditional learning environment the teacher is usually held responsible for the learning that occurs and immediate performance using acquired competencies may or may not be expected of the learner as part of the formal learning experience. Consequently, a competency-based learning environment puts new performance demands upon learners. Little attention has been given to identify strategies for helping learners (and learning facilitators) make this critical adjustment. In Chapter 11, Kenneth Pierce describes a strategy that has been successfully used to assist both faculty members and learners at Holland College, Prince Edward Island, Canada, a community college setting. The strategy is also useful to any individual who faces a need to make extensive adjustments to accommodate change in their life.

Karen Gorsline, et al., present the details, and an in-depth explanation of how the Human Resources Department of the Bank of Montreal developed a competency model for the role of Human Resources Relationship Manager. Developing the competency model, however, and explaining it to the affected employees does not generate sufficient impact to cause performance improvement. As the chapter title suggests, ways needed to be found to move the competencies included in the model "off the page" and "into the people." They accomplished just that at the Bank of Montreal. To do so, they created a workshop that helped participants make the competencies "real" in their daily job lives and in the performance of their role. The bulk of Chapter 12 is devoted to a description of the steps that were taken, and the outcomes that were realized during the implementation. The authors present liberal examples of documents they produced and used to bring the competencies to the people in highly meaningful ways.

As you read and think about each case, you must remember that competency work is—in practice—"never finished." Work in the competency arena is dynamic rather than static. As you will discover from reading the case chapters, organization leaders tend to initiate competency work in an area of their organization that will have immediate "strategic significance." This is not a surprising finding, given the rapid change that organizations must manage in today's highly competitive global marketplace.

In closing, I want to thank each of the case authors for their individual and collective contributions to this book. Without their hard work and long-term commitment to the goals of the project, this book would not have been produced. I also want to acknowledge, with thanks, the assistance in recruiting case authors that was provided by Ms. Marilyn Steinthal and other staff of the International Quality and Productivity Center.

David D. Dubois, Ph.D.
Editor

David D. Dubois, Ph.D., is President of Dubois & Associates and author of the highly regarded book *Competency-Based Performance Improvement: A Strategy for Organizational Change* (HRD Press, Amherst, Mass., 1993). Dr. Dubois can be contacted at Dubois & Associates, P.O. Box 10340, Rockville, MD 20849-0340; (301) 762-5026.

1.
COMPETENCY-BASED CURRICULUM DESIGN IN TECHNICAL SKILLS TRAINING

Michael O. Brousseau — Senior Organization Development Consultant

Background

Introduction

The accelerating rate of change in world economic conditions has created enormous pressure on business and industry to become more competitive. Over the past decade, American business has responded to the challenge by making major investments in technology, restructuring, reengineering, and (ultimately) downsizing, all in attempts to become more productive. And yet despite these efforts, many businesses are sadly reporting that their investments have not paid off as expected (Robinson & Robinson, 1995).

According to management consultants Hamel and Prahalad (1994), these approaches have not produced the results expected because they represent misguided solutions for what is really required to survive a rapidly changing, 21st century economy. The keys to being productive in the future will not be found in the old Tayloristic responses of the past, but rather in the strategic development and application of the organization's "brainpower" and "intellectual capital." According to this prevailing view, an organization's competitive strengths are the collective learnings of its employees, particularly their ability to assimilate and direct their knowledge to the core processes of the business (Prahalad & Hamel, 1990). The organization's only real competitive advantage, therefore, is the collective knowledge and competency of its workforce.

In response, organizations are being urged to tap into their largely ignored and massively underdeveloped human resources by transforming themselves into "knowledge-creating" companies (Nonaka, 1991) or, more specifically, to adopt the "learning organization" as a way of developing a competitive advantage. A learning organization is one that is founded on a principle of "continuous learning," which is the systematic approach applied to increase learning in an organization so as to enable the organization to respond more effectively to change (Watkins & Marsick, 1993). From this behavior arises the definition of a learning organization as one which is "skilled at creating, acquiring, and transferring knowledge, and at modifying its behavior to reflect new knowledge and insights." (Garvin, 1993, p. 80)

This case study chronicles the efforts of one company to transform the culture and the climate of the organization into a learning organization by adopting a strategy for organizational change based on David Dubois' *Competency-Based Performance Improvement*, published in 1993. This study is unique because of its emphasis on involving groups (self-regulating teams) through the process of planning and directing a competency-based learning and training system to meet the performance requirements of the workplace.

The Company

The organization featured is a petrochemical company employing approximately 500 people. It is a division of a North American company involved in the distribution of natural gas services and petrochemicals. The plant under study was constructed in the late 1970s to meet domestic requirements for energy and chemical products. By the mid 1980s the plant saw a sharp decline in demand for its products. To rationalize the future of the plant, the organization turned its attention to new opportunities in the international marketplace. In order to compete globally, the plant required significant upgrading to match the production capabilities of newer facilities being built around the world. The new technology and business strategy proved successful for the company, which reported record profits through the late 1980s.

Key Issues and Events

The 1990s brought a new set of challenges. The continuing emphasis on new technology increased the complexity of the facility. The technical knowledge and capabilities of the operating personnel were stretched to capacity and the traditional methods of training were slow in responding to the constant demands of the workplace. Benchmarking studies conducted as part of a continuous improvement effort identified new opportunities to upgrade the performance of the facility.

In 1994 the organization began a corporate reengineering effort whose purpose was to take advantage of the benchmarking studies by changing the business policies and controls, systems and technology, and organizational relationships and business practices, so as to enable the plant to compete in the context of the evolving business environment. The early efforts at reengineering focused on the hard or technical processes and encouraged cross-organizational involvement across the divisions. These processes represented the more concrete and easiest to change. The more difficult to change and less concrete would prove to be the infrastructure or people systems such as training and development, measurement systems, management systems, and reward structure.

Reengineering the business processes ultimately led to a restructuring of the organization. In restructuring, the organization chose to reduce the levels of management and adopt a team-based style of management referred to as self-regulating teams (SRTs). An SRT by design is "a functional group of employees (usually between 8 and 15 members) who share the responsibility for a particular unit of production. The team consists of trained individuals who possess the technical skills and abilities to complete all assigned tasks. . . . Each team member possesses a variety of technical skills and is encouraged to develop new ones to increase job flexibility and value to the team." (Torres & Spiegel, 1990, p. 3)

To support the need for the development of new technical skills required by the SRTs, a strategic initiative designed to develop the competencies—knowledge, skills, and behaviors—was launched. Termed a "learning and growth initiative," it had a clear-cut purpose: to transform the company into a learning organization in order to create the best environment to foster continuous learning and allow people to reach their full potential.

The strategic priority for learning and growth was, therefore, to increase the learning power of the organization by focusing on core competencies necessary for success. The focus needed to be on the development of a total learning system that emphasized performance improvement and value-added solutions to the organization's needs. To accomplish this strategic initiative, the traditional role of training and development, with its emphasis on classroom training and instructional development, would need to be transformed into one of facilitating and coaching learning opportunities to the line organization.

Competency-Based Learning and Training

Traditional training practices have typically proven to be less than adequate at meeting the needs of the reengineered business organization (Pepitone, 1995). The conventional methods of training grew out of the same principles that fit the way in which business has been managed in the past, with complex hierarchies, employees managed within disciplines, and responsibility and decision making in the hands of a few senior managers. As a result, training became institutionalized as a staff function and motivated training practitioners to promote training solutions more as a function of their own existence rather than to meet any real business needs.

What is required is a new paradigm for training—one that adds value to the business by transforming learning experiences into performance-based outcomes. The achievement of such a transformation requires a completely new view of training. This view includes activities such as linking learning needs to strategic business objectives; planning management involvement in defining and clarifying learning deficits; planning learning interventions that are integrated with job performance; scheduling learning interventions for high payoff; and creating structures for support of critical activities before and after learning events.

Competency-based learning and training (CBL&T) is a process that can integrate learning events into the ongoing operations of the business. The key to CBL&T is systems thinking, the assumption that training has an interdependent, dynamic relationship with other business processes and the total organization. This view is very much in contrast to the prevailing view of training as a separate, secondary function that produces programs and learning that may not transfer to the workplace. Competency-based training systems design is a methodology of defining what is to be taught and how it is to be taught, and of determining the most effective media for delivery. The result is a performance-based curriculum design that guides the development of a total system of training within the context of a given job or category of position. This ensures that all training works together to produce the desired results by providing employees with all the knowledge and skills needed to do their jobs.

CBL&T is guided by a set of beliefs and a philosophy about the way training is perceived and structured within the organization. Effective learning and training is part of everyone's job. Everyone is responsible for managing his or her learning and cultivating the knowledge and skills that support the business goals of the company. This means that individuals must assume responsibilities such as:

- Determining the level of knowledge and skill set required

- Relating training goals to business needs

- Finding time for learning

- Deciding on activities, materials, resources, and equipment for learning

- Estimating one's own level of progress

- Managing results so that learning increases and is transformed into added value to products and services

People who hold managerial or supervisory roles have additional responsibilities over and above planning, facilitating, coaching, and evaluating the overall and integrated results of learning in the workplace. Those responsibilities are shown in the following list.

- Translate strategic priorities into training solutions

- Identify key learning needs of individuals and business functions

- Manage the key contextual factors that affect the training process

- Integrate training technologies with nontraining methods of performance improvement

- Manage post-learning interventions to reinforce applications of training on the job

- Integrate learning into the work process so that employees learn while they work

- Measure the efficiency of the training process to improve results and reduce costs

CBL&T is, therefore, more than a process for structuring training; it is a situational approach to learning designed to add value to the organization in the form of improved performance or productivity. The construction of a CBL&T process requires an integrative approach to planning, with the key stakeholders directly involved in the training process.

Planning Partners

Conventional wisdom suggests that it is necessary to involve people in planning change, to secure their buy-in and to further ensure eventual success. In reality, however, involving everyone directly in the planning process makes the process too cumbersome to get off the ground. An alternative is to develop the planning process with the involvement of team members so as to promote team-based actions and learning that will eventually support the goals and objectives of the project. This is the approach that we chose.

The first steps in the planning process began with a meeting between the training facilitator and members of the senior management to clarify management's expectations for a CBL&T system. It was agreed that senior management would act as the steering team throughout the project. The roles and expectations of the steering team were defined, and a charter for the project was prepared and communicated to the organization. The charter outlined the purpose of the project, roles and responsibilities of team members, and expected accomplishments, and provided an estimated time frame. A project team leader was identified, who in turn selected 8–10 members of the target population to become part of the project team. The project team leader and members would in time identify additional resource people from the functional areas to serve as partners during the various stages of analysis, design, and development of the project. The project team structure and the role of the steering team and facilitator are shown in Figure 1.

FIGURE 1: Competency-Based Learning and Training Project Leadership

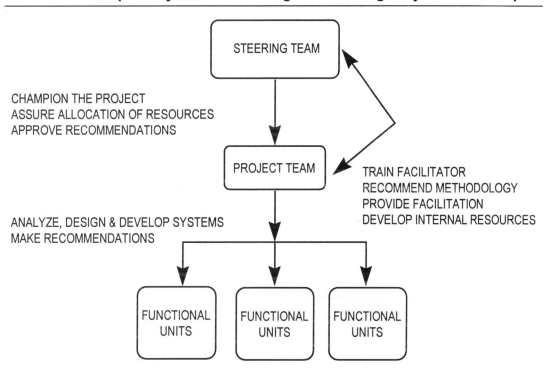

STEERING TEAM

CHAMPION THE PROJECT
ASSURE ALLOCATION OF RESOURCES
APPROVE RECOMMENDATIONS

PROJECT TEAM

TRAIN FACILITATOR
RECOMMEND METHODOLOGY
PROVIDE FACILITATION
DEVELOP INTERNAL RESOURCES

ANALYZE, DESIGN & DEVELOP SYSTEMS
MAKE RECOMMENDATIONS

FUNCTIONAL UNITS

FUNCTIONAL UNITS

FUNCTIONAL UNITS

IMPLEMENT APPROVED DESIGNS
PARTICIPATE IN EVALUATIONS

Target Population

To create a manageable project, the steering team, in consultation with the facilitator, made a decision to restrict the program to a specific number of job areas that had high value to the organization's business and operating plans. Based on this criteria, the operations area of the plant was selected as a "candidate" for a pilot project. This area represents the core of the production facility operating 24 hours a day, with five crews rotating on 12-hour schedules. The workforce consists of senior operating technicians (150) who are well educated (averaging two to three years of post-secondary education, many with technology degrees).

Front-End Needs Analysis, Assessment, and Planning

The foundation for success in a competency-based learning and training strategy must be well prepared before any learning interventions take place. If the project is to be a success, it must be able to show that the training activities are linked to business results. Following this assessment, training leaders and work group supervisors can work together to plan an effective training strategy, deliver reliable learning interventions, and collaborate to support trainees and other stakeholders to achieve and sustain improved job and organizational performance.

The first task of the project team was to develop a series of process workflow diagrams similar to those prepared in the earlier business-reengineering activity. The purpose of developing these diagrams was to establish a visual model that could clearly identify how the work gets done and ultimately make sense in terms of the connection to the strategic intent and purpose of the business. The strategic connection to the business was developed through a process referred to as a "performance results framework." The framework is basically a method of linking performance to the business strategy. Strategic business goals and measures were identified and linked to the performance expectations of the teams. Team objectives were translated into individual objectives with suitable measures of performance.

The next step in the planning process was (1) to meet with the steering team and share the outcome of the performance results framework for its consensus, and (2) to continue the needs assessment process by conducting a performance analysis. The latter was basically an exercise at clarifying the job outputs that needed to be improved in order for the key processes to work effectively and produce the desired quality outputs. To guide the analysis, Rummler and Brache's (1990) Human Performance System framework was used to determine the cause of poor performance and the appropriate corrective action. Figure 2 is an example of a Human Performance System and the key performance variables examined.

FIGURE 2: The Human Performance System

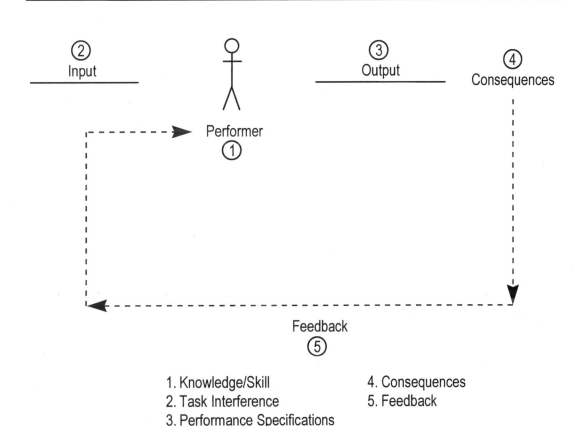

1. Knowledge/Skill
2. Task Interference
3. Performance Specifications
4. Consequences
5. Feedback

During the process of analysis, performance problems were identified and solutions to eliminate them were developed. The problems associated with the lack of knowledge and skill were listed and prepared for the next phase of the process.

Competency Model Development

The next major series of activities involved determining the competencies (tasks) involved in the separate job functions. Commonly referred to as an occupation analysis, this process can be carried out using any one of several techniques; the more common ones are the Modified Task Analysis Approach, the Critical Trait Approach, and the Situational Approach (Zemke, 1989). After careful review and consideration, the project team selected the DACUM (Norton, 1985) process. DACUM, or "**D**eveloping **A** **C**urriculum," is a relatively new and innovative approach to occupational analysis. It has proven to be a very effective method of quickly determining, at relatively low cost, tasks that must be performed by persons employed in a given job or occupational area. The profile chart that results from the DACUM analysis is a detailed and graphic portrayal of the duties and tasks involved in the occupation or job being studied. The DACUM process operates on the following three premises:

1. Expert workers are better able to describe/define their jobs than anyone else.

2. Any job can be effectively and sufficiently described in terms of the tasks that successful workers in that occupation perform.

3. All tasks have direct implications for the knowledge and attitudes that workers must have in order to perform the tasks correctly.

The benefit of using a process like DACUM is in the versatility of the completed product. DACUM profile charts can also be used for curriculum development, training needs assessments, worker performance evaluations, and competency test development.

The suggested steps for conducting a DACUM process are as follows:

1. Assemble a group of 8–10 job or role experts who are familiar with the job or role.

2. Brief the panelists on what DACUM is and why it is carried out.

3. Assemble panelists in a room and ask them to proceed in round-robin fashion to list activities typical of what they do. List work activities on 8½ × 11 sheets posted on the wall, one activity per sheet. Continue this "work activity generation" stage until panelists run out of work activities to list.

4. Take a break and cluster the work activities into logical order.

5. Reconvene the panel and ask the panelists to review the selected categories and add, delete, or modify them.

6. Print the chart and use it as the basis for curriculum development. (Norton, 1985)

To facilitate the DACUM analysis, the operations area was broken down into five functional areas and separate analyses were conducted for each area. The HR facilitator guided the panel members through two days of work to complete a profile chart of each of the areas under study. The completed charts were distributed for confirmation and feedback through the functional team membership. Figure 3, on the following page, shows a typical profile chart for one of the job functions studied.

The next step involved verifying the initial listing of task and duty statements. Verification consisted of asking the functional SRT members who did the work to confirm whether the tasks listed were actually those performed (technically accurate), whether the tasks listed represented the important tasks performed, and whether the functions listed included all the important tasks performed. The outcome of the DACUM and verification process produced an exhaustive list of tasks per functional area that needed to be prioritized for training emphasis. Each of the identified tasks were rated on a scale of difficulty, importance, and

FIGURE 3: Example of Profile Chart

FUNCTION: MATERIAL FLOW

DUTIES/RESPONSIBILITIES: (B) OPERATE PRESSURE STORAGE FACILITIES

◄ ∙∙∙∙∙∙∙∙∙∙∙∙∙∙∙∙∙∙∙∙∙∙∙∙∙∙∙∙∙∙∙ **Tasks** ∙∙∙∙∙∙∙∙∙∙∙∙∙∙∙∙∙∙∙∙∙∙∙∙∙∙∙∙∙∙∙ ►

Monitor N2 blanketing system on spheres B-1	Line up Methanol to Fuel Gas GA-9103 B-2	Line up 52 bullet to Fuel Gas FA-8301 B-3	Line up 52 bullet to Well 3 B-4	Startup Fuel Gas booster pumps GA-8301 B-5
Line up GA-9156/9197 to LPG Co-cracking B-6	Line up GA-9156/9197 to Fuel Gas Header B-7	Startup L.P.G. Co-cracking System B-8	Shutdown L.P.G. Co-cracking System B-9	
Adjust 52 bullet pressure to Flare 11 B-1	Purge L.P.G. System with N_2 to 52 Bullet B-12	Blow down Level Column on 52 Bullet B-13		
Shutdown 53/54 Propylene System B-16	Swing 53/54 Bullets to C3 loading B-17	Startup GA-9130/S Pumps B-18		
Line up C3 to Pilot Gas B-21	Line up C3 Fuel Gas B-22			
Shutdown GA-9820/S Pumps B-26	Drain bottom water off 21/25 Spheres B-27			
Shutdown Sphere 26 system B-31				
Transfer C4 from Olefins to Sphere 26 B-36				

frequency in terms of performance. The final list of tasks for training development would be controlled by the length of the training program and the allocated budget.

The documented outputs from all the analysis meetings were then reviewed with the steering team. The purpose of this examination was to share with the leadership the results of the DACUM analysis and the priority list identified for training purposes. Input was also sought from the steering team on any additional core, leadership, team, and personal skills required to support the business function. The project scope, estimated time table, and budget constraints were also prepared as guidelines for the curriculum design process to follow.

Curriculum Planning

Curriculum planning consisted of mapping all the training requirements identified by the analysis groups into a curriculum structure or design document. The intention of the planning process was (a) to produce a master blueprint for the entire training product line, and (b) to ensure that the voice of the customer was reflected while maintaining instructional integrity. The project team met with the various functional teams for one-day meetings to review the information and the guidelines established by the steering group and to begin the process of developing curriculum plans. The basic steps included:

1. Analyze the verified competencies.

2. Translate the competencies into objectives.

3. Sequence performance objectives.

1. Analyze the Verified Competencies

After the review session with the steering team, the next phase of activity was to generate with the analysis teams a list of skill and knowledge statements for the prioritized tasks. By definition the focus was on what the learner must be able to do to perform effectively and what the learner must be able to know to do the job. To perform successfully in an occupation, people are generally expected to display three types of job-related behaviors: (a) psychomotor, (b) cognitive, and (c) affective (Bloom, 1956). Psychomotor behaviors involve the physical manipulation of tools, objects, and so forth. Cognitive behaviors involve the physical processing of information and decision making. Affective behaviors

FIGURE 4: The Relationship Between Function and Behavior

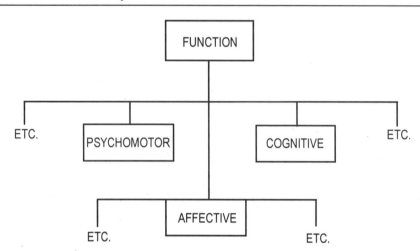

involve visible actions that communicate emotional tones toward people, data, and things. Figure 4 shows the relationship between function and behavior.

Historically, vocational educators and trainers in business and industry have focused on psychomotor skills and the knowledge base associated with those skills. As a consequence, curriculum development efforts have tended to ignore or downplay the importance of affective behaviors in the instructional development process. Pucel (1989) has argued that affective behaviors are critical to effective performance and therefore require the same curriculum development and evaluation emphasis as psychomotor tasks. The process of identifying skill and knowledge statements included Pucel and co-researchers' Occupational Affective Behavior Analysis instrument (Pucel, Jensrud Quetler, Damme, & Warner, 1992) to gather affective information for each of the tasks under study.

2. *Translate the Competencies Into Objectives*

Each competency statement was translated, in writing, into a measurable performance objective. The recorded performance objectives had a twofold purpose: to serve as additional guidelines for the design of instructional materials, and to serve as a basis for developing tests to evaluate learner achievement. The objectives, written in Mager (1984) style, are precisely stated:

- Performance required (activity to be performed)

- Conditions under which it is performed

- Criteria to be met

3. Sequence Performance Objectives

The purpose of this step was to develop a hierarchy, or tree, of the training content to be developed. Performance objectives to be handled by training were organized into related groups. Each group represented a training module. Within each module, the learning objectives were sequenced in order to develop the instructional progression from fundamental skill and knowledge to highly specific job skills. Figure 5 shows the relationship between the basic components to be developed and their relationship to the hierarchy of job levels.

FIGURE 5: Basic Components and Hierarchy of Job Levels

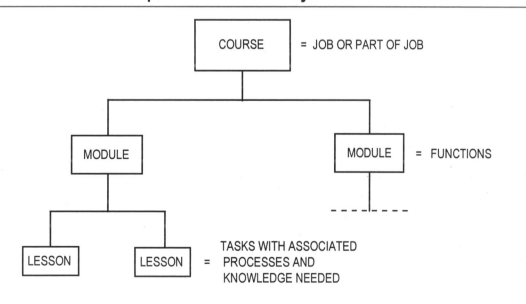

The visual diagram became an important communication tool with the organization. The diagram served as a "course map" so organizational members could see what was being proposed for development and also comment on gaps and overlaps in the curriculum plans.

Learning Intervention Design and Development

The curriculum plan continued to serve as the blueprint to guide the design and the development of the various training products required and to optimize the training investment for bottom-line business impact. It involved organizing all the training content into important groupings called modules. Existing training materials were examined to determine what was currently available and/or could be adapted to fill the needs. Specification sheets to guide the development of the modules were prepared.

The following steps were taken:

1. Develop content specifications.
2. Develop criterion-referenced tests.

1. Develop Content Specifications

Developing content simply meant identifying and categorizing the relevant subject matter to be included in the development of the instructional materials. Subject matter experts familiar with the tasks under consideration were consulted. To keep the inventory of information manageable and related to the specific objectives, only essential and helpful information was listed. Essential information consisted of the absolute minimal content that the curriculum must contain in order for the training to meet previously stated objectives. The next category, helpful information, related to content that supplemented the essential. Learners could be brought up to the expected level of performance by trainers simply presenting the essential information; adding helpful information, however, provided further background so the learners could better understand the nature of the task and its relationship to the job.

2. Develop Criterion-Referenced Tests

Prior to the development of instructional materials, criterion-referenced tests (CRTs) were developed for all the terminal and enabling objectives listed in the content specifications. As part of the overall competency-based learning and training strategy, the steering team specifically requested that (a) test items be developed for all terminal performance objectives, and (b) the objectives be related to performance requirements. Test items were written in terms of observable behavior and were intended to convey essentially the same type of information:

1. What the learner/trainee will do (the skill to be performed)

2. The specific conditions (or "givens") under which the skill will be performed

3. The criteria (or standards) of performance that must be achieved in order to demonstrate competence in the skill

Steering Team Review

The completed design package was presented to the steering team for their review and sign-off. The package included a budget justification for personnel, equipment, and supplies. The purpose of the review was to obtain the steering team's feedback and approval of the design blueprint to allow development of materials to proceed. A secondary goal of the review was to update the project timetable and delivery of completed products. Priorities were established for the development and acquisition of materials required to support business goals and strategies.

Development

Instructional development on a large project can be very time-consuming and demanding. Since the organization lacked sufficient skilled instructional developers and the production capabilities to develop all the materials required, a decision was made to outsource the development. The design blueprints were assembled and proposals were tendered to a number of off-site developers for competitive bids. The proposals upon return were reviewed with the project team for completeness, and questions were clarified with the vendors. The successful bidder was awarded a contract for the development of the first year of training requirements. Roles and responsibilities were clarified with the developer, and quality assurance standards and production schedules were prepared and agreed to.

Evaluation

The purpose of competency-based learning and training is, of course, to bring about learning. To know whether the instruction being developed will be successful in bringing about the performance desired on the job requires careful attention to the subject of evaluation.

Two types of evaluation—formative and summative—are important to the success of this project. A formative evaluation plan guided the analysis, design, and development of the training materials. The goal of formative evaluation was to improve the instructional materials prior to the delivery of the training. The process was structured in such a way that it also provided important information on possible oversights in needs analysis, analysis of objectives, or the tests themselves, or in faulty sequencing or instructional strategies. Pilot tests of the completed training materials were conducted with small groups, and the learners' in-training progress and attitudes toward the training were assessed. The purpose of the evaluation plan was therefore to remedy these situations while the instructional materials were being formed.

A summative evaluation is planned for a later date. The purpose of the summative evaluation will be to measure how well the learners are performing the assigned tasks on the job. Performance tests to compare on-the-job performance before and after training will be developed. This information will be used to maintain or change training materials as needed to affirm the instructional integrity of the program.

Summary

This case study has described a competency-based curriculum design approach for developing technical skills training to support self-regulating teams. The primary feature of this case study was the involvement of the learner throughout the process of competency modeling and the design of the instructional materials to support continuous learning. As such, the emphasis of this project was on learning, not simply on instruction. This approach departed from traditional instructional systems development and involved a project team and learners through the processes of program planning, course design, evaluation procedures, and documentation.

Competencies derived from the occupational analysis were converted into key results areas and performance measures to be used by the team to track their performance. Learning became driven by individual learning plans and team responsibilities directed at performance expected on the job.

An investment in training has been made by this company. Employees understand why training is important; management has established a supportive environment to allow for the transfer of learning to take place and is prepared to continue its support of learning and training. Performance is being measured at all levels of the organization in terms of value-added product and service to the company. The self-regulating teams featured are continuing their efforts toward business process improvement by focusing on their key responsibility areas and utilizing the CBL&T system to pursue continuous learning opportunities. The organization's goal of becoming a learning organization has gotten off to a good start.

References

Bloom, B. S. (Ed.). (1956*). Taxonomy of educational objectives—Handbook I: Cognitive domain.* New York, NY: Longman.

Dubois, D. D. (1993). *Competency-based performance improvement: A strategy for organizational change.* Amherst, MA: HRD Press.

Garvin, D. A. (1993). Building a learning organization. *Harvard Business Review, 71*(4), 78–91.

Hamel, G., & Prahalad, C. K. (1994). *Competing for the future.* Boston, MA: Harvard Business School.

Mager, R. F. (1984). *Preparing instructional objectives.* Belmont, CA: Lake Publishing.

Nonaka, I. (1991). *The knowledge-creating company.* In R. Howard & R. D. Haas (Eds.), *The learning imperative.* Boston, MA: Harvard Business School.

Norton, R. E. (1985). *DACUM handbook.* Columbus, OH: Ohio State University, The National Center for Research in Vocational Education.

Pepitone, J. S. (1995). *Future training. A roadmap for restructuring the training function.* Dallas, TX: AddVantage Learning Press.

Prahalad, C. K., & Hamel, G. (1990). The core competencies of the corporation. *Harvard Business Review, 90*(3), 79–91.

Pucel, D. J. (1989). *Performanced-based instructional design.* New York, NY: McGraw-Hill.

Pucel, D. J., Jensrud Quetler, T. J., Damme, S., & Warner, D. (1992). *Performance-based occupational affective behavior analysis (OABA): Implementation and supporting research.* St. Paul, MN: University of Minnesota, Minnesota Research and Development Center for Vocational Education.

Robinson, D. G., & Robinson, J. C. (1995). *Performance consulting: Moving beyond training.* San Francisco, CA: Berrett-Koehler.

Rummler, G. A., & Brache, A. P. (1990). *Improving performance: How to manage the white space on the organization chart.* San Francisco, CA: Jossey-Bass.

Torres, C., & Spiegel, J. (1990). *Self-directed work teams: A primer.* San Diego, CA: University Associates.

Watkins, K. E., & Marsick, V. J. (1993). *Sculpting the learning organization.* San Francisco, CA: Jossey-Bass.

Zemke, R. (1989). Job competencies: Can they help you design better training? In H. Gillespie (Ed.), *Performance technology.* Minneapolis, MN: Lakewood.

About the Contributor

Michael O. Brousseau, Ph.D., is Manager of Organizational Learning for the organization featured in this case study. He acted as the designer and facilitator throughout the course of this project. His background includes 12 years of involvement in organizational and instructional systems redesign to improve business results.

2.
COMPETENCY MODELING AT MOTOROLA
Using Competency Modeling to Develop Technicians at Motorola Semiconductor Products Sector

Jeremie Hill Grey, Ph.D. — former LATG/East Valley Group Training Manager
Sarabeth Simpson — former CPSTG Group Training Manager

ADDITIONAL CONTRIBUTORS:

Jennifer Fox Kennedy, M.S. — LATG/East Valley Senior Instructional Designer
Susan Tou, M.Ed., M.B.A. — Training and Development Manager/ACT Operations

In 1992 the Motorola Semiconductor Products Sector began a major technician-training project that has become a model for competency-based curricula within Motorola. This chapter provides a history and description of that project, with an explanation of methodology and results. The last stages of the project were implemented in January 1997.

Background and Strategic Organizational Profile

With approximately 150,000 employees worldwide, Motorola, based in Schaumburg, Illinois, remains one of the largest and oldest of American high-technology corporations. Founded in Chicago in the 1920s by Paul Galvin, Motorola initially manufactured radios and radio equipment and over the years has expanded this role to include computers, cellular phones, pagers, aerospace, and a host of other technologies and products. At the heart of all of the products are the computer chips manufactured by the Semiconductor Products Sector (SPS) headquartered in Phoenix, Arizona. SPS alone employs 50,000 engineers, technicians, and manufacturing and support personnel worldwide, and has large-scale U.S. operations in Arizona, Texas, California, Virginia, and North Carolina, and global operations in France, Scotland, Germany, Japan, Singapore, Hong Kong, China, Taiwan, and many other locations.

The Galvin family is still actively involved in Motorola's management, and despite the tremendous growth of the past few years, the family has succeeded in retaining the company's commitment to its people, to long-term employment, and to family values. Employees have responded with a loyalty exceptional in the high-tech world.

Because of the stability of employment with Motorola and the long length of service typical of the employee population, career and skill development assume major importance within the human resources (HR) function. Every Motorolan is required to complete a minimum of 40 hours of training per year. To meet this requirement, SPS employs approximately 300 training personnel worldwide, in addition to the corporate services of Motorola University (MU). Many of these training specialists are involved at various levels in educational counseling and production of curricular roadmaps and guidelines, as well as scheduling, training, and record keeping.

Aside from the cultural requirements of the organization, intense competition among high-tech companies to recruit talented engineers and technicians requires that training specialists within SPS play an active role with local technical schools, community colleges, and universities. Assuring that these schools understand the current and future skill requirements of the Motorola workforce is a major objective for the semiconductor training organizations because of the heavy concentration (in excess of 20,000) of Motorola employees in the Phoenix valley. However, prior to the onset of the project discussed in this chapter, there was no methodical system for keeping schools advised of the company's skill requirements, which were increasing in number and complexity.

By the early 1990s, the skill levels and versatility requirements of technicians had grown exponentially, as did the population (an increase of 30% in three years). Our then-current vehicles could not adequately support the demands generated by such growth. Problems included the following:

- Technician training and promotional matrices, established years before, were obsolete and incomplete, and the career path was unclear for the many types and levels of technicians.

- At a time of increased emphasis on performance management and career counseling, supervisors and managers of technicians had inaccurate and incomplete information, and could not adequately counsel their employees.

- Existing technicians were trained in a single discipline and were working to sustain current processes and equipment.

- Our search for the right set of skills and the training to support them had been relatively unfocused and inconsistent.

- The constant introduction of new equipment and processes was placing pressure on a workforce already stretched in terms of skill and capability.

Because of these problems, many of the company's needs were not being addressed, including the need for technicians who

— were familiar with process as well as equipment

— could operate at a higher level of performance and initiative

— could manage their own learning and skill development in a fast-paced environment

A series of management interviews and meetings beginning in 1992 made it clear that we had to focus on two major goals: (1) the internal development of multiskilled, versatile, and adaptable technicians, and (2) the support of skills acquisition and maintenance through a series of curricula and human resource systems.

Target Populations and Their Needs

The customers for this project were identified as hundreds of operators within the Phoenix factories who desired to become technicians, over a thousand technicians in SPS's Phoenix facilities, and the supervisors and managers of both groups. The target populations were concentrated in the Phoenix Valley, but management and project team members recognized even at the onset that our programs and materials might be validated and used elsewhere in our worldwide sector. (This forecast has proven to be accurate, as our models and methods have been validated and used in Beijing, Europe, and—with adaptations—in other sectors of the company.)

Operators

Operators were primarily high school graduates with little or no technical academic education. Most of the operators had acquired semiconductor manufacturing skill through on-the-job and classroom training in the factory, and had a limited knowledge of electronics or equipment maintenance, both of which are absolute prerequisites for a successful transition to the job of technician. Besides electronics and equipment skills, they also needed general education in report writing, development and delivery of presentations, and statistical process control, as well as team process, to enhance their value as operator team members and to help them move into the more skilled and responsible position of technician.

Many training programs designed to meet these more generic needs were available internally through Motorola University. These courses closely paralleled offerings in local community colleges, but were shorter and more concentrated because of business needs; they also were not accredited—an issue that we needed to address. As well as requiring a minimum of 40 hours of training per employee per year, Motorola encourages employees to earn degrees and advanced degrees, and actively supports attendance at accredited colleges and universities through an educational assistance program that reimburses employees for tuition. The requirements to earn a technical two-year degree, however, are formidable for employees working full time. We resolved to obtain college credit for our internal Motorola courses wherever possible to reduce redundancy in internal Motorola and external community-college requirements, and, by extension, the time and effort required of our operators in work towards the degree.

Technicians

The second segment of the target population—existing technicians—were, for the most part, graduates of technical schools and community colleges, with two-year technical degrees. Most had substantial job experience. A number of these had been promoted internally over the years without having completed degrees, and their technical backgrounds required strengthening. An additional consideration were the large numbers of technicians whose degrees had been granted or whose training was acquired many years before, and who were threatened with obsolescence. Several hundred of them required skill assessment and updated training to sharpen and renew their technical skills.

A second skills area also became a matter of concern. Project members suspected at the outset what our needs assessment later substantiated: that the most important skills of technicians were not technical in nature, but rather communicative, with team leadership skills included. When called to address a problem, technicians had to rely upon the verbal reports and explanations of operators and supervisors within the area. These skills played a key role in cycle-time reduction and accuracy of diagnosis and repair. Interpersonal skills, communication, and questioning/problem-solving techniques were therefore essential for technicians at all levels, in addition to technical skills.

Supervisors and Managers of Operators and Technicians

The last segment of the target population included the supervisors and managers of operators and technicians, who were charged with performance evaluation and skill development for their employees. These individuals needed to have a full understanding of the skill requirements, the career paths and options, and the compensation and promotional policies for operators and technicians; they also needed job aids to help them during employee conferences.

Information About the Planning Partners

To address the above needs, we assembled the Technician Council, a cross-functional team charged with carrying out this program and providing ongoing supervision of the program when implemented. In time, this group became the Manufacturing Education Council. The Council was led by senior manufacturing managers and supported by SPS training managers and instructional designers, and consisted of various representatives from the factory groups and HR specialists.

Representatives From Factory Groups

We initially invited factory managers to name appropriate representatives for each major organization

— to make experts available for data collection purposes

— to provide an interface between the council and the organizations

— to ensure that each organization was properly represented in all decisions

— to ensure acceptance of the project when it came time for implementation

Organizations frequently provided more than one member, including the manufacturing manager, the technician manager, one or more production supervisors, and master technicians. Over time, the membership became more self-selecting because of the dedication and time commitment required, but the representation of each organization, particularly for voting and other decision-making activities, became the standard method of operation.

Human Resource Representatives

Equally important to the Council's operation were the HR specialists who supported it. Employee-relations personnel from each major organization were involved, as were several dedicated compensation representatives from SPS organizations in the Phoenix Valley. These individuals were essential because a number of HR systems and procedures had to change or be implemented in order for the project to be successful. The Council members early on adopted a full-systems approach to the project and were very much aware that no training program could successfully change performance without support from the compensation and performance management systems. Given the multi-year duration of the project, the membership was remarkably dedicated, attending monthly or bimonthly meetings and joining sub-teams for specific task accomplishments as they were required.

Priorities and Plans

Even before the completion of a formal needs assessment, the project's complexity was obvious. The massive scope required that it be done in phases, with implementation at the completion of each phase. Assessing our resources, we reasoned that we should adopt a continuous improvement philosophy, in which we would move toward our goals in increments, identifying and achieving specific priorities established by the organization. Our needs analysis and council input identified the following as those priorities:

- Developing a new model of technician within the manufacturing area, with the specific intent of creating curricula to develop operators (who already had experience in the factory) into this category of technician, thereby building on existing skills and creating a career path for those with the initiative to pursue it

- Upgrading the skills of the existing technician population by developing competency models for each of five technician types, and the various levels (beginning and advanced) within each

- Developing curricula to support the renewal and development of each type and level of technician

- Collaborating with local colleges to create appropriate educational programs and degrees, thereby making efficient use of existing resources, supporting our community, and encouraging our people to earn degrees

- Gaining college accreditation for internal Motorola courses, including both Motorola University generic courses (where appropriate), and specific Semiconductor training courses

- Clearly delineating career paths and promotional opportunities, so employees and their supervisors would be able to take responsibility for career development

- Implementing the training and development programs successfully. Counseling employees for technician careers and training had traditionally been a function of the Training Department. Cycle time, cost-effectiveness, empowerment, and the need for managers to understand and support the process for appropriate performance management and individual development dictated that this responsibility pass to the operations groups. Providing tools and resources to help managers and employees assume this responsibility became a major goal of the Council.

- Ensuring that compensation and other (e.g., recruiting and employment) systems supported the change in performance expectations

The Technician Project progressed through a number of distinct phases:

1. Creation of the Technician Council and identification of procedures and goals; initial data collection and analysis

2. Development of a competency model for a new technician function for the development and transition of operators into technicians. This phase included development of new job descriptions and promotional hierarchies and obtaining management approval for them.

3. Development of the curriculum to support the new category of technician, including a key partnership with Mesa Community College (MCC) to develop a degree tailored to our needs and grant college credit for internal Motorola training programs

4. Creation of competency models for five other categories of existing technicians, including accomplishments, competencies, requisite skills and knowledge, and existing resources for training and development

5. Revision of job descriptions, promotional criteria, performance management tools, and a host of compensation issues designed to support the adoption and implementation of the new system, including: revised job descriptions and a compensation/promotional system to reward development and attainment of further degrees; development of publications defining career paths, curricula, and promotional requirements, and other resource material

6. Creation of a workshop for supervisors and managers of experienced technicians, to be used in the implementation phase

The phases of the project were not discrete, and frequently overlapped. Because of the group's size, the project's complexity, and the expertise required, a sub-team approach was used based on the phase of the project. Small teams addressed particular elements of the project.

Phase One

Creation of the Technician Council; Identification of Procedures and Goals

During the formation of the Council, members defined its mission to guide the development of tools and procedures for the improved performance, training, and development of operators and technicians, and identified as the first priority the creation of a new functional type of technician. Members representing each organization participated in identifying the characteristics and requirements of the desired function, which were later used in the development of a competency model and a job description. The Council also established regular meeting dates (twice monthly for the duration of the project) and the desired format and procedures of meetings. We also established a preliminary development schedule with milestone dates and achievements.

Initial Data Collection and Analysis

Project team members knew that the depth of data collection and analysis at the beginning of the project would substantially affect the value of the resulting project, and carefully designed the data collection and analysis methods to ensure quality data. Using a systems approach, we designed a general collection of data regarding our current functional conditions, or "as is."

Step 1—Scoping the Project

Our first step was to scope the project by identifying the current types and levels of operators and technicians in the Phoenix area, and the numbers within each category. We first identified the sites and organizations we wished to include, and then used a matrix form (see Figure 1) to record information from the personnel database, along with the job code numbers we had used to access the information. We identified three major types of operators at four levels. We also identified six distinct functional types of technicians, finding that the vast majority of techs were found in three principal classifications. One type contained so few individuals that we combined it with another type. The majority of technicians were at an intermediate to advanced level in terms of grade. Because the job titles and numbers of occupants are proprietary information, only the format appears in Figure 1.

FIGURE 1: Matrix of Target Populations

Type of Tech	Type 1	Type 2	Type 3	Type 4	Type 5
Level One	# of type	# of type	# of type	# of type	# of type
Level Two	# of type	# of type	# of type	# of type	# of type
Level Three	# of type	# of type	# of type	# of type	# of type
Type of Operator	Type 1	Type 2	Type 3		
Level One	# of type	# of type	# of type		
Level Two	# of type	# of type	# of type		
Level Three	# of type	# of type	# of type		
Level Four	# of type	# of type	# of type		

Step 2—Assembling Documentation

Our next step was to assemble all available documentation on these two major populations. The documentation included current job descriptions, compensation guidelines, promotional hierarchies, and training road maps within the various operations groups. We then created a high-level skill matrix based upon the documentation (particularly job descriptions), listing available data and comparing job data for all of the related operator and technician categories to determine a clear progression.

Because the existing documentation was created primarily for compensation purposes, task and skill progressions were listed at a level that was far too general for competency modeling or training development. In addition, the information typically addressed minimal skill and performance requirements for the various jobs, and we were interested in engineering performance of a higher level. The information did, however, create a framework for the project and identify what research remained to be done. This matrix provided us with a reasonable understanding of the current minimum skill requirements for these categories, and the current progression from one level to the next, and gave us the general parameters for our new technician category.

The Council reviewed the existing information and identified gaps and inconsistencies, which were subsequently addressed. Two heavily edited samples of the document appear in Figures 2 and 3. The first deals with generalities about the particular job descriptions, including purpose, entry-level requirements, and general abilities. Proprietary issues prevent us from listing it in its entirety. The second example, in Figure 3, shows the format for comparing actual technical responsibilities as listed in job descriptions and other compensation documents. Again, proprietary issues preclude us from including much detail.

FIGURE 2: Compiling and Comparing Existing Job Data

Grade	Operator Type1 Level 1	Operator Type1 Level 2	Operator Type1 Level 3	Operator Type2 Level 1	New Entry-Level Technician
Purpose:	Operate and monitor automated/ computerized probe equip. to test die or train to learn wafer	Perform single or limited variety direct labor tasks in a wafer-processing area	Perform wafer-processing tasks either as a gen-eralist performing tasks in diffusion, metals, backlap and polish; or as a specialist performing tasks	Perform multiple wafer-processing tasks, perform minor equip. adjustments/ repair and isolate	Perform a variety of mfging tasks to — process product — maintain — repair — verify complex semiconductor processing equip. — sustain and improve yield — sustain and improve quality standards
Activities/ Duties:					
Skills and Abilities:	Basic entry-level	More abilities	More abilities at a higher level	Greater no. of abilities at a higher level	Greater no. of abilities at a higher level

FIGURE 3: Technical Skills Progression Matrix by Level From Existing Job/Function Data

Grade	Operator Type 1 Level 1	Operator Type 1 Level 2	Operator Type 1 Level 3	Operator Type 2 Level 1	New Entry-Level Technician
Education and Qualifications	Minimal →	→	→	→	Highest
Set-Up	2. Set up and make adjustments to automatic production equipment. 7. Check equipment settings against specs. 10. Input data in computer equipment to prepare for process, assembly, or test operations.	2. Set up and make adjustments to automatic production assembly equipment (e.g., bonding equipment, coil winding). 9. Connect meters or other electronic test equipment to product (e.g., frequency counter, current meter, power meter) prior to beginning test operations. 10. Input data in computer equipment to prepare the equipment for process, assembly, or test operations.	2. Set up and make adjustments to automatic production equipment. 10. Input data in computer equipment to prepare for process, assembly, or test. 12. Prepare or use caustic or corrosive solutions according to set formats or methods.	3. Set up and make adjustments to material processing equipment (e.g., tapping or polishing machine, crystal plating machine, screen printer, mask aligner, silicon grinder, solder flow machine plating tank, walking beam, ovens, marking equipment). 5. Adjust controls to obtain proper environmental conditions (e.g., thermostats, air controls, oven settings). 6. Ensure the pumps, filters, hoses, etc., are connected correctly and in working condition. 7. Check equipment settings against specs before beginning operation. 10. Input data in computer equipment to prepare the equipment for process, assembly, or test operations (e.g., load program tape, complete basic data entry). 12. Prepare or use caustic or corrosive solutions according to set formulas or methods (e.g., acids, cyanides, bases).	1. Interpret flow diagrams, schematics, blueprints, product specs, etc., to ensure proper machine or equipment set up. 2. Set up and make adjustments to automatic production equipment. 3. Set up fabrication equipment (e.g., forming or cutting machines, drill press). 4. Calibrate or adjust electronic inspection or testing equipment (e.g., oscilloscope). 7. Set up computer-controlled systems associated with process, assembly, or test operations.
Material Processing/ Equip. Apps.					
Assembly					
Inspection					
Test					

Phase Two

Development of a Competency Model for a New Category of Technician

After reviewing the data, the Council members were ready to begin development of the new functional category and job description. Because of the need to define a new category, and the emphasis on performance management and skill development, members of the SPS training team proposed the use of competency modeling for this project.

The competency-based curricular approach had been introduced to the corporation's instructional designers in 1992 by a team led by Motorola University (MU) Design Manager Ken Hansen and Engineering Competency Center designer Bob Aron. Starting out with competency-based methods similar to those used in other organizations, this team—the Competency-Based Curricular Team—defined terms and adapted methods to Motorola's specific needs.

The competency-based approach had particular value for Motorola because of the size and complexity of the corporation. Job descriptions and titles varied from sector to sector and group to group, making comparison of training needs between and among groups difficult. Functions, however, remained relatively common across the corporation, provided standard terminology, and so eliminated confusion. The MU-led team resolved to define competencies only by function, and not by job, thereby eliminating conflicting job titles and descriptions and building on our commonalties.

All work was based on the concept of output or accomplishment as defined below. Essentially, the team identified the outputs or accomplishments of organizations (i.e., various functional operations groups), and then determined what competencies would be necessary to produce those outputs or accomplishments. Next, competencies were broken down into knowledge and skill clusters. The following standard set of definitions were critical to the MU-led team's efforts.

Accomplishment/Output	A discernible output of a business operation, initiative, technology, or organizational role which requires specific competencies.
Competency	The ability to perform to a defined criteria. The organizing principle is structured around knowledge, skills (or skill clusters), and values determined through analysis that support functions within a business. Competencies usually occur at two levels: novice or expert.
Curriculum	A listing of competencies required to attain a business objective or accomplishment, the knowledges and skills required to execute them, and the resources available to learn them; NOT a list of courses, although these may be attached to the curriculum as part of the available resources for learning.

Within SPS, we further adapted the MU team methods, incorporating tools and techniques that we had used in our specific areas. Our modifications were largely based upon the work done by Geary Rummler within SPS in preceding years, and involved the use of the Rummler competency model format. We selected this tool for a number of reasons:

1. The format lends itself well to group process and would provide a mechanism to create consensus on a function that was, after all, not yet existing and, therefore, a model in the truest sense.

2. The information elicited in the completion of this model would include action, criteria, and enough detail to build performance objectives and subsequent curriculum. We needed to develop both, as well as to create new job descriptions and promotional hierarchies and to obtain management approval for them.

3. The SPS technical community had some previous experience with this modeling method and was comfortable with it.

A sample annotated competency form is shown in Figure 4.

FIGURE 4: Sample Annotated Competency Form

TARGET POPULATION: Technician Type 1   **LEVEL: Level 1 (separate sheet for each level)**

SMEs/Focus Group Members: (names of those from whom we took data and their groups)

OUTPUT/ACCOMPLISHMENT: (listed from the interview data collection, and prioritized; these were validated using group process)

Competencies (Prioritized)	Measures	Standards	K/S/A	Resources
1. Major activities or activity/task groups essential to the output or accomplishment of the area; tasks are subsets of the competencies. 2. Competency —Task —Task —Task 3. 4. 5. 6. 7. 8. 9.	1. Necessary to write performance objectives and to know how the project affects the bottom line and performance management	1. Necessary to write performance objectives, and for evaluation and performance management (especially with government or safety regulations)	1. Knowledge, skill, and attitude or attribute requirements by competency	1. These are known documents, training materials, or programs currently in use, generated by the job, or important in some way to the outputs and tasks.

When these models were complete, we had detailed analysis data and were able to
• write performance objectives
• match objectives to existing programs
• set up program evaluation
• nail down the gaps
• create specific job aids
• engineer current performance based on current best practices
• use scenario/contingency/futures planning to determine how they were likely to change and what we had to plan/train for

Developing and Refining the Model

Council representatives and master technicians spent several sessions developing and refining the model for our new technician function. SPS training specialists led the group through the process, identifying (1) outputs or accomplishments, (2) the competencies required to execute those outputs or accomplishments, (3) measures (both functional performance and business measures), (4) standards, and (5) the knowledge, skills, and attributes required by each competency. After several iterations, we had built a model of the perfect technician in the new category, and had obtained consensus within all the represented groups. The first page of this competency model is shown on the following page, in Figure 5.

Phase Three

Development of the Curriculum to Support the New Category of Technician

When the competency model for the new category of technician was complete, instructional designer Susan Tou began the process of converting the information into performance objectives. This was done by stating the action required of the technician, the circumstances under which it had to be done (conditions), and the criteria against which it would be measured. Following completion, Council members reviewed the objectives and noted any minor revisions that were necessary.

The Critical Role of Performance Objectives

Performance objectives were important to our process because we needed a vehicle to communicate our training requirements for technicians to our local community college district, which was anxious to partner with us. Advanced American educational institutions (colleges and universities) are frequently accused of being unresponsive to the needs of industry. In some cases this may be true, but generally we believe that they simply have another context for

FIGURE 5: Competency Model for New Technician Function

Competency Model: New Entry-Level Technician Category
East Valley/ Phoenix SPS

Accomplishment: Set Up Equipment

Competency	Key Measures	Standards	Knowledge/Skill

1.0 Set up/operate automatic equipment
1.1 Adjust computer-controlled systems
	1.1 • Quality
	   — Accuracy of adjustments
	   — Accuracy of approach; follow correct method
	• Timeliness
		1.1 • Meet process specs
		• Follow manufacturer's recommended method
			1.1 • Analytical skills
			• Understand basic computer operating system
			• Understand specifications
			• Use design skills per vendor/manufacturer/ department
			• Use data entry skills
			• Interpret adjustment data

1.2 Make mechanical adjustments to production equipment	1.2 • Quality
	   — Accuracy of adjustments
	   — Accuracy of approach
	   — Maintain yield and process control
		1.2 • Meet process specs/tolerances
		• Follow manufacturer's recommended method
		• No negative effect on yield
		• Meet SPC parameters
			1.2 • Understand SPC concepts
			• Use SPC tools
			• Understand vendor's equipment
			• Use basic hand tools
			• Understand basic electricity
			• Understand and use basic mechanics

1.3 Verify calibration and/or adjust production equipment	1.3 • Quality
	   — Accuracy of verification
	   — Accuracy of method/sequence
		1.3 • Meet tolerances
		• Meet specs
		• Meet SPC parameters
		• Meet manufacturer's specs
			1.3 • Use SPC tools
			• Understand calibration
			
			Equipment
			• Understand basic electronics
			• Use design skills per vendor

understanding requirements and often do not have enough familiarity or access to industry to gather the information they require to be responsive. We needed to present our requirements to them in a logical way that they recognized and could respond to. Educational institutions generally state their performance/ curricular requirements in the form of objectives, and we hoped that presenting the information in this way would allow us to match our needs with their current offerings. The objectives, when compared with the objectives of the community college's current offerings, would also allow us to identify any gaps and tell us what had to be developed. A sample of these objectives, which were keyed to the competency model, appears in Figure 6. The objectives have been edited to remove any material that might be considered proprietary or confidential.

FIGURE 6: Sample of Performance Objectives

New Entry-Level Technician Curriculum Performance Objectives

SET-UP

1.1   The technician will accurately adjust computer-controlled systems on the line to meet process specifications and the manufacturer's recommended method in a time-efficient manner.

    1.1.1   The technician will use analytical skills to determine the type of adjustment required on a piece of equipment and the appropriate remedy.

    1.1.2   The technician will understand and be able to use basic computer operating systems appropriate to his/her area.

    1.1.3   The technician will explain set-up and operation specifications for computer-controlled systems in his/her area.

    1.1.4   The technician will understand and explain the design of _____.

    1.1.5   The technician will correctly enter data into the computer-controlled system appropriate to his/her area.

    1.1.6   Given a warning on the computer screen that equipment is out of adjustment, the technician will correctly interpret adjustment data and perform corrective action.

(continued on next page)

FIGURE 6: Sample of Performance Objectives *(concluded)*

1.2   The technician will use the manufacturer's recommended method to make accurate mechanical adjustments that meet process specs and tolerances to maintain yield and process control and meet SPC parameters.

    1.2.1   The technician will recall, understand, and apply SPC concepts and tools.

    1.2.2   The technician will identify the characteristics and understand the operation of vendor's equipment, including _____.

    1.2.3   The technician will demonstrate ability to use basic hand tools, including

        _____.

    1.2.4   The technician will recall and explain basic safety principles of electricity, including

        _____.

    1.2.5   The technician will recall and describe basic principles of mechanics, including

        _____.

1.3   The technician will accurately verify the calibration of, and make accurate adjustments to, production equipment to meet the manufacturer's specifications and/or the department's specifications or tolerances.

    1.3.1   The technician will recall, understand, and apply SPC concepts and tools.

    1.3.2   The technician will understand the purpose and use of calibration equipment.

    1.3.3   The technician will recall, explain, and be able to apply basic electronic theory and application.

    1.3.4   The technician will use design skills to _____.

    1.3.5   The technician will correctly interpret manufacturer's specifications to adjust production equipment as appropriate to the department.

1.4   The technician will correctly use fabrication equipment for equipment modification/repair to meet/exceed original manufacturer's design and maintain integrity of the equipment.

The performance objectives approach proved to be very successful. The Technology faculty at Mesa Community College used the performance objectives to identify appropriate current offerings and to outline new courses that would be required. Working with us and our Technician Council, faculty members developed and implemented a new degree program. Faculty members also reviewed the objectives of existing Motorola University and Semiconductor Products Sector training courses, and granted college credit (following evaluation) for our Motorola programs. Students enrolling in the program from Motorola were individually evaluated and could receive up to a quarter of the required degree credit for training they had received through Motorola. The chairman of the Technology Department, Gary Lyon, worked within Motorola plants during summer vacations to counsel individual technicians, meet with their managers and supervisors, and tour technical areas. His presence and close association with our technical population guaranteed MCC's understanding of our needs, facilitated communication, and assured technician access to appropriate counseling.

Ancillary Benefits: Computer Labs and Learning Labs

Upon review of our objectives with Mesa Community College officials, it became apparent that one clear requirement would involve the use of state-of-the-art computer equipment and software. MCC did not have access to this hardware or software. We approached our senior manufacturing management for assistance, and they subsequently granted MCC the hardware and software required for a computer laboratory of 30 workstations to be installed at the MCC campus (near several large Motorola plants). We also laid the foundation for the creation of a large learning lab with similar equipment at one of our major plants. Employees thus had access to equipment and materials both at the MCC campus and at their work sites.

Another requirement for our students would be a solid foundation in electronics. Matching our objectives with a vendor of learning software, we were able to find self-paced, interactive, basic electronics instructional software available on laser disk, and we set up several workstations at various plants to make this instruction available on a 24-hour basis for our employees.

Certification Levels

We arranged that at specific points in their completion of the MCC curriculum, employees would receive certificates as an added incentive to keep going. The first two certificate levels, which exemplify the program developed by Mesa Community College, appear in Figure 7.

The Implementation Process

When we had completed our new functional category and the curriculum to support it (Motorola's list of required competencies and MCC's degree curriculum to support them), we began a gradual implementation process, one major organization at a time. MCC agreed to hold classes on Motorola sites whenever practical to reduce the time and travel required of our employees. Our organizations set up selection criteria for candidates desiring to enter the program, and frequently provided incentives in the form of some release time from work and tuition assistance to encourage attendance. Managers and supervisors were coached to provide support for attendance. Approximately 200 employees are currently enrolled in the program.

Simultaneously, our HR compensation members on the Council obtained approval for the new job description and a promotional hierarchy. These were announced to organizations and explained to employees. Successful completion of our new curriculum (the competency model and available resources within Motorola, and the MCC degree program at the community college) was required to attain the new functional grade, so employees were given a clear goal and an incentive for completing the program.

Phase Four

Creation of Competency Models for Existing Technicians

When we had completed and implemented our new technician category, we turned our attention to the development of those hundreds of employees already

FIGURE 7: Sample of MCC Program

Certificate Levels I and II:
Associate of Applied Science Degree in Electromechanical Process Technology

ENTRY-LEVEL TECHNICIAN CATEGORY

Certificate Level I		Hours
ELE 101	Mathematics (Intro Alg)	3
ENG 101	Freshman English	3
Any	Oral Communication	3
substitute	*MGT 113 Managing Conflict (MU* .5 unit*	*up to 3*
	MGT 202 Effective Presentations (MU) 1 unit	
	MGT 201 Effective Meetings (MU) 1 unit	
	HRD 108 Effective Listening (MU) .5 unit	
	TCH 330 Interaction for Techs (MU)	
	TTT 101 Instructor I (MU) 2.5 units	
Any	Computer Skills	2
substitute	*3 Mac courses or 3 IBM PC courses*	*2*
	Co-op credit for production systems	*1*
ELE 100	Concepts of Electricity/Electronics	3
ENG 111	Technical Writing	3
DFT 114	Machine Trades/Blueprint	3
		20

Certificate Level II

ELE 105	Math (Nit Alg/Trig)	5
GTC 181	Fluid Power	3
ELE 111	DC Circuit Analysis	4
ELE 112	AC Circuit Analysis	4
GTC 185	Electromechanical Devices	3
ELE 131	Digital Logic & Digital Circuits	4
		23

*MU = Motorola University

classified as technicians. We had studied entry-level requirements during the previous process, and had all of the appropriate data. We needed data on technicians classified as intermediate or advanced.

Information Interviews

To enhance performance or to engineer improved performance, it would be necessary to understand the current best practice for each of the technician categories. Essentially, we wanted to "clone" the performance of our best technicians by identifying what they did well and establishing requirements and training programs to help other technicians attain that same level of performance. We asked the organizational representatives on the Council to identify for us three expert performers within each organization, and then conducted information interviews to identify precisely what the experts did and how they did it, and the organizational issues that would have to be resolved to enable other people to learn and apply those skills.

We identified 26 best-expert technicians from nine organizations within SPS, representing various functional technician groups (Types 1 through 5), and arranged to interview them for two- to four-hour periods. Selection criteria for these subject matter experts (SMEs) appear below.

Selection Profile for Subject Matter Experts (SMEs)

- Top 10% of ranking and rating group in each of five technician areas

- Instructors for technical training courses

- Reputation by supervisor and peers (and employees, if applicable)

- Between 5 and 25 years' experience with the company.

A semistructured interviewing questionnaire/protocol was developed. We used a funneling approach for the questions, moving from a generic level of information dealing with general roles and responsibilities, and becoming increasingly more specific about duties, expert and nonexpert performance, training methods, critical incidents, and barriers to performance. A similar protocol is shown in Appendix A. Probing questions have been added to illustrate the process. Instructional designer Mary Jane Thome conducted the interviews.

Data Analysis and Summary

Following information interviews, data were sorted and analyzed using naturalistic technique (e.g., we clustered and prioritized like information). A data summary was presented to the Technician Council for review. A number of issues that had surfaced during the interviews were referred to appropriate departments for resolution. For instance, we became aware that new hire technicians were frequently placed on third (graveyard) shift by themselves, without a mentor or anyone to answer questions. This practice was reviewed by the Council; then appropriate recommendations were sent to the Employment and Employee Relations departments for corrective action, and supervisors in at least some areas were encouraged to assign new hires more appropriately.

Competency Modeling and Creating Performance Objectives

The information that resulted from the interviews, when added to the job data we had collected in the earlier phase of the project, gave us a broad framework for the project and information on what comprised current best performance. We then began the competency modeling process for each of five types of experienced technicians, drawing on our information to create preliminary models. The Technician Council developed new competency models for expected performance for each of these five types of technicians in a series of sessions. The competency models answered the questions: What does the technician do? How do we know he or she has done it well? What knowledge and skill does he or she need to do it? An example of the model for Technician Type 1 is shown on the following page, in Figure 8.

When the models for all five types of experienced technicians were completed, instructional designer Jennifer Fox Kennedy began a process similar to the one we had used in the first phase of the project—using the data in the competency models to create performance objectives for each of the five types.

FIGURE 8: Sample of Competency Model for Technician Type 1

Sample Competency Model: Technician Type 1

Competency	Measures	Standards	Knowledge/Skills
1.0 Set up, design, adjust, and operate the process and equipment. **Tasks** 1.1 Set up and adjust the equipment[10] 1.2 Modify equipment to meet special maintenance needs[7] 1.3 Make equipment improvements to improve availability, capability, and yield[8] 1.4 Set up computer interface to equipment[20] 1.5 Set up and adjust the equipment from a computer[20] 1.6 Maintain or improve quality of the process[13] 1.7 Set up and perform PM[4,5] 1.8 Design equipment parts using a computer[23]	1.0 *Performance Measures* (Level 3): • Certification tool for installation, set up, and configuration tasks • Certification tool for operational tasks • Accuracy of approach • Quality • Maintain process control • Cp/Cpk • Uniformity of results from equipment to equipment • Uptime (Availability) *Business Measures* (Level 4): • Product yield • Cost per product	1.0 • Meets process specifications • Meets fab environment specifications • Meets safety specifications • No negative yield impact • Meets department and area goals • Vendor procedures and specifications • Meets performance requirements • Meets customer's equipment requirements • Meets product cost goals • Meets quality goals	1.0 a) Analytical/problem-solving skills[7,8,10] b) Know equipment (operation, internal functions, parameters, and outcomes)[7,8,10,13] c) Know process (set up specifications, parameter entry into control panels, parameter entry into recipes, and how parameters impact critical outcomes)[8,10,13] d) Know safety procedures[7,8,10] e) Interpret technical documents (manuals, electrical and mechanical schematics, procedures, specifications)[7,8,10,35] f) Interpret test results[2,7,8,10] g) Know basic math and statistics h) Mechanical and electrical knowledge and skills[7,8,10,4,5] i) Know electrical and mechanical test equipment usage[2,7,8,9,10] j) Know SPC[8,9,10,13] k) Know computer programming, usage, and data access[20] l) Know computer interface protocol drivers and cable wiring[20] m) Know equipment interface protocols SECS-I/II and GEM[20]

FIGURE 9: Sample of Performance Objectives for Technician Type 1

(Objectives Created from and Keyed to the Competency Model)

1.1.0 Set-Up and Operation
The Technician will accurately <u>set up</u>, <u>adjust</u>, and <u>operate</u> the process and related equipment to meet process specifications, yield, and SPC parameters using internal specifications and vendor procedures.T1.0
Common skills and knowledge used in all set-up tasks 1.1.1 through 1.1.8

1.1.0.a Analytical and Problem-Solving Skills (Refer to 1.3.0, 1.3.1, 1.3.2, 1.3.3 Troubleshooting and Repair tasks.)

1.1.0.b (and 1.1.0.c) Equipment and Process Knowledge

    1.1.0.b1 The Technician will draw a block diagram showing the major equipment functions internal to the process in his/her area and label operator entry points for parameter set-up and adjustment.

    1.1.0.b2 Training operators and technicians (See 1.5.3.1 Communications.)

    1.1.0.b3 The Technician will demonstrate equipment/process knowledge by selecting key parameters used in the process within his/her area, from a list of parameters used throughout the wafer fabrication process.

    . . .

1.1.0.d Safety Knowledge (Refer to 1.9.0 Observe and Conform to Safety Procedures.)

1.1.0.e The Technician will locate and apply vendor and other documentation required to set up, adjust, troubleshoot, and repair equipment in his/her area.

These objectives were subsequently reviewed and validated by the Technician Council; then performance objectives were added to our resource lists and given to Mesa Community College's Technology Department. MCC used them, as they had done previously with the entry-level category, to match Motorola's requirements with existing MCC courseware and to identify gaps that had to be filled by the development of new courseware.

The performance objectives were, of course, keyed to the competency models. Figure 9 shows a sample of the performance objectives written for Technician Type 1. A sample of *The Resource Guide for Technicians*, published within Motorola, appears in Figure 10. We have also included the document that shows the matching process (Motorola's performance objectives to MCC learning objectives) with Mesa Community College courses, in Figure 11. The courses are abbreviated in this document.

FIGURE 10: Sample of the Resource Guide for Technicians

Resource Guide for Technician Type 1

1.0 Set-Up and Operation

Accomplishment: The Technician will accurately *set up, adjust,* and *operate* the process and related equipment to meet process specifications, yield, and SPC parameters using internal specifications and vendor procedures.

Competencies	Objectives	Resource/Intervention
1.1 Set up and adjust the equipment.	1.0 The Technician will use analytical skills and specifications to determine appropriate adjustments to make during set-up procedures on normally functioning equipment (non-troubleshooting). 1.1.1 The Technician will perform set-up procedures from existing specifications and/or vendor procedures. 1.1.2 The Technician will enter process set-up parameters into controls on equipment panels. 1.1.3 The Technician will enter process set-up parameters into computer-controlled process recipes or computer-based control screens (where applicable). 1.1.4 The Technician will verify normal operation of the process and take appropriate action to diagnose abnormal conditions or malfunctions. 1.1.5 The Technician will verify normal operation of the process and if unsafe conditions are present, take action as specified in safety procedures. 1.1.6 The Technician will be able to operate the process to produce products which meet or exceed equipment and product specifications. 1.1.7 The Technician will perform *equipment/process set-up and operational certification tasks* on an equipment/process specific operational simulator covering tasks for the equipment in his/her area.	Courses, rotational programs, internships, and training programs are listed here for each item.

FIGURE 11: The Matching Process

Match of Courseware for Technician Type 1

Equipment Set-Up	Course Match	Standards	Course Match
1.0 Set up, design, adjust, and operate the process and equipment.	GTC, MSC, ATC, VTM, CLT	1.0 a) Analytical/problem-solving skills[7,8,10] b) Know equipment (operation, internal functions, parameters, and outcomes)[7,8,10,13] c) Know process (set-up specifications, parameter entry into control panels, parameter entry into recipes, and how parameters impact critical outcomes)[8,10,13] d) Know safety procedures[7,8,10] e) Interpret technical documents (manuals, electrical and mechanical schematics, procedures, specifications)[7,8,10,35] f) Interpret test results[2,7,8,10] g) Know basic math and statistics[8,10] h) Mechanical and electrical knowledge and skills[7,8,10,4,5] i) Know electrical and mechanical test equipment usage[2,7,8,9,10] j) Know SPC[8,9,10,13] k) Know computer programming, usage, and data access[20] l) Know computer interface protocol drivers and cable wiring[20] m) Know equipment interface protocols SECS-I/II and GEM[20]	1.0 a) GTC, MSC b) ATC, VTM c) ATC d) PWB e) CMS, ATC f) GTC, MSC g) MSC h) GTC i) ATC, GTC j) MSC k) CLT l) CLT, ATC m) CLT, VTM
1.1 Set up and adjust the equipment[10]			
1.2 Modify equipment to meet special maintenance needs[7]			
1.3 Make equipment improvements to improve availability, capability, and yield[8]			
1.4 Set up computer interface to equipment[20]			
1.5 Set up and adjust the equipment from a computer[20]			
1.6 Maintain or improve quality of the process[13]			
1.7 Set up and perform PM[4,5]			
1.8 Design equipment parts using a computer[23]			

Developing a Curriculum

Mesa Community College worked with instructional designer Jennifer Fox Kennedy and the SPS Technician Council to develop a detailed curriculum/course listing for our experienced technicians based upon our competency models, our objectives, and the course matches we had produced. Again, as with the new entry-level technician category we described earlier, MCC granted up to 25% of degree credit to those who had completed internal Motorola training programs that were similar to MCC courses. A sample of the completed Motorola/MCC course listings appears in Appendix B.

Phase Five

Revision of Tools

From the beginning of the Technician Project, HR specialists played an active role in the Technician Council, assuring that the compensation and employee relations issues raised during the project were addressed effectively and efficiently. Their work, particularly in the compensation arena, contributed substantially to the success of the project and its subsequent implementation. Instructional designers originated the project, performed data collection and analysis, and produced the curricular tools. Competency-based curricula, however, is only as effective as the organizational systems that support them. Compensation specialists and managers Christine Florez, Murlene Jefferson, and Jane Maxson, and Sector Testing Manager Karen Mattimore, developed the mechanisms for adoption and institutionalization.

Job descriptions were revised throughout the project to support new performance models. Our compensation specialists conducted a large-scale survey of managers and supervisors to identify key compensation issues/barriers, and developed strategies to overcome them. The career paths that they identified, and the compensation/promotional system they developed to reward development and attainment of further degrees, were extremely valuable to the project.

Karen Mattimore and the Sector Testing Group provided a key link for the overall project by condensing the competency models into one- to two-page employment profiles and guidelines. Our instructional designers were primarily concerned with the training and development of existing employees. The Testing Group, however, focused on employment and orientation of new Motorolans. As a result of the profile job aids produced by this group, Motorola SPS recruiters received sufficient information to successfully hire candidates that either matched our new performance models or had the ability to quickly achieve the profiles.

Our employee relations specialists, particularly Helen Marvin, provided key communication interfaces with operations management, and provided a first line of defense for employee questions about the changing technician requirements and opportunities. They worked closely with the compensation specialists and Technician Council members to develop booklets containing descriptions of programs, promotional requirements, contact information, and other data for the successful implementation of the technician project.

The Technician Project was the first of many forays for SPS Training into competency-based curriculum, and taught us an invaluable lesson that we have subsequently applied to other functional curricular projects: Human resources support is absolutely essential for the implementation of the overall performance system. HR representatives can and must be key members of the project team.

Phase Six

Creation of an Implementation Workshop for Supervisors and Managers of Experienced Technicians

Our final task for the Technician Project was to ensure a thorough and successful implementation of the competency models, curricula, and revised HR policies and procedures. One last tool remained to be developed—a workshop for managers and supervisors (and the HR specialists who support them). The workshop explained the project, clearly defined the goals and strategies, and walked supervisors and managers through changes in expectations, job descriptions, and compensation, training, and promotional procedures. It also provided tools for career planning and performance management, based on the competency models we had developed, to encourage managers and supervisors to evaluate technician performance in a manner consistent with the overall models. Instructional designers developed the workshop in conjunction with the Technician Council. Implementation was to occur in early 1997, in conjunction with a major communication effort to advise technicians of the changes and opportunities.

Evaluation

When we began the project and formed our Technician Council, one of our first activities was to establish mission and objectives. These are listed below with the status opposite each.

Objectives	Results
1. Developing a new model of technician within manufacturing —creating curricula to develop operators —providing a career path	1. Model developed and implemented —curricula built and implemented —career path identified and published
2. Upgrading the skills of the existing technician population by developing competency models for each of five technician types, and the various levels (beginning and advanced) within each	2. Competency models built for five types of technician, with consideration of beginning and advanced within each
3. Developing curricula to support the renewal and development of each type and level of technician	3. Curricula to support each type and level of technician developed and published
4. Collaborating with local colleges to create appropriate educational programs and degrees, thereby making efficient use of existing resources, supporting our community, and encouraging our people to earn degrees	4. Collaboration established; programs and degrees complete and implemented
5. Gaining college accreditation for internal Motorola courses, both MU and SPS*	5. College credit granted for internal Motorola courses (both MU and SPS) up to 25% of degree

Objectives	Results
6. Mapping career paths and promotional opportunities, so employees would be able with their supervisors to take responsibility for their own career development	6. Career paths identified and promotional guidelines published; managers and supervisors working with technicians to counsel and coach
7. Implementing the programs successfully; providing tools and resources to assist managers and employees to assume responsibility for counseling for training and career development	7. Programs established; publications and other tools written and published; final implementation 1/97
8. Assuring that compensation and other (e.g., recruiting and employment) systems supported the change in performance expectations	8. Compensation systems in place for both new tech category and experienced tech types and levels; performance management expectations communicated

*MU = Motorola University
 SPS = Semiconductor Products Sector

Final implementation and communication of the program was completed in January, 1997. All other action items were completed. Two hundred Motorola employees were registered in the initial curriculum for the new category of technician, and experienced technicians were expected to begin registration and classes with the final implementation in 1997.

Level One evaluation (participant reaction) was positive and continuously monitored by both the Council members and Human Resources. Level Two (learning) was measured by the Mesa Community College courses, which contained tests and measures. The pass rate served as an indicator for Level Two. Level Three (subsequent performance on the job) was not yet being measured because our employees were still in the educational pipeline. Level Four (organizational change) had not yet been addressed at the end of 1996.

Conclusions

The Technician Project was the first of many large-scale functional curricular projects undertaken by Semiconductor Product Sector Training, and provided the foundation of the methodology that has been used for subsequent projects. Key curriculum projects are now complete, including the First-Line Leader (with a corporate-wide supervisory curriculum), Mid-Level Manager Curriculum (Motorola University), SPS Software (a project comprising 18 distinct models for different functions within the software discipline), SPS Engineering (10 functions within the semiconductor engineering discipline), and projects focusing on five key HR functions and on semiconductor operators.

We learned a number of valuable lessons about competency-based curricula during the course of this project, which we have summarized below.

- Project teams must be cross-functional, and at a minimum must include

    — members from each organization to be affected by the project
    — technical experts
    — instructional designers, or other training specialists
    — human resource specialists in compensation and employee relations

- These functional projects tend to be huge in scope, and thus take commitment, time, materials, and skilled labor over many months.

- Success depends upon quality data and detail during the data collection phase, and sound project management.

- Using a complete systems approach ensures not only quality training, but the human resources policies and procedures (including performance management and compensation) to implement, reward, and sustain performance. Organizational design and development groups tend to benefit from these projects as well, as the projects address major organizational issues.

- Technical personnel within a corporation tend to like this methodology because of its logical and thorough approach. On one occasion, when SPS training specialists attempted to take methodological shortcuts to expedite development, Technical Council members sharply reined them in. Members had learned the system, and intended that we follow all the proper steps. They view this method as a technical process like any other and have learned that with the proper tools and methods, performance can be engineered, just like products.

The competency-based methodology we employed is becoming a standard for development among our education and training councils. The various councils are chartered to maintain the competency models specific to their areas. For example, the Technician Council that initiated this project has expanded its charter and become the Manufacturing Education Council, with focus on technicians, first-line leaders, and direct labor.

During this project, and as a result of it, the Technician Council members learned performance technology methodology and collaborative skills, built strong relationships, widened their networks, influenced their management teams, and took ownership of many responsibilities traditionally reserved for the HR function. This project was therefore an important developmental experience for those SPS employees who participated in it. We have every hope that competency-based curricula will become the Motorola standard over the course of the next few years.

Acknowledgments

Many people contributed to the success of the Technician Project, among them the following:

Compensation specialists Jane Maxson and Murlene Jefferson provided us with expert support for several years. The project experienced a major break-through when Christine Florez, who had long represented the employee relations arena, became a senior compensation manager for SPS in Phoenix. Her aggressive support for changes in the compensation system to accommodate a competency-based curricular approach was key to the project's success. Motorola University's support was also crucial during the second half of the project, as it supplied instructional design assistance and negotiated with Mesa Community College (MCC) for college credit for internal Motorola training programs. Key

MCC representatives were Ken Schultz, who initiated the interface between Motorola and the Community College; Technology Department Chairman Gary Lyon; and Professor Jim Harter, who compared Motorola's specific requirements in the form of performance objectives with Mesa Community College's Technology Program objectives and designed a new MCC curriculum for us.

APPENDIX A

Information Interview Protocol—SME

This semi-structured information-interview format is designed to be used during a two- to four-hour information session with subject matter experts. The questions are intended to elicit information on a variety of key training/skill issues for performance improvement. Interviewers should refrain from adding interpretative comments, and should check frequently for accuracy of information by repeating responses and asking clarifying/probing questions to attain maximum data. Careful notes should be kept and confidentiality assured. Respondents should be told that they will never be quoted as individuals, and that all data will be presented in summary format. Explain the protocol to respondents before beginning the interview.

Please remember that we are interested in function rather than job description. Job descriptions may be very inaccurate. Note any discrepancies that become obvious during the course of the interview, so that we may resolve any issues.

Demographic Data

Name:

Grade:

Title:

Date:

Location:

Shift:

Date of Hire:

1. What would you say are the major outputs, accomplishments, or outcomes of your functional area? This may include products, processes, services, or a variety of other items.

2. (a) What would you describe as the major roles in your area of responsibility (Type 1 Technician)?

   (b) Please prioritize them in terms of importance to your functional area.

(c) Please describe how each relates to the outputs, accomplishments, or outcomes of your functional area.

(d) Which role takes up the most time? How do you know which role is expected of you, and at what time?

3. (a) Please tell us about the specific responsibilities of each of your major roles, including duties and tasks.

(b) Please prioritize them in terms of importance to the role. Which occupy the majority of your time? About what percentage of the average day do you spend on them?

— What makes you start doing each?

— What makes you stop?

— Do you interact with anyone while you do that? If so, who? How does his or her role differ from yours?

— Is there any documentation that you use while you're doing that? If so, may I have a copy?

(c) How critical are these responsibilities to the success of your functional area? Can you give examples of why they would be important (critical incidents)?

4. Please name three to five behaviors that you think represent effective or successful types of technician behavior. Can you give me specific examples? How do you know if a person in your functional area is well trained or a good performer? What things would you expect to see him or her do or produce?

5. Can you think of three to five behaviors that you think represent ineffective or unsuccessful technician behaviors? Specific examples?

6. (a) How would you know if a person was an exceptional performer? What might this person do differently or better than an average employee?

(b) You have been identified as an expert or exceptional performer. What causes your boss/peers to see you this way? Are there activities that you do differently or more often than your colleagues?

7. (a)   How are people in your functional area currently trained or brought up to speed in terms of their roles and responsibilities? What skills or knowledge are essential to a new technician? Just entering the field? Experienced, but just entering the job or function here?

    (b)   Recall when you first started in this position. What were some of the major problems you had to deal with as you settled into your job or function? Start with the most difficult. Did someone help you with that? If so, how? What do you think might have made a difference?

    (c)   Are job aids, specialized hardware or software tools, training materials, or courses currently available for training new people in this function? If so, please identify them for us.

    (d)   Do you have copies of, or literature about, these tools or programs?

    (e)   Do you have suggestions on how to train new hires better or differently?

8. (a)   What kind of training do experienced employees in your functional area currently receive?

    (b)   Do you have copies of, or literature about, these programs?

    (c)   Do you have suggestions on how to develop experienced employees in this function? Please be as specific as possible.

    (d)   How do you know if a person in your functional area is inadequately trained or having performance problems? What things would you expect to see him or her do or produce? What might this person do differently than an average employee?

    (e)   How is retraining or performance coaching handled now? Can you think of examples?

9. (a)   What key changes or trends are occurring in your functional area now?

    (b)   Do you foresee any major changes in the way the function is currently performed? What would cause this change, and in what time frame would it occur?

    (c)   Are skill requirements going to be significantly different as a result of these changes? If so, how?

    (d)   How would an employee acquire these new skills or this new knowledge?

10. Can you tell me what kinds of training you have had?
    — What was the most valuable?
    — What was the least valuable?
    — What was missing?

11. What groups of people do you spend the most working time dealing with? Can you give me three examples of effective or successful interactions with these folks? Three examples of ineffective or unsuccessful interactions?

12. What is your reporting structure? From whom do you receive the most direction? Can you tell me what technician behaviors are most often rewarded? Can you provide examples?

13. Have you had any experience in working with teams? What types, how often, under what circumstances? Who led the team?

APPENDIX B

Experienced Technician Education and Training Model
(Engineering Operations)
for Technician Type 1, Technician Type 2, Technician Type 3,
Technician Type 4, and Technician Type 5

In the following model, the education and training resource of Motorola University/SPS Training, OJT/Vendor Training, and Mesa Community College are teamed to form a troika of resources to support the career ladder of the experienced Technicians Types 1 through 5, including and beyond the level of the Associate of Applied Science degree. The model blends these three education and training resources to facilitate the development of Grade-Level Attributes and Position Competencies.

Category	Grade-Level Attributes		Position Competencies	
Institutional Courses (512 Hrs. Total)	Interpersonal Skills (ISK)	40 Hrs.	Area of Technical Concentration (ATC)	192 Hrs.
	Mentoring and Training Skills (MTS)	28 Hrs.		
	Communication Skills (CMS)	16 Hrs.	General Technology (GTC)	64 Hrs.
	Organizational Awareness (ORA)	12 Hrs.		
	Physical Well-Being (PWB)	16 Hrs.		
	Computer Literacy (CLT)	16 Hrs.		
	Math/Science (MSC)	128 Hrs.		
	Total Hours:	**256 Hrs.**	Total Hours:	**256 Hrs.**
Other Training			Vendor Training/Mentoring (VTM)	**192 Hrs.**

- Grade-Level Attributes comprise the body of knowledge and skills universally required to effectively function at the senior level.
- Position Competencies comprise the set of knowledge and skills required to have self-reliance in a specific senior technician position.
- Institutional Courses are those courses taught by MU/SPS, MCC (or other community colleges), universities, and engineering societies (IEE, SME, ASQC, etc.)

Grade-Level Attributes
(256 Hours of Institutional Course Work)

Interpersonal Skills (40 Hrs.)

Take any combination of courses totaling a minimum of 40 hours.

Subject Code	Hours	Course Title
MGT 106	16	Effective Interactions w/Employees
MGT 330	16	Interaction
HRD 104	16	Understanding People
HRD 108	4	Effective Listening
TCH 203	8	Managing Team Conflict
TCH 330	16	Interaction for Technicians
WFD 101	6	Understanding the Diverse Workforce
WFD 303	4	Preventing Sexual Harassment
WFD 340	8	Female/Male Communication Strategies
WFD 510	32	Efficacy Seminar for Nonexempt Women
WFD 580	32	Efficacy Seminar for Men

Mentoring and Training Skills (28 Hrs.)

Take any combination of courses totaling a minimum of 28 hours.

Subject Code	Hours	Course Title
MGT 201	16	Effective Presentations
MGT 330	16	Interaction
MGT 360	4	Building a Foundation of Trust
MGT 365	4	Expanding Your Team's Capabilities
MFG 350	24	Manufacturing On-the-Job Training Skills
WFD 104	4	Mentoring in a Modern Workforce
WFD 105	8	Mentoring Work—Skills for Partnerships

Communication Skills (16 Hrs.)
(Written—Verbal—Nonverbal)

Take any combination of courses totaling a minimum of 16 hours.

Subject Code	Hours	Course Title
HRD 108	4	Effective Listening
HRD 300	16	Problem Analysis and Decision Making
MGT 201	16	Effective Presentations
PDE 512	16	Technical Writing
PDE 540	16	Basic Business Communications Skills
PGM 413	24	How to Write Winning Proposals
PRD 102	18	Reading Refinement for Nonexempt

Organizational Awareness (12 Hrs.)

Take any combination of courses totaling a minimum of 12 hours.

Subject Code	Hours	Course Title
MGT 218	24	System Thinking: Skills for the Learning Organization
MGT 240	8	Life Management (Life, Time, Self)
MGT 360	4	Building a Foundation of Trust
MGT 365	4	Expanding Your Team's Capabilities
MFG 335	8	Technology Awareness
PEQ 110	1	Protection of Proprietary Information
WFD 100	4	Working with Diversity
WFD 101	6	Understanding the Diversity Workforce
WFD 400	26	Workplace Interaction Training—Teams

Physical Well-Being (16 Hrs.)
(Stress Management — Safety)

Take any combination of courses totaling a minimum of 16 hours.

Subject Code	Hours	Course Title
HRD 128	16	Managing Personal Growth (Nonexempt)
HSP 202	8	Stress Management
MGT 240	8	Life Management (Life, Time, Self)
PER 118	8	Professional Excellence
PER 200	8	Working in a Changing Environment
SAF . . .		See Safety Training Matrix in MU Catalog
WEL 101	4	Self Care
WEL 102	4	Healthy Heart

Computer Literacy (16 Hrs.)

Take any combination of courses totaling a minimum of 16 hours.

Subject Code	Hours	Course Title
IBM 501	8	DOS, Hard Disk Management
IBM 504	8	Windows Orientation
IBM 514	8	Windows Advanced User
IBM 525	8	Word for Windows: Level 1
IBM 526	8	Word for Windows: Level 2
IBM 527	8	Word for Windows: Advanced
IBM 540	8	Excel Worksheets
IBM 545	8	Excel Database and Graphics
IBM 546	8	Excel Advanced
IBM 547	8	Excel Power User

(continued)

Computer Literacy (16 Hrs.) *(continued)*
Take any combination of courses totaling a minimum of 16 hours.

Subject Code	Hours	Course Title
IBM 563	8	dBase IV Introduction: Level 1
IBM 564	8	dBase IV Introduction: Level 2
IBM 565	8	dBase IV Advanced
IBM 580	4	LAN Overview—Novell
MAC 500	8	Macintosh Orientation in System 7
MAC 504	8	Macintosh Advanced User
MAC 520	8	MS Word: Level 1
MAC 521	8	MS Word: Level 2
MAC 540	8	Excel Worksheets
MAC 542	8	Excel Database and Charts
MAC 543	8	Excel Advanced
MAC 544	8	Excel Power User

Mathematics/Science (128 Hrs.)
Take any combination of courses totaling a minimum of 128 hours.

Subject Code	Hours	Course Title
ENG 234	24	Design of Experiments: Practical Approach
ENG 244	40	Advanced Statistical Applications
ENG 474	10	Improvement Curve Analysis
SPC 388	24	Statistics II
SPC 390	24	Nonparametric Comparative Experiments
SPC 392	16	Full Factorial Experiments
SPC 394	16	Fractional Factorial Experiments
SPC 396	4	Component Search
SSG 102	8	Utilizing the Six Steps to Six Sigma
CHM 151	64 MCC	General Chemistry I with Lab
CHM 152	64 MCC	General Chemistry II with Lab
CHM 230	64 MCC	Fundamental Organic Chemistry with Lab
CHM 260	48 MCC	Fundamental Biochemistry
ELE 201	48 MCC	Technical Calculus I
MAT 155	48 MCC	College Algebra/Functions
MAT 160	48 MCC	Plane Trigonometry
MAT 220	80 MCC	Analytic Geometry and Calculus
MAT 223	64 MCC	Calculus with Analytic Geometry I
MAT 224	64 MCC	Calculus with Analytic Geometry II
PHY 111	64 MCC	General Physics I
PHY 112	64 MCC	General Physics II

Position Competencies
(256 Hours of Institutional Course Work)
(192 Hours of Vendor Training/Mentoring)

Area of Technical Concentration for Type 3 Technician (192 Hrs.)
Take any combination of courses totaling a minimum of 192 hours.

Subject Code	Hours	Course Title
EDN 003	24	Ion Implantation Technology
EDN 040	20	RF Fundamentals
EDN 041	24	ENI RF Generators (Advanced)
EDN 045	70	Vacuum Technology
MFG 460	24	Intro to Programming Robots
MFG 465	16	Intro to Machine Vision
ELE 221	64 MCC	Linear Solid-State Devices
ELE 241	64 MCC	Microprocessor Concepts
ELE 243	48 MCC	Microprocessor Applications
GTC 181	48 MCC	Introduction to Fluid Power
GTC 209	48 MCC	Automated Manufacturing (Intro to PLC)
GTC 272	48 MCC	Sequential Process Control (PLC/Robot)

Area of Technical Concentration for Type 4 Technician (192 Hrs.)
Take any combination of courses totaling a minimum of 192 hours.

Subject Code	Hours	Course Title
EDN 003	24	Ion Implantation Technology
EDN 040	20	RF Fundamentals
EDN 041	24	ENI RF Generators (Advanced)
EDN 045	70	Vacuum Technology
MFG 460	24	Intro to Programming Robots
MFG 465	16	Intro to Machine Vision
ELE 221	64 MCC	Linear Solid-State Devices
ELE 241	64 MCC	Microprocessor Concepts
ELE 243	48 MCC	Microprocessor Applications
GTC 102	48 MCC	Machine Processes
GTC 181	48 MCC	Introduction to Fluid Power
GTC 209	48 MCC	Automated Manufacturing (Intro to PLC)
GTC 272	48 MCC	Sequential Process Control (PLC/Robot)
WLD 101	48 MCC	Welding I

Area of Technical Concentration for Type 1 Technician (192 Hrs.)

Take any combination of courses totaling a minimum of 192 hours.

Subject Code	Hours	Course Title
EDN 003	24	Ion Implantation Technology
EDN 005	24	Ion Implantation Basic
EDN 040	20	RF Fundamentals
EDN 041	24	ENI RF Generators (Advanced)
EDN 045	70	Vacuum Technology
EDN 047	16	Metalization
EDN 049	16	Diffusion/Oxidation
EDN 051	8	Basic Plasma Etching
EDN 053	8	Wet Etch
EDN 055	16	Chemical Vapor Deposition . . .
ENG 147	24	Plasma Etching
MFG 460	24	Intro to Programming Robots
MFG 465	16	Intro to Machine Vision
ELE 221	64 MCC	Linear Solid-State Devices
ELE 241	64 MCC	Microprocessor Concepts
ELE 243	48 MCC	Microprocessor Applications
GTC 181	48 MCC	Introduction to Fluid Power
GTC 209	48 MCC	Automated Manufacturing (Intro to PLC)
GTC 272	48 MCC	Sequential Process Control (PLC/Robot)

Area of Technical Concentration for Type 4 Technician (192 Hrs.)

Take any combination of courses totaling a minimum of 192 hours.

Subject Code	Hours	Course Title
EDN 047	16	Metalization
EDN 049	16	Diffusion/Oxidation
EDN 051	8	Basic Plasma Etching
EDN 053	8	Wet Etch
EDN 055	16	Chemical Vapor Deposition . . .
EDN 062	20	Statistics Decision Tree
QCT 143	48 MCC	Introduction to Quality Assurance
QCT 153	48 MCC	Statistical Quality Control
QCT 275	48 MCC	Management Concepts for Quality Control
XXX . . .		Courses in Quality through local ASQC

Area of Technical Concentration for Type 2 Technician (192 Hrs.)
Take any combination of courses totaling a minimum of 192 hours.

Subject Code	Hours	Course Title
EDN 003	24	Ion Implantation Technology
EDN 005	24	Ion Implantation Basic
EDN 040	20	RF Fundamentals
EDN 045	70	Vacuum Technology
EDN 046	16	Basic Microlithography
EDN 047	16	Metalization
EDN 049	16	Diffusion/Oxidation
EDN 051	8	Basic Plasma Etching
EDN 053	8	Wet Etch
EDN 055	16	Chemical Vapor Deposition . . .
ENG 147	24	Plasma Etching
CHM 130	64 MCC	Fundamental Chemistry with Lab
CHM 151	64 MCC	General Chemistry I with Lab
MAT 155	48 MCC	College Algebra/Functions

General Technology for Technician Type 1–5 (64 Hrs.)
Take any combination of courses totaling a minimum of 64 hours.

Subject Code	Hours	Course Title
EDN 017	32	Microlithography (Advanced)
EDN 043	24	Basic Vacuum Practices
EDN 046	16	Basic Microlithography
EDN 056	32	Microlithography (Intermediate)
EDN 063	10	Fundamentals of Material Technology
HRD 244	40	Semiconductor Fundamentals
DFT 252	48 MCC	Computer Aided Drafting I
TQM 201	32 MCC	Total Quality Management
TQM 230	32 MCC	Teamwork Dynamics

Vendor Training/Mentor Program for Technicians Type 1–5 (192 Hrs.)

The 192 hours in this portion of the senior Education and Training Model have been allocated to the organization (at whatever level is appropriate) for mentor programs of one-on-one training. Also, the need for vendor training is provided for in this 192 hours.

References

Aron, R. (Ed.). (1993). *Motorola University competency-based curriculum team: Summary report and presentation.* Phoenix, AZ: Motorola University.

Rummler, G. A., & Brache, A. P. (1990). *Improving performance: How to manage the white space on the organization chart.* San Francisco, CA: Jossey-Bass.

About the Contributors

Jeremie Hill Grey, Ph.D., former Group Training Manager for the Logic and Analog Technologies Group, Motorola Semiconductor Products Sector, received her doctorate in educational media from the University of Arizona. Dr. Grey has 20 years of professional experience in training and development for high-technology companies, including curriculum design and development (especially competency-based curriculum), instructional design and development, training administration, and documentation/publications. She previously managed training or publications groups for Intel Corporation, The Singer Company (Software and Aerospace), and served Motorola for six years as Development Manager and later Group Training Manager of a major technology group in the Phoenix area. Still a Phoenix resident, she is now a senior consultant for the Learning Consortium.

Sarabeth Simpson, former Group Training Manager for the Communications, Power, and Signal Technologies Group, Motorola Semiconductor Products Sector, received her undergraduate degree from Arizona State University. Ms. Simpson has served Motorola for 27 years in a variety of HR management positions, including Training and Development, where she became interested in learning labs and competency-based curriculum. She is currently the Director of Human Resources for Sector Support Operations in the Semiconductor Products Sector.

Jennifer Fox Kennedy, currently Senior Instructional Designer for Motorola Semiconductor Product Sector Training (LATG), received her M.S. in instructional systems at Florida State University, where she was a student of Walter Dick and Roger Kauffman. Ms. Kennedy has authored competency-based curricula for a variety of functions, including technicians, leadership, occupational health, human resources, and engineering, and was a major contributor in SPS's development of the competency-based methodology.

Susan Tou, currently Training and Development Manager for ACT Operations in Motorola's Semiconductor Product Sector, received her B.S. in engineering from the University of Michigan, an M.Ed. in instructional design from Purdue University, and her M.B.A. from Arizona State University. Ms. Tou spent some years as an instructional designer for Motorola SPS, during which she worked with competency-based curriculum and organizational design and development. The combination of engineering background, instructional design, and business made her particularly valuable to the development team on this technical project.

3.
IDENTIFYING AND REWARDING COMPETENCE
Introducing a Competency-Based System Into the Defense Mapping Agency, U.S. Department of Defense

Curt Dierdorff — former Director of Human Resources, DMA
Pam Lobdell-Brunger — Assistant Director, Human Resources Plans and Analysis, NIMA
Regina Millard — Director of Human Resources, NIMA

This chapter describes competency-related transitions within the Defense Mapping Agency (DMA), a combat support agency of the U.S. Department of Defense (DOD) with a proud heritage of providing the U.S. military forces and others with quality mapping and geodetic products.

Background

In the late 1980s, the DMA faced a sea change in the technology used to produce and deliver its products when a fully automated, digital production system was introduced into the organization. The technological solutions were unique to the mapping and geographic information services industry. While not initially a major focus, the transformation of workforce competencies was soon recognized as a key to achieving the full benefits of this $2.5 billion capital investment. New competencies were needed to exploit the major advances in computer technology, expert systems, telecommunications, large database systems, and electronic distribution of information to field organizations.

Lessons learned from the DMA's experience provides human resource practitioners with valuable information about how to introduce a competency-based system into a large high-technology organization.

Organizational Environment

The DMA is the primary source of worldwide mapping products for the U.S. and allied forces. In 1996, it became part of the National Imagery and Mapping Agency (NIMA). It offers an extensive array of products and services, including detailed topographic paper maps, digitized terrain-elevation data and terrain-image maps, and bathymetric contours of the ocean floor. Success on the battlefield requires reliable geographic and intelligence information, and the agency gives the military a distinct advantage in this area by supplying timely and accurate information about, and products for, the environment in which the forces must train and fight. With the increasing sophistication of navigation, weapons, and command and control systems, the DMA's support job has become ever more demanding.

The agency's predominant occupations are thus scientific and technical; among them, cartography, geodesy, geology, astronomy, oceanography, remote sensing, photogrammetry and optics, and computer sciences. This bundle of professional skills contributes to the DMA's core business competency: to deliver world-class geographic information to add value to war fighting and peace-keeping military operations. It should also be noted that while the principal customers for DMA products and services are the U.S. armed forces, the agency also provides nautical charts, marine navigation data, and worldwide air-navigation-safety products for civilian, military, and other uses.

Key Issues and Events

Change Comes to Military Mapmaking

In the late 1980s, the DMA faced a number of major changes that required a new approach to HR management. They included the following:

- The entire production workforce of over 4,000 employees needed to relearn their jobs because of major changes taking place in the technology. Manual processes were being replaced by automation, and the craft dimension of the work, which many employees found satisfying, seemed to be disappearing.

- Customer expectations for speed and accuracy were increasing as new technology made production processes more efficient.

- A prolonged period of downsizing had begun, which required major cuts in infrastructure and support organizations, as well as in production organizations with obsolete technology. (In 1987 DMA employment levels reached nearly 9,500 civilian and military personnel; by 1995, those levels had dropped to around 7,500.)

- With a reduction in the number of supervisors (the ratio of employees to supervisors increased from 10:1 to 16:1), employees would have to develop the ability to resolve technical problems on their own. Thus greater employee empowerment became an issue of concern.

The HR Challenge: Redefining the Workforce-Management Systems

Gary Hamel and C.K. Prahalad, in their 1994 book, *Competing for the Future*, point out that "competence represents the synthesis of a variety of skills, technologies, and knowledge streams" (p. 214). They further note that integration of competencies leads to core competencies (for example, Federal Express' ability to integrate the competencies of bar-code technology, wireless communication, network management, and linear programming led to a core competency of package routing and delivery). Particularly in 1989, the DMA experienced a major change in the individual competencies and technologies used to perform its work; in effect, its core competencies were changing, and it was vital that adjustments be made in the selection, compensation, training, and incentives for its production workforce.

In that same year, the DMA's leadership noted several disturbing trends which, if not addressed, posed a threat to the agency's ability to meet customer requirements and achieve the transition to the new production system.

First, the attrition rate among the main mission occupations was nearly twice the rate for professional employees in other parts of the federal government. Given the major investment being made in recruitment and training, this was an expensive problem. Attrition also threatened the continuity of operations. Each year from 1986 to 1989, approximately 350 professional employees left the agency. It was estimated that the average cost to replace a fully qualified professional cartographer was over $44,000 when all recruitment, separation, and learning-curve costs were considered. The total cost of attrition was estimated to be well in excess of $10 million each year. Unfortunately, attrition was especially high among employees with less than five years' experience. This group possessed the most recent academic training in computer science, which formed the basis for the mapping systems of the future.

Second, a survey of workforce attitudes indicated some special problems among the production workforce. It was theorized that this revealed a condition that not only affected the attrition rate, but likely reflected a lack of alignment between employee and organizational goals as well. Among the indicators from the survey were the following:

Topic	Score Among Production Workers*
Job Challenge	2.9
Job Reward	2.1
Organization of work	2.3
Goal Integration	1.9
Decision-Making Practices	1.8
Influence and Control	2.3
Satisfaction Index	3.0

* Note: the survey results were measured on a 5-point scale, with 5 being the highest score (most satisfied).

These results clearly indicated a high level of dissatisfaction with the content of the work, the way the work was organized, and the degree of influence workers had over their daily activities. Consequently, the level of employee integration of organizational goals was very low. Further, when asked about various HR processes, employees indicated that they were most dissatisfied with promotional practices, pay, and career development opportunities. Focus groups held after the survey indicated that professional employees generally felt that job design did not use their competencies, and that their only opportunity for advancement was to pursue a management position. This often resulted in excellent professionals moving into management against their wishes, with the resulting loss of, for example, a good scientist and gain of a poorly motivated supervisor.

Addressing this problem created two distinct challenges for HR leaders. The first was systemic: the federal civil-service system. The second was program design: developing a system that would challenge the best technical minds and motivate them to pursue goals consistent with the organizational objectives.

The First Challenge: The System

Civil-service systems are historically driven by a bias for consistency, equity, and compliance, even at the expense of degradation in mission capability. Such was the system used to determine the job classification (compensation) and hiring practices of the DMA's professional mapmakers. The federal classification system is position-oriented. Generally, grades are determined by evaluating the duties and responsibilities of the position against centrally developed standards, rather than by evaluating employee competence and results. After considerable study and debate, the HR team agreed to propose a "value-added" concept that more closely linked personal competence and broad professional perspectives to more challenging assignments and improved compensation. The intent was to create incentives for increased employee competence and to encourage employees in these ways:

- Expand employee understanding of the overall production process, not just individual task assignments.

- Enhance employee ability to diagnose and resolve technical problems. This was especially important in view of the planned reduction in supervisory personnel, which created a need for employees to be more self-sufficient.

- Increase professional competence to develop improved production methods and procedures. The quality improvement process was starting to take root in the agency, and the notion that employees were the best source to solve production problems within their work areas was an emerging point of management emphasis.

Another issue concerned federal promotion practices, which tend to place a premium on length of experience as contrasted with accomplishments. Established practices and procedures at the DMA did little to differentiate between high performers and those who had merely done an adequate job. The thought of moving to a system that based promotions on the ability to perform critical job functions, rather than length of experience, was threatening to many. Early on, the agency's HR specialists and management officials realized that the emphasis on results in lieu of tenure would be a source of dissatisfaction among those who benefited from the old system.

The Second Challenge: Program Design

In addition to these systemic issues, the challenge of how to develop a better approach had to be confronted. A decision was made to create significant opportunities for mapping professionals to grow into more challenging and rewarding jobs by establishing a certification program. The program would provide for an increase in job responsibilities along with an increase in compensation. Four objectives were established:

1. To enhance recruitment and retention of high-quality professionals in production organizations

2. To encourage professional development by providing promotional opportunities based on broader skills

3. To systematically develop a well-trained, flexible, and adaptable work-force capable of responding to rapid and dramatic shifts in workload, priorities, and technological changes

4. To shift position-design strategy for production positions by broadening work assignments and providing greater professional challenges

The program's development and its results are discussed in the remainder of this chapter.

Certification Program Development

Teams of subject matter experts from production organizations, along with HR experts familiar with job analysis, were established to identify the critical duties and competencies to be used for certification. Eight different positions were established based on the mapping processes involved in the production organization. The major duties of the certified positions, which differed from the regular production positions, included dealing with nonstandard technical problems; developing new procedures and techniques to resolve production problems; performing quality assurance and approving final product release; and training other personnel on the technical aspects of the work. Three competencies were identified as being critical:

1. Ability to Produce Mapping, Charting, and Geodetic Products

2. Ability to Communicate

3. Proficiency in Performing Production Duties

1. Ability to Produce Mapping, Charting, and Geodetic Products

This competency included demonstrated experience in performing the end-to-end production process for each product. "End-to-end" was defined as all tasks or sub-tasks associated with delivering a product specific to the division's production requirement. The emphasis on end-to-end production knowledge encourages employees to develop broader competencies. This enables the organization to be more flexible in responding to rapidly changing customer requirements. This competency was worth a total of 35% of the total certification score. There were three major skill areas involved in this competency:

- **Product Knowledge** (e.g., terrain analysis products, digital feature analysis data, and topographic maps)

- **Knowledge of the Production Process** (e.g., planning, preprocessing, data collection, models review, post-processing, and control generation)

- **System Knowledge,** which included the systems that support map production (e.g., Digital Extraction Segment, Product Generation Segment, AS-11 Workstations)

The highest point total was awarded to those professionals who could demonstrate the ability to do end-to-end production of more than two products.

2. Ability to Communicate

This competency was worth up to 15% of the total certification score. The intent here was to ensure that senior professionals had the skill to articulate technical issues clearly to their peers and to experts who would be involved in correcting technical problems with the production system. Also, there was a need to communicate in a training environment. The measurement of this competency was demonstrated by proven examples of successfully communicating technical information in a job setting. Examples of the types of communication expected included training sessions and technical briefings.

3. Proficiency in Performing Production Duties

The third and final competency was worth 50% of the total certification score. The heavy weighting of this competency was based on the realization that there would be many people who demonstrated the technical proficiency to perform end-to-end production. DMA senior leadership believed that demonstrated past performance was the most important predictor of success in the new positions. The sources of information to measure this competency were the annual performance appraisals employees received while serving in production positions. Three appraisals were used to guard against anomalies such as someone receiving a lower rating because he or she had been reassigned and was experiencing a learning curve in the new position. To receive the top score, an employee's most recent rating had to be outstanding (5 on a 5-point scale) and the other two ratings had to be at least highly successful (the rating immediately below outstanding). Performance ratings for production positions were typically based on quantity and quality of work, as well as interpersonal behavior and support of agency goals and objectives.

A number of employees objected to the use of performance appraisals as a measure of their qualifications. They contended that the appraisals were too subjective and did not measure those elements which were most important to the new positions. After review, DMA leadership concluded that the appraisals were indeed valid predictors of success in the new positions. As a result of this decision, the appraisal process is now taken much more seriously, and employees are more inclined to challenge ratings with which they disagree. While this increased attention to appraisal decisions was traumatic to some supervisors, it opened up communication about job expectations and led to more rigor in the appraisal process.

The Certification Process

A four-step process was used to determine who would be certified. First, the employee completed an application that asked specific questions about his or her ability to produce mapping, charting, and geodesy (MC&G) products, his or her ability to communicate, and the results of the last three performance appraisals. Next, in step two, the application package was transferred to the first-line supervisor, who was asked to validate the information. This was a level of empowerment and responsibility previously unknown to first-line supervisors, and one that some supervisors were reluctant to assume. In step three, the package was reviewed by the next two levels of supervision, who had a simple concurrence or nonconcurrence responsibility. Then in step four, the final packages were sent to a certification panel, consisting of technical experts in the line of work and an HR expert, who determined which candidates met the certification criteria. A minimum score of 85 out of 100 possible points was necessary for certification.

Following the first round of certification, an evaluation was conducted to determine whether the certification approach needed further refinement. Some employees continued to be concerned about the weight given to the performance appraisal. Some managers felt that the technical competencies were not sufficiently rigorous to ensure only the best employees were selected. Also, there were rumors that newly certified employees were not actually performing the higher-level duties they were being paid to perform.

The evaluation included the administration of a questionnaire to all certified employees regarding their experiences with the process and their skills utilization after certification; an in-depth job audit of a random sample of certified professionals to determine if they were performing the higher-level work; and interviews with senior managers of production departments to gauge their acceptance of the program. The results of this effort indicated the following:

- **Questionnaire Results.** A total of 440 responses were received. Certified employees surveyed indicated they were performing the duties of their new positions. Further, employees were positive regarding the increased opportunity to advance and the increased utilization of their skills. They expressed some concern about the weight given to performance appraisals as compared with other factors.

- **Job Audit Results.** All employees were found to be performing duties at the appropriate level of complexity and responsibility. Employees in one department, where the leader was acknowledged as being deficient in leadership skills, had difficulties understanding the difference in assignments between the certified professionals and the other production employees. The solution offered was to promote everyone to avoid the difficult task of differentiating between assignments. This was not feasible because of the increased costs and the limited amount of higher-level work to be performed. Eventually the department manager moved to another position, and stronger leadership resulted in improvements in employee perceptions.

- **Production Department Manager Interviews.** The production departments' leaders were generally very positive about the certification program. They expressed the belief that the program contributed to mission accomplishment by encouraging broader skill development, assisted in achieving the increased supervisory ratio, and formed the basis for a technical career track for highly competent employees who were not inclined toward careers as managers. Their main concern was that the certification process needed to be repeated soon to meet ongoing staffing needs.

As a result of the evaluation, DMA senior management approved another round of certification. There was concern about the number of people who would be certified and whether some controls should be established on the percentage of certified professionals. The concern was driven by two considerations: cost and the amount of higher-level work available. After examining the work, it was determined that the number of certified professionals could not exceed 33% of the total nonsupervisory production workforce. Based on the Department of Human Resources' analysis of the work during the job audits, it was believed that there was sufficient work to support this number; the number was also consistent with the earlier cost-estimates. As a result of the second round of certification, the population of certified professionals increased from 350 to nearly 700, with one production facility nearly achieving the maximum 33% provided by the staffing model.

Certification Program Audit

In August 1992 the certification program was audited by the U.S. Office of Personnel Management (OPM) in response to persistent complaints by a group of employees who, due primarily to narrow careers and average performance, were unable to compete effectively for the higher-level positions. They were especially vocal about the fact that employees with less total years of experience were being certified primarily because of their performance records. This, of course, was consistent with the original goal to establish a strong link between performance and advancement. While OPM found the program to be basically sound, they recommended a further review of the selection criteria to reexamine the issues raised by employees who were not successful under the existing criteria.

Certification Program Revisions

The program review was initiated by conducting 13 focus group discussions with a total of 180 employees. The focus groups included some employees who were not certified the first time, and, consequently, some of the focus group discussions were quite emotional. The focus groups yielded two key issues related to competencies. First, there continued to be a concern about the weight given to performance appraisals. Second, the focus group participants felt that experience needed to be given more weight.

In response to this data, Human Resources recommended that a working group be formed to address the two issues. The working group consisted of mid-level managers from production departments; HR experts; and professional psychometricians from George Mason University's Psychology Department who specialized in competency-based systems. The result of this work was a restructuring of the certification criteria. These changes strengthened the technical competencies, added leadership competencies, and improved the measurement tools. The new model had three elements:

1. Technical Competencies (40%)

2. Leadership Competencies (40%)

3. Performance Record (20%)

1. Technical Competencies

The original approach included one technical profile for each production department, and the rating decision as to whether the employee met the technical competency was binary (yes or no). The new approach developed technical competencies for each production function. Each competency was defined very specifically and was designated as an *essential* or *desirable* competency. The revised process required that certification candidates jointly complete the technical competency portion of the application with a sponsoring supervisor.

The candidate's proficiency level was evaluated for each competency, based on standardized definitions and using this rating scale:

0	No experience
1	Novice
2	Developmental/Apprentice
3	Journey Level
4	Distinguished
5	Expert

To receive further consideration for certification, the candidate had to have demonstrated, and had to achieve, level 4 or 5 evaluations for *all* essential competencies. Individual scores were combined to achieve a total score for the Technical Competency portion of the evaluation. The scoring methodology of the Technical Competency assessment not only provided a way to establish minimum technical-competency requirements for further consideration, but also established additional distinction among eligible candidates.

The technical competencies were very specific and were designed to demonstrate ability to complete major product of system-specific production phases keyed to organizational operations. For example:

- **Source Package Generation:** Creates source package of rectified imagery, native maps and charts, geographic names, grids, projections, and boundaries utilizing a program-management-segment computer system. Ensures all source material is provided in the package and that all information is correct.

- **Vertical Elevation Generation:** Creates vertical elevation files on the UNISYS computer system. Transfers files to the VAX using the hyperchannel system.

2. Leadership Competencies

A major change in the process was the identification of seven leadership competencies that are critical to successful performance at the senior professional level. These competencies, developed with the assistance of industrial psychologists from George Mason University, are listed below and are followed by their definitions.

Certification Leadership Competencies

Problem Solving

Coaching

Organizational Skills

Team Goals

Personal-Interaction Skills

Verbal Communication

Written Communication

- **Problem Solving.** Recognizes problems and knows what is necessary and whom to contact to resolve them. Troubleshoots to avoid encountering problems, and takes the initiative to gather relevant information to solve those problems. Investigates, documents, implements, and evaluates the success of solutions.

- **Coaching.** Is willing to help and/or instruct individuals on work activities. Openly communicates and shares knowledge with co-workers. Volunteers to train new employees on products, processes, systems, and/or functions.

- **Organizational Skills.** Successfully organizes time to cope with multiple assignments and competing priorities. Meets production deadlines and must be able to shift back and forth from one product/process to another. Is able to organize tasks to handle crisis situations.

- **Team Goals.** Focuses on organizational goals and promotes collaboration and teamwork as the preferred means to achieve those goals. Is aware of what needs to be done, identifies and accomplishes the action required, communicates and cooperates with team members in problem resolution, and supports team decisions.

- **Personal-Interaction Skills.** Works well with others. Is able to adapt to changing personnel, is open-minded, and gives thought to others' ideas. Is able to compromise.

- **Verbal Communication.** Communicates complex issues in understandable terms. Demonstrates an understanding of concepts. Is able to adapt messages to varying expertise levels.

- **Written Communication.** Provides well-organized, thorough, and clearly written instructions. Uses appropriate terminology, grammar, and punctuation. Clearly documents what has been accomplished.

For each of the leadership competencies, applicants were now required to identify specific achievements demonstrating these abilities. For each achievement they had to address the questions:

— What was the problem or objective?

— What did you actually do, and when?

— What was the outcome or result? (In addition, applicants had to assess the extent of their contribution to the achievement—minimal, moderate, or high.)

Applicants were also asked to give the name, address, and telephone number of someone who could verify the achievement.

A rating scale was developed for each of the seven leadership competencies. The format for the rating scale is shown below:

General Behaviors	RATING LEVELS	Specific Accomplishments
Behaviors are defined for levels 5, 3, and 1.		Sample accomplishments are described for levels 5, 3, and 1.
	5	
	4	
	3	
	2	
	1	

Rating panels were established to evaluate the applicant's submissions for each competency. Emphasis was given to demonstrated linkage between experience and the accomplishment anchors, and statements that easily tie the candidate's accomplishments to a specific point on the anchor scale were required. If an applicant's accomplishments did not "fit" on the scale but were comparable in terms of evidence to the general behaviors desired, credit was given and documented as such.

3. Performance Record

Performance was retained at the wish of the DMA's senior leadership and because previous literature-research results validated past performance as a good predictor of future performance. Some minor adjustments were made to use four ratings instead of three, and required that performance at higher grade levels be given more weight than ratings given for performance at lower grade levels.

Validation

To validate the new competencies, "dry runs" were conducted at each production facility. Generally, the dry runs identified some needs for rater training, but the participants believed that the new competencies and rating process were superior to the previous certification process.

Since the program revision, over 100 MC&G professionals have been certified.

Certification Program Results

The results of the process are quite positive, with over 800 employees certified as senior professionals. While this represents less than 33%, it is a considerable investment in increased labor costs. Prior to the initiation of the certification program, it was theorized that the increased costs of the certification program would be recovered from attrition and the elimination of the costly replacement of fully qualified employees with new hires. The estimated cumulative cost of the certification program from 1990 through 1994 was approximately $11 million. The additional cost to increase the compensation of supervisors to reflect their new role and maintain pay alignment was estimated at $4.5 million. Savings from a 50% reduction in staff through attrition over the same five-year period was estimated to be $25 million.

At approximately the same time as the certification program was developed, an initiative was underway to improve the leadership capabilities of line managers at all levels at the organization. While it is not possible to allocate the degree of impact of the professional certification program on attrition, as compared with the leadership development initiative, there were some very positive outcomes. The attrition rate among MC&G professionals dropped by nearly 50% between 1989 and 1991. This lower level of attrition has been sustained in the following years through 1995, as had been predicted.

When the workforce was resurveyed in 1993, there were significant improvements in the perceptions of employees about working for the DMA. The following areas are indicative of responses to questions directly related to the certification program.

— Employees expressing satisfaction with their jobs increased from 73% to 84%.

— Satisfaction with the organization increased from 54% to 74%.

— Satisfaction with pay increased from 54% to 73%.

— Satisfaction with opportunities to get ahead increased from 41% to 77%.

— Employees' perception that the organization has an interest in their welfare and satisfaction increased from 32% to 68%.

The University of Michigan's Rensis Likert Institute, which analyzed the survey under contract with the DMA, summarized the results in this way:

The pattern is one of substantial improvement since the previous survey. . . . The guidance system is much improved, and jobs are seen as now more challenging and economically rewarding. The work is felt to be better organized than it was four years ago. As a result, goal integration is much improved, as are satisfaction with the job, the organization, pay, and chances for getting ahead in the future. The organization is clearly on the right course.

The Lessons Learned

Those responsible for leading the introduction and evolution of the certification intervention believe there are a number of lessons that are important to successfully addressing cultural and core competency changes of this nature.

1. Be very clear about the goal and the need for change. State the goals in terms of mission results.

2. Ensure that top management is prepared to "own" the change.

3. Early and constant communication with stakeholders is vital.

4. Try to clearly understand who gains and loses, and be candid about these effects—explain why.

5. Don't let the barriers overwhelm the need for action. There will always be those who discourage change. If it is the right thing to do, just do it.

6. Get expert help with competency measurement if help is not available internally. Internal experts must establish their credentials.

7. Don't hesitate to make changes—it is very difficult to get a major change effort perfect the first time.

8. Measure the results frequently and keep all stakeholders advised of how it is going.

9. Keep the experts about the work involved throughout.

10. Understand the cost-benefit factors.

The use of a competency based approach to selecting and rewarding senior technical people at the Defense Mapping Agency was a culture change that led to a number of positive outcomes, as discussed above. The lessons learned clearly demonstrate the need to consider the change management issues as well as the technical issues around defining and measuring competencies. Creating an accepting climate for adopting a competency-based approach must address costs and benefits at both an organizational and an individual level.

References

Hamel, G., & Prahalad, C. K. (1994). *Competing for the future.* Boston, MA: Harvard Business School Press.

About the Contributors

Curt Dierdorff is a consultant and principal partner in CD HR Services, located in Fairfax, Virginia. He has been working in the general area of HR transformation for a number of clients. Prior to his current work, he was the Director of Human Resources for the Defense Mapping Agency (DMA) for seven years. He was awarded Presidential Rank awards by Presidents Bush and Clinton for his work while at DMA.

Pam Lobdell-Brunger is the Assistant Director for Human Resources Plans and Analysis, National Imagery and Mapping Agency (NIMA). Ms. Lobdell-Brunger has worked for many years on competency-based systems, and is currently working with Regina Millard to implement a competency-based system for NIMA.

Regina Millard is the Director of Human Resources for NIMA. She has held this position since 1996. She is actively involved in implementing a competency-based human resources system for NIMA.

4.
COMPETENCIES AT THE ROCK
Creating a Competency-Based Integrated Human Resources System for Prudential HealthCare Group–Western Operations

Michele Bina, M.A.— Principal Consultant, Michele Bina and Associates
Juhlin Newkirk, Ph.D. — Consultant-Partner

Background

Introduction

In April 1994, Prudential HealthCare Group (PHG)–Western Operations embarked on a unique, fast-paced organizational change effort: the PHG–Western Operations' Competency Project. The project's stated purpose was "To implement a competency-based human resources system that would complement PHG's desire to produce a major cultural change and be able to support management decision-making in compensation, performance planning and appraisal, training and development, selection processes, and human resource strategic planning."

While the change effort's overall goal was to develop the competency-based system, its driving force was the urgent need to develop within 12 months a competency assessment process for all employees. The data resulting from this process was to be used in compensation decision-making during 1995. This driving force and other factors made the PHG–Western Operations' Competency Project unique from the start, as shown in the following description:

- Competency development was driven by the introduction of a new compensation program that included competency-based performance factors.

- Competencies were developed for 15 out of 18 major job families simultaneously within a six-month period.

- The competency assessment process was multiple-rater and conducted through an on-line system.

- Competency development involved a large proportion of job holders, both to increase the accuracy of the results and to facilitate acceptance of the competency assessment process and a competency-based integrated human resources (HR) system.

About Prudential HealthCare Group–Western Operations

The Prudential Insurance Company of America (The Prudential along with its subsidiaries, the Company) is one of the largest diversified financial-services institutions in the world; based on total assets, it was the largest insurance company in North America as of December 31, 1994. With capital close to $10 billion, the Company's primary business is to offer a full range of products and services in three areas: insurance, investments, and home ownership for individuals and families; healthcare management and other benefit programs for employees of companies and members of groups; and asset management for institutional clients and their associates. Employing nearly 100,000 people worldwide—and with a sales force of approximately 19,000 agents, 3,400 insurance brokers, and 6,000 financial advisors—the Company insures or provides other financial services to more than 50 million people worldwide.

One of the Company's primary businesses, the Prudential HealthCare Group (PHG), is a national healthcare company. PHG was divided into four geographic regions of operations: Western, Southern, South Central, and North Central. In PHG–Western Operations, as nationally, the business focus was on expanding market growth while managing administrative costs. One of the key strategies for growth in PHG was the ongoing planning development of quality managed care in Prudential's nationwide system of health maintenance organizations (HMOs). For 1995, in a challenging and competitive business climate, PHG–Western Operations managed healthcare for over 800,000 customers or members. Due to the tremendously competitive business climate, especially in California, the region continually focused on operational standards and cost-effectiveness while increasing market share. It was the business climate and PHG–Western Operations' strategic focus that led to the implementation of multiple strategies: process reengineering, reevaluation of market approach, and the development of a new compensation plan for its 2,700 employees (referred to within PHG as "associates").

Front-End Needs Analysis, Assessment, and Planning

Strategic Organization Profile

1. Why Competencies

As mentioned earlier, the development and application of competencies was driven by the introduction of PHG's compensation plan. The new compensation plan, originally introduced in January 1994, was a strategy to compete more effectively for and through people in a changing and demanding business environment. The new plan's objectives were the following:

- Tie pay more closely to the external market and to what competitors paid

- Create a more efficient environment in which the organization used all the skills the associates had to offer

- Create a culture in which career development could occur laterally (across job families) as well as vertically. Because of the company's previous salary-level system, employees usually would not consider a job move unless it led to a "higher-level" job. This created a level-focused, not flexible, approach to career development.

2. Purpose of Competencies

As a result of the new compensation plan's design, competencies became a key element in making associate-base-pay decisions, along with market survey data on the associate's job. With competencies now introduced into the organization through the new compensation plan, it was possible to pursue what the divisions of Human Resources and Organizational Effectiveness had envisioned from the start: a more comprehensive application for competencies in the form of a competency-based integrated human resources system.

Consequently, the overarching objective of PHG–Western Operations' Competency Project was to support Prudential's desire for cultural change through the development and implementation of competencies in the areas of compensation, performance management, recruitment and selection, training and development, and HR strategic planning (succession planning). These were the Competency Project's deliverables:

- Identification of job competencies that were reliable and valid for 15 of 18 job families

- An on-line, automated system of competency assessment using multiple-rater assessment and producing individual, summary, and statistical reports

- A process for competency- and performance-based performance appraisal and planning

- A system of competency- and performance-based compensation decision-making

- Recommendations and action plans for the integration of competencies into other key HR areas

Overall Definition of the Competency Project

1. Information About the Planning Partners

To support the development and implementation of competencies as part of the new compensation plan, PHG–Western Operations established a special team for competency design as part of its larger Compensation Team. The Competency

Design Team was led by Michele Bina, at the time a senior consultant in the PHG–Western Operations Organizational Effectiveness Division. The Compensation Team had members representing all major divisions and levels within the organization. The Competency Design Team worked closely with the Compensation Team, which was simultaneously addressing other issues related to base and incentive pay within the new compensation plan. Technical and planning support for the Competency Project were provided by outside consultants.

2. Key Issues and Events

To determine the degree of cultural change that would result from this project, an analysis was conducted by the Competency Design Team to assess current HR processes within PHG–Western Operations. The results showed that the implementation of competency-based HR practices would require significant changes in current management practices. It also demonstrated that there was substantial variation in HR processes and decision making throughout the organization. The summary below highlights the existing HR practices prior to this project.

- Performance expectations were often unclear, narrowly focused, and inconsistent from one division to another.

- Many job descriptions were obsolete or nonexistent.

- Performance was primarily measured through tracking of results or subjectively or both. Accurate comparison of the performance of different job holders was only possible for production-type jobs.

- Performance appraisals were done manually by a single rater (supervisor) on the employee's hiring anniversary date. Different forms were in use throughout the organization, and performance appraisals were not always completed prior to compensation decision-making. Managers typically presented the completed appraisal to the employee and asked for a reaction.

- The reward and compensation system was an internally driven merit-based compensation plan that had no external benchmarks for pay. There were no defined job families or salary ranges. Pay decision-making practices among managers were subjective and inconsistent. An incentive compensation plan existed only for exempt (management and professional) employees.

- Training and development needs were defined subjectively. Technical training for the same or similar jobs was created and delivered independently by each area. Basic leadership training and career development was provided by generic programs.

- There were no guidelines for developing selection criteria for jobs.

On the basis of this information, the Competency Design Team began planning the development and implementation of a competency-based integrated human resources system that would be applicable for the organization. Project planning considered the following organizational questions:

- *Project Objectives.* What were the long- and short-term objectives of the Competency Project?

- *Competency Model.* What competency definition, identification process, and assessment model would fit the needs of the organization?

- *Project Scope.* What would the immediate application for competencies look like? By when? What would longer-term competency applications look like? By when?

- *Project Constraints.* What impact would anticipated additional organizational activities (such as process reengineering) have on the competency work? What risks would the Competency Team need to consider that might hinder the development and implementation of competencies and the on-line assessment system?

- *Project Approach.* What would be the phases of the project? What project activities needed to occur in parallel? What was the critical path?

- *Project Resource Requirements.* What external expertise would need to be hired to maintain the reliability and validity of the competency identification process? What internal resources would be needed before, during, and after implementation of competencies? What technology (equipment, expertise) would be needed?

Priorities and Plans

A comprehensive project plan was developed by the Competency Design Team and outside consultant firm, Apple Consulting, and was broken into three phases:

- Phase 1: Identification of Competencies

- Phase 2: Competency Assessment Pilot

- Phase 3: Creating a Competency-Based Human Resources System

The major steps and timelines for each phase are shown in Figure 1.

In addition, to ensure that associates and management understood competencies and the impact of implementing competencies, a comprehensive communication and education plan was developed. The overarching strategy was to provide communication using multiple channels (e.g. electronic mail, newsletters, presentations) in "just-in-time" fashion. The Organizational Effectiveness Division became a key agent in designing and disseminating the appropriate information. Communication began in September 1994 during Phase 1 of the project. The key steps (in chronological order) in this extensive process of communication and education were as follows:

1. In September 1994, an introductory communication was sent to all managers by electronic mail. This communication contained an explanation of competencies and their use in the new compensation plan and a brief overview of the Competency Project.

FIGURE 1: Competency Identification Project Design

Step I—Identification of Competencies

Task	1994						1995								
	Jul	Aug	Sep	Oct	Nov	Dec	Jan	Feb	Mar	Apr	May	Jun	Jul	Aug	Sep
Management Interviews conducted Documentation gathered	██	██	██	██	██	██									
Focus groups (25 conducted region-wide—200 associates)			▦	▦	▦	▦									
Competency ID Survey Administered (750 associates)			▨	▨	▨										
Communication Activities/Plan	▒		▒			▒									

Step II—Pilot of Competency Assessment Process

Task	1994						1995								
	Jul	Aug	Sep	Oct	Nov	Dec	Jan	Feb	Mar	Apr	May	Jun	Jul	Aug	Sep
Orient Pilot Participants (750 associates)							██								
Administer Competency Assessment Survey							▦	▦							
Report/Apply Survey Results									▨						
Communication/Education Activities/Plan				▒	▒	▒	▒	▒	▒						

Step III—Implementation of Competencies—Integrate into Comp/HRD

Task	1994						1995								
	Jul	Aug	Sep	Oct	Nov	Dec	Jan	Feb	Mar	Apr	May	Jun	Jul	Aug	Sep
System Designed/Developed and Maintained				██	██	██	██	██	██	██	██	██	██	██	██
Tie into Professional Development/Training												▦	▦	▦	▦
Tie into Selection Process												▨	▨	▨	▨
Tie into Performance Appraisal											▒	▒	▒	▒	▒
Tie into Compensation										▩	▩	▩	▩	▩	▩
Communication/Education Activities							▥	▥	▥	▥	▥	▥	▥	▥	▥

2. Memos were delivered monthly to all PHG–Western Operations associates explaining competencies and the purpose of the Competency Project, and providing an overview of the competency identification and implementation procedures.

3. Communication of the pilot process (Phase 2 of the Competency Project) occurred prior to the pilot and was delivered to all associates in late 1994. The pilot results were communicated to all associates in May 1995.

4. Competency Education sessions were held at all geographic sites within the region beginning in January 1995. One thousand four hundred PHG–Western Operations associates, including management, attended 50 separate sessions. The purpose of these sessions was to explain the concept of competencies and to provide an overview of the use of competencies in the new compensation plan and how competencies would be assessed (multi-rater on-line).

5. A competency presentation was provided to all management personnel at the February 1995 regionwide Leadership Conference. The purpose of this presentation was to provide all managers with a comprehensive overview of competencies and the competency identification process.

6. In February 1995, management information packages were delivered to all 300 managers and team leaders. These information packages contained competencies for each job family in their division/team and instructions on how to discuss competencies with their staff. Managers were asked to distribute the appropriate competencies to each associate at this time and to discuss the competencies with them.

7. In May 1995, copies of a competency administration manual were sent to all 300 managers and team leaders. This manual explained the competency assessment process in detail, outlined the actions required of managers and all participating associates, and provided reference information.

8. Throughout May 1995, Competency Orientation sessions were held for all PHG–Western Operations associates, including management. These sessions provided information on how to select raters, complete the competency assessment survey, and interpret competency results. In addition, each associate received a copy of the competency assessment survey appropriate for his or her job.

9. Beginning in the second quarter of 1995, special management staff meetings were held at all sites, during which the process for competency implementation was discussed in detail with each site-management team.

10. Performance Evaluation and Compensation Decision-Making training sessions for management were held throughout the summer of 1995.

11. In addition, throughout the Competency Project a competency-update newsletter was published and distributed regularly to all associates.

12. Management coaching sessions were held in key division in an attempt to prepare managers for the competency assessment.

Detailed Description of Competencies Application

Competency Model Development

After reviewing the literature and competency models used by other organizations, the Competency Design Team decided that the PHG–Western Operations Competency Model would be based on these definitions:

- Competencies are the underlying knowledge, skills, and attributes necessary to successfully perform a job.

- Competence can be demonstrated at four levels of proficiency for each competency. The generic definition of each level of proficiency is given below. (Also, behavioral definitions were written for each competency item, as shown in the sample of a competency survey item provided later in this chapter.)

1. **Exceptional.** This person is viewed as demonstrating consistent expertise in this performance area. In addition, this person is seen as sharing expertise with others, thereby positively shaping others' performance in their work environment. This person's behavior consistently has a positive impact on the production of the entire work unit.

2. **Highly Competent.** This person is viewed as highly effective in this performance area. This person will also occasionally guide others to improved performance in this area.

3. **Effective.** This person is viewed as applying satisfactory knowledge and skills to create fully acceptable performance in this area.

4. **Less Than Effective.** This person is viewed as learning knowledge and skills in this performance area. Or this person is viewed as not demonstrating knowledge and skills or appropriate job behavior in this area.

In addition, the team decided that job performance standards would need to be defined by managers by operationalizing the competencies to explain job-specific performance requirements.

Phase 1: Identification of Competencies

Beginning in June 1994, meetings were held with key managers to gather any existing job descriptions and job information and to define preliminary job families based on that information. Fifteen job families containing the jobs held by almost all employees were selected for competency identification; the remaining three job families were to be addressed after the completion of the first round of competency assessments.

Competencies were identified by through a multiple-step procedure consisting of:

1. Management meetings

2. Focus groups

3. Competency identification surveys

First, the impact of the current business direction and objectives on competencies was examined and meetings were held with managers to identify job families. Then, focus groups were held for each job family to identify the knowledge, skills, and attributes (KSAs) required to successfully perform the jobs in that family. Focus group participants represented the range of jobs in the family and were selected by managers to fit selection criteria: participants had to be experienced high performers who could articulate the KSAs required for their jobs. Because some job families represented many associates, and as it was preferable to have several geographic locations participate in the process, 25 focus groups involving 200 employees were conducted regionwide.

Focus group participants were asked to identify what were the critical roles and responsibilities of their jobs given the current business direction of the organization. They were then asked to identify, based on those critical roles and responsibilities, the KSAs required to successfully perform their jobs. The information generated by these focus groups was then compiled into lists of the KSAs required for each job family. The KSA lists were grouped into categories such as Communication or Technical Skills; when the same KSAs were identified for different job families, care was taken to word them identically.

The third step was to administer a version of the competency identification survey for each job family to select the KSAs that were considered critical or very critical for job success by a cross-section of 750 experienced job holders with adequate or high performance levels (28% of all associates) and their supervisors. Those KSAs that were rated as critical or very critical for job success by 75% or more of participants in each job family were used to develop competency statements.

Competency statements were written for each job family and grouped into categories. Again, where the same competency appeared in more than one job family, care was taken to create identical competency statements. Behavioral definitions of the four levels of proficiency were then written for each competency statement and competency assessment surveys created for each job family. A sample survey item is shown in Figure 2.

FIGURE 2: Sample Item—Competency Assessment Survey

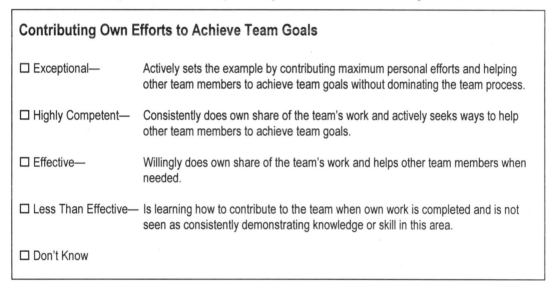

Contributing Own Efforts to Achieve Team Goals

☐ Exceptional—   Actively sets the example by contributing maximum personal efforts and helping other team members to achieve team goals without dominating the team process.

☐ Highly Competent—   Consistently does own share of the team's work and actively seeks ways to help other team members to achieve team goals.

☐ Effective—   Willingly does own share of the team's work and helps other team members when needed.

☐ Less Than Effective— Is learning how to contribute to the team when own work is completed and is not seen as consistently demonstrating knowledge or skill in this area.

☐ Don't Know

Interestingly, core competencies that applied to all 15 job families were identified in four areas: Communication, Personal and Work Management, Teamwork, and Customer Focus. Six other competency areas were also identified for various job families.

The competency identification procedure was followed by the review and approval of the competency assessment survey for each job family by the appropriate management teams.

Phase 2: Competency Assessment Pilot

The purpose of Phase 2 was to test the *process* for competency assessment and results feedback, *not* the competencies themselves. Pilot groups consisted of intact work groups chosen to represent strategically critical job families (such as underwriting, provider relations, and leadership). Pilots were conducted in five divisions in Northern and Southern California. One hundred and thirty-five associates participated in the pilot as "ratees"—those whose competencies were assessed. An additional 390 associates participated as raters who assessed the ratees.

All pilot participants attended special Competency Orientation sessions to learn about rater selection and the competency assessment and feedback process. The ratees selected their raters, pending management approval, during their orientation session. Each ratee chose two work-team members and two internal customers, as well as his or her supervisor. In addition, ratees were to complete a self-assessment as part of the pilot. After being approved by the ratees' managers, raters attended separate Competency Orientation sessions to learn about the new assessment process and their role as raters.

Each ratee and his or her manager simultaneously received a detailed report of the assessment results and were asked to schedule a meeting to discuss this feedback.

The competency assessment pilot process was evaluated by interviewing 25% of those assessed after the pilot to evaluate reactions to the process and to obtain recommendations for improvement. Feedback was solicited on the Competency Orientation sessions, rater-selection procedure, rater education, content and completion process of the competency assessment survey, and the feedback discussion between ratee and his or her direct supervisor. Overall feedback was very positive. The major improvement suggested was to better prepare managers for the feedback discussion. The subsequent management training programs on the use of competencies in performance appraisal and the new approach to performance management helped to address this concern.

Phase 3: Creating a Competency-Based HR System

By early 1996, less than two years after the initial introduction of competencies, competencies at the Rock were well on their way to being integrated into the HR processes for training and development, recruitment and selection, and performance management, as well as compensation. The following describes how competencies were applied to each of these HR areas.

Compensation

As part of the new process for compensation, all of PHG–Western Operations associates' performance-appraisal dates were changed to a new Focal Point Review period running from June to September. For hourly employees this meant that performance evaluations and the accompanying pay raises would no longer occur on their hiring anniversary dates. Focal Point Review became a means by which the organization managed pay raises that in part were reliant on current market-survey data.

In mid 1995, during the Focal Point Review period, approximately 2,400 PHG–Western Operations associates were assessed for their job competencies using a multiple-rater approach. To maintain accuracy and confidentiality of rater information, the assessment process occurred through an on-line mainframe system application. In order to produce an overall evaluation of each person, associates selected five raters in addition to themselves: their immediate manager, two peers, and two internal customers. (Self-Rating was not included in the overall consensus scores.)

Shortly after the on-line rater information was collected through a back-end PC-based system, competency profiles were generated for each associate describing how well the associate performed overall and in each of his or her competency areas (see Figure 3).

The results of the competency assessment were then used in combination with the performance results to determine overall base-pay for each associate. Specifically, 40% of the salary decision was based on competency results and the remaining 60% was based on performance results.

Performance Management

In mid 1995, to assist managers in the new approach to compensation decision making, a new performance appraisal form, one that included competency-data results, was designed. However, the development of a new appraisal form was insufficient to make an effective impact on individual and team performance. With a proposed plan by the Organizational Effectiveness Division, the PHG–Western Operations Executive Team agreed to move forward with in-depth competency integration for the region. The first HR area (after compensation) to be addressed was performance management.

The overall plan for integrating competencies into this region's performance management process involved developing a comprehensive system of performance management. The new system included three essential elements: performance planning, performance coaching/ongoing feedback, and performance appraisal. Prior to this, the organization had no clear and consistent system of individual performance management.

With the new system developed, an implementation plan was created by Organizational Effectiveness to introduce it to PHG–Western Operations managers. Local HR managers (one designated to each major geographic site in the region) played key roles in the system's actual implementation. Specifically, the following key steps were taken:

1. A special training program was provided to all PHG–Western Operations management in which the new performance appraisal form and the new process for performance management was introduced.

2. Competency profiles and information from 1995, collected as part of the Focal Point Review process, were used to create more comprehensive 1996 performance plans. Once again, to ensure the performance management system was being utilized consistently throughout the management ranks, special training sessions were provided in first quarter 1996 to all PHG–Western Operations management. The focus of this training was on performance planning and coaching.

FIGURE 3: Sample Competency Profile

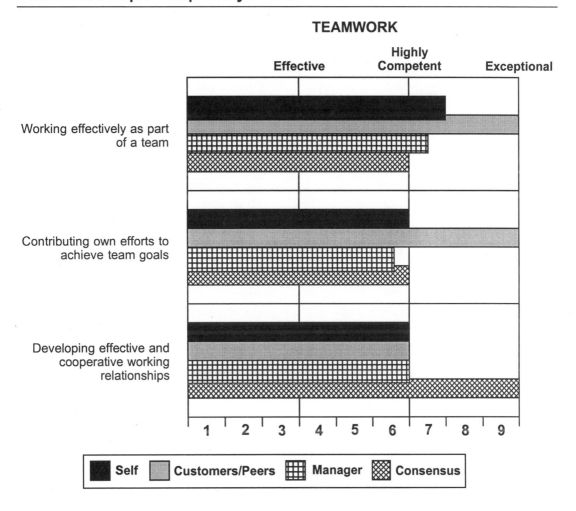

TEAMWORK

| | Effective | Highly Competent | Exceptional |

Legend: Self | Customers/Peers | Manager | Consensus

3. To ensure that associates were developing the *necessary* competencies, the organization chartered Organizational Effectiveness in partnership with the Hay McBer Group to enhance and, in essence, to validate the competency model developed in 1995. The purpose of the validation study was to identify "differentiating" competencies. Differentiating competencies were defined as those critical competencies needed by the organization to be successful currently and in the future.

    The validation study used a method that went beyond the traditional task-analysis approach used in 1995. The method, pioneered by David McClelland in the 1970s, empirically identifies what makes a person a superior performer in a particular job in a specific organization, and the process for competency modeling can predict which competencies are essential to achieving long-term success and effectiveness in a position or a team in a specific organization.

    To validate the Prudential HealthCare Group–Western Operations' competency model, a six-step procedure was used:

    - **Step 1—Planning:** The project was planned and a review of Prudential HealthCare competency materials was performed.

    - **Step 2—Education:** The Behavioral Event Interviewing Workshop was conducted for a group of PHG–Western Operations representatives in order to guarantee the transfer of technology and to allow those individuals to participate in the data-gathering phase of the project.

    - **Step 3—Data Collection:** Using the competency data and definition, data was collected through a series of 34 behavioral event interviews (BEIs) with managers, supervisors/team leaders, and front-line associates. In addition, a team BEI was conducted with a reengineering pilot team to identify the competencies demonstrated by this team, such as addressing decisions, problems, issues, and other concerns.

- **Step 4—Benchmarking:** An extensive database of empirically developed competency models was accessed to benchmark the "best practices" of other high-performing organizations with customer service orientations.

- **Step 5—Data Analysis and Model Development:** The information collected was analyzed and the results of the initial analysis were compared to the 1995 PHG–Western Operations' competency model to identify discrepancies and overlaps. Any critical competencies identified through the benchmarking were also added at this point.

- **Step 6—Presentation of the Refined Competency Model:** By February 1996 the model had been presented to key managers for approval (see Figure 4).

Recruitment and Selection

Simultaneous to the development of a new compensation plan and competencies, PHG–Western Operations was engaged in examining the extent to which they would reengineer key work processes. The focus of this initiative was the redesign of a key customer process (member engagement and service delivery) and implementation of a new team-based organization design by mid 1996. Because of the initiative's impending *potential* organizational impact, critical HR efforts were refocused to assist in the reengineering implementation. Selection and development of new teams and team members became an important human resource need. To effectively address this need, a new process for competency-based interviewing and selection was designed by the divisions of Human Resources and Organizational Effectiveness and implemented by the local HR managers in mid 1996.

These were the key implementation steps:

1. With the new selection process designed, a special "train-the-trainer" session was conducted for all HR managers and Organizational Effectiveness consultants in the region.

FIGURE 4: 1996 PHG–WO Competency Model

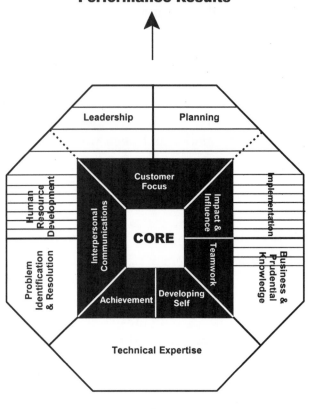

PHG-WO Competency Model

Performance Results

Leadership | Planning

Human Resource Development

Customer Focus

Impact & Influence

Implementation

Interpersonal Communications

CORE

Impact & Teamwork

Business & Prudential Knowledge

Problem Identification & Resolution

Achievement

Developing Self

Technical Expertise

Competency-Based Performance

- Core competencies for all associates

- Competencies required (in addition to core) for team/ operation leadership

- Competencies requires (in addition to core) for various other occupational groups

2. Certified in the new interviewing program, the local HR managers conducted Interviewing and Selection training sessions for management throughout the first half of 1996.

3. Organizational Effectiveness consultants worked with Human Resources to supplement the training as well as to assist in the selection of new team members for the reengineered teams.

Training and Development

Competencies had already been introduced through the areas of compensation and performance management before they were integrated into the region's training and development function. However, in early 1994, a strategic plan for training and development had been developed in Organizational Effectiveness that focused on four critical objectives:

1. The development of a learning organization through the design and implementation of a competency-based framework for training curriculum and development.

2. The development of an effective technical-training system. This system included the development of a regionwide "Training Consultant Network," consisting of division trainers.

3. The design of a career development system using a special development program as the cornerstone.

4. Creating a process for management development that supported the organizational development of teams as well as building management competencies.

The definition of competencies for the region assisted greatly in the achievement of these objectives. Conversely, as training strategies were already in place, competencies were more easily integrated into key HR processes.

As a first step towards integrating competencies into the training and development system at PHG–Western Operations, a resource guide was piloted that addressed each identified competency area. Figure 5 presents an excerpt from this guide. Learning interventions included self-study and on-the-job activities.

Second, competencies were integrated into the existing system of career development by providing information about job families, the types of jobs each job family contains, and the competencies required for each job family, utilizing the employee's multi-rater competency feedback data as a career planning tool. Consequently, associates could identify other jobs or job families that require the same competencies as their current job, and were able to identify the competencies they needed to develop or demonstrate (or both) in order to compete effectively for a job requiring different competencies than their current job.

FIGURE 5: Excerpt—Training and Development Resource Guide

Competency Area: Personal and Work Management	
(Subskill: Managing work to meet goals, deadlines, and other commitments)	
Overview:	The following information and resources will help you to prepare a detailed plan with resources required for each task, to structure flexibility into proposed plans, and to set deadlines and dates for each activity. Also you will be able to organize your responsibilities more effectively.
Workshops:	"Working Smarter"—Innovative Information Techniques, Inc. "Time Management"—Franklin Program available in-house.
Self-Study:	*Project Management with Larry Johnson*—video available in OE Library
Readings:	*Manage Your Time, Manage Your Work, Manage Yourself* by Douglas & Douglas *Getting the Job Done! Managing Project Teams and Task Forces for Success* by Randolph
OJT Activities:	Volunteer to manage projects with tight but reasonable deadlines. Take breaks from complex assignments by working on less strenuous tasks for short times. Ask for specific feedback on how well you managed a project and if there were any complaints or praise about your work. Document successes and failures so that you can be more aware on your next project.
Other Suggestions:	Find a role model/mentor at work or in a community group. Watch what they do and ask for feedback on how you work.

Third, division trainers were taught how they could utilize the competency information to conduct training needs assessment and to design and evaluate training. Division trainers met quarterly via the Training Consultant Network to participate in professional development and to discuss ways to improve the quality and effectiveness of their training efforts.

Plans for 1996 for training and development included work in two other key areas: competency-based leadership development and team development. A Leadership Development Program was designed to develop management competencies to satisfy short-term organizational objectives as well as long-term strategic planning. Team development processes consisted of redesigned team-based technical training and interpersonal-skills training programs and processes.

Evaluation

Several evaluations were done on the competencies and the competency assessment process. In addition, a variety of other measures were piloted to evaluate the impact of the Competency Project on the effectiveness of human resource management behaviors and processes.

Evaluation of the distribution of competency ratings and rater deviation was provided by statistical reports produced by the outside consulting firm, Apple Consulting, as part of the competency assessment process. Although some managers had been concerned that competency ratings would be skewed toward high scores, the results indicated a basically normal distribution of ratings. In addition, although this was the first time the competency assessment process had been used, no significant rater deviations were identified. If there had been significant rater deviations, follow-up interviews would have been held to determine if the deviation was caused by the rater not understanding the process, by the rater using different performance-level criteria, or by other factors.

Assessing the validity of the competencies was also a concern. Two concurrent validation studies began in late 1995: statistical validation and differentiating competencies validation. A revised 1996 competency model was a result of the methodology described earlier (see the "Phase 3," Performance Management section, and Figure 4). Several competencies were added to the model:

- **Achievement**—Setting goals and achieving standards of excellence

- **Developing Self**—Improving one's skills so as to contribute more effectively

- **Impact and Influence**—The ability to impress and persuade others within and outside one's team

In addition to the associate core competencies, several new team and operational leader competencies were defined. These included:

- **Leadership**—Holding others accountable

- **Developing Others**—Actively coaching others towards results

- **Planning and Implementation**—Focusing on achieving business objectives by communicating with and motivating others

- **Business and Prudential Knowledge**—Developing solutions to broad business issues

Assessment of associate perceptions of the effectiveness of the performance management application of competencies was done through the 1995 all-associate opinion survey. PHG–Western Operations has been conducting annual all-associate surveys since 1993 to assess progress in effecting cultural change. Several questions in the September 1995 survey provided feedback on the impact of this project. Forty percent of those completing the survey agreed or strongly agreed with the statement "The new multiple-rater competency assessment system used for performance appraisal is more objective." In addition, 17.4% agreed or strongly agreed that "The effectiveness of the performance appraisal discussion with my manager improved as a result of the multiple-rater competency assessment." Given that 41.5% of associates had not yet had their performance appraisal discussion with their manager, we believe that positive responses to this item would have been higher if the survey had been conducted later in the year.

It was projected that the competency-based integrated human resource system would confer these benefits:

- Administrative savings of $360,000 in annual recruitment and selection costs due to 5% reduced turnover for PHG–Western Operations

- Improved associate competency ratings indicating a higher level of performance results

- A better-aligned performance management system that focuses associate performance on business objectives and direction

- Increased return on investment in training expenses as a result of improved development planning

- Higher levels of associate satisfaction in career development opportunities in the organization

Conclusions

Lessons Learned

There were four critical lessons learned during the development and implementation of competencies at Prudential HealthCare Group–Western Operations.

1. The Competency Project time frame was extremely condensed. This required additional expertise and people resources to meet the compensation implementation requirements.

2. Because competencies were linked to compensation, there was a high employee need for ongoing communication and education from managers. However, because of multiple organizational priorities, many

managers lacked the time and resources to prepare employees for the compensation and competency implementation. In retrospect, additional communication and education could have taken place for management. Because of the condensed time frame for implementation, there was little preparation time, and as a result, managers often felt ill equipped to answer their staff members' questions about the process.

3. Because competencies and the compensation plan were developed simultaneously, associates had a tremendous amount of complex information to process in a relatively short time (six to eight months). This often resulted in confusion and frustration.

4. The automated on-line competency assessment system was developed in six months. More testing time was needed to work out the glitches. However, by 1996 the on-line system had been redesigned for national competency implementation.

Issues on the Horizon

The business climate in PHG–Western Operations' region continues to be highly competitive and volatile as new healthcare groups develop quickly and change rapidly. In this region, as in the rest of PHG, continuous business initiatives are underway to make it possible to serve the customer more effectively. As a result of these concentrated efforts, there have to be organizational structural changes and many changes in management requirements, including different roles and resulting competencies.

Acknowledgments

The overall success of PHG–Western Operations' Competency Project was due in large measure to the personal involvement, commitment, and support of a great number of people. The following were highly influential in contributing to this success: Keith Apple of Apple Consulting, Inc., Guerneville, California; The

Hay McBer Group; Competency Design Team members; the internal System Design and Implementation Division staff; the dedicated Human Resources and Organizational Effectiveness teams; and the PHG–Western Operations Executive Team, led by CEO Kathy Swenson.

References

DuBois, D. (1993). *Competency-based performance improvement: A strategy for organizational change* (pp. 70–113, 119–147). Amherst, MA: HRD Press.

Robinson, D. (1989). *Training for impact* (pp. 33–62, 85–131, 255–279). San Francisco, CA: Jossey-Bass.

Rummler, G. A., & Brache, A. P. (1995). *Improving performance: How to manage the white space on the organization chart* (pp. 79–114, 198–220). San Francisco, CA: Jossey-Bass.

Spencer, L., & Spencer, S. (1993). *Competence at work: models for superior performance* (pp. 246–275). New York, NY: John Wiley & Sons, Inc.

Spencer, L., Spencer, S., & McClelland, D. (1994). *Competency assessment methods* (pp. 8–20). Boston, MA: Hay McBer Press.

About the Contributors

Michele Bina, M.A., was Project Manager and Senior Consultant for the design of Prudential's two competency models and the application of those models to key HR processes. She is currently principal of Michele Bina and Associates, her own Glendale, California-based firm, which provides management services in competency development and human and corporate training and development. Ms. Bina has held training management positions in several industries, including banking, insurance, retail, and healthcare. Her specialty area is the design and implementation of 360-degree on-line behavioral assessment and competency development programs. She mentors others in training and organizational development through regular publications and workshops sponsored by several national associations.

Juhlin Newkirk, Ph.D., was External Senior Consultant with Prudential throughout the planning and implementation of the Competency Project. She is currently principal of her own firm, which is located in Atlanta, Georgia. Her firm provides services in the areas of large-scale organizational change, performance improvement, and team development. Her work has served organizations of all sizes and in a variety of industries, including education, healthcare, financial services, manufacturing, and nonprofit business. Ms. Newkirk brings extensive corporate experience to her consulting assignments, including management and staff positions in major companies such as Transamerica Occidental Life and Kaiser Permanente.

5.
A COMPETENCY MODEL FOR HUMAN RESOURCES

Debra L. McDaniel, SPHR — Senior HR Associate, Eli Lilly and Company

Background

Eli Lilly and Company was established in 1876 in Indianapolis, Indiana, to specialize in ethical drugs. The term *ethical* was used to describe Lilly medications so that customers could differentiate between Lilly products and the pills and potions that were brewed and sold by pitchmen, often at sideshows. Contrary to this practice, the new pharmaceutical company developed and produced high-quality medications that were dispensed to patients on the recommendation of a physician.

Over the years, the company expanded so that pharmaceuticals were no longer the only products sold. Specialized agricultural chemicals, cosmetics, and medical instruments and diagnostic products were added to the portfolio.

For most of its first hundred years, the company was run by three successive generations of the Lilly family. They established the company's core values of *respect for people, integrity,* and a thirst for *excellence,* which continue to guide the behavior expected of the company and its employees. Today, at the close of the twentieth century, Eli Lilly and Company employs more than 20,000 people in over 100 countries around the world, and strives to be the global leader in helping people worldwide live healthier, more productive lives.

Strategic Organizational Changes

The New Mission

In recent years, dramatic changes have occurred in the global healthcare marketplace, requiring the company to reinvent the business to respond to and anticipate customers' changing needs. Around the world, countries are rapidly improving the quality of healthcare for their citizens, and healthcare providers and payers are as concerned about cost as they are about quality. At the same time, upward pressures continue to exert force on the costs of bringing a new drug to market.

To maintain its competitive edge in the next century, the company must respond to this new environment by providing customers with innovative products *and* comprehensive solutions to their healthcare problems. The new mission at Lilly is to create and deliver innovative pharmaceutical-based healthcare solutions that enable people to live longer, healthier, and more active lives.

Strategic Focus

The change in the company's mission has led to the definition of three dimensions of strategic focus:

1. Achieving breakthrough advances in targeted disease categories

2. Expanding the company's global presence

3. Building and improving the company's critical capabilities

Recent company initiatives reflect at least one and sometimes the interaction of all three strategic dimensions.

The new strategy has required the company to focus its resources, resulting in separating its medical devices and diagnostics businesses from the core pharmaceutical business, as it had previously done with its cosmetic company. It has also expanded its presence in new global markets, acquired new businesses with needed technologies, and collaborated with other corporations on new pharmaceutical products and healthcare solutions.

Significant changes have taken place in the company's leadership and employee population as well. New board members, retirements and replacements of senior executives, globalization, and a voluntary early-retirement program have dramatically changed the composition of the organization.

These environmental and internal changes have greatly influenced the creation of a new strategic direction for the company. The strategy combines assumptions about the environment, the mission of the organization, prioritized initiatives needing implementation, and the values that guide expected behavior.

To accomplish the strategy, the company must strive for preeminent organizational effectiveness (POE). This phrase suggests that to be a world leader in the pharmaceutical industry, the company must restructure itself in a way that will enable every employee to serve the customers efficiently and effectively.

The Role of Human Resources

For the restructuring to be successful, the global Human Resources (HR) organization must transform itself into a strategic business partner within the company. Consequently, HR has begun to make the transition from a more traditional "personnel" function to one which provides quality solutions in the management of people that will enable the company to achieve POE.

This transition has brought a new dimension to the HR strategy. The HR Council, whose members include the vice president of Human Resources and an HR representative for each area of Lilly, continuously updates the HR strategy to support the strategic direction of the company.

HR Strategy

The new strategy is a combination of six key elements: Partnership, HR Processes, Competency, Operating Principles, Decentralization, and Management

Process. Initiatives that support each of these elements are in process. Those supporting the Competency element are the focus of the remainder of this chapter.

Within the Competency element of the strategy, two different roles are defined for the 200-plus members of the global HR organization. HR account managers are intended to:

— develop strategic business partnerships with their line areas

— facilitate necessary changes

— represent employees in resolving issues

— implement HR processes

The role of Global Staff members is to:

— provide deep technical knowledge in HR

— develop and deploy global HR guiding principles

— facilitate global replication of best HR practices

— provide expertise in applying HR processes

In combination, these roles are designed to contribute to the achievement of the corporate strategy through superior performance in the functions that are specialties of Human Resources.

To expedite the development of the new HR organization and to define the performance expectations for account managers and Global Staff members, it became necessary to identify the causes of superior job performance in HR. In response to this need, the HR Council sponsored a pilot project to create a competency model for the HR Account Manager role. Models for the Global Staff areas would follow, if appropriate.

The Competency Modeling Project: Initial Steps

Process and Team Selection

A team leader who holds a master's degree in industrial relations and several years of experience in the Human Resources organization as assigned by the HR Council to lead the project. Work began with an extensive literature search on identifying competencies for HR. The literature revealed many definitions of *competency* and described several different modeling processes.

The criteria used to select a modeling process required that the model do the following:

- Support the future needs of the organization

- Focus on the results that would help achieve the company's strategy

- Identify the competencies that cause superior performance

A modified version of the process being taught by Linkage Incorporated (1994) was created to guide the development of the Account Manager competency model. The process modifications are described later in this chapter, in the section on data collection.

An eight-person team, including account managers and Global Staff members, was appointed to build the competency model. The educational background and work experience of the team members varied significantly. The continuum ranged from those with HR graduate degrees and more than ten years of HR work experience to others with non-HR degrees and few years of HR experience. The diversity of the group was intended to provide a variety of perspectives in building the model and to develop competency-modeling expertise in the team members.

The project was expected to take approximately 30% of the team leader's time and 11% of the team members' time over three months.

Team Training

The project began with a one-day training session conducted by the team leader. The training included an overview of the project followed by skill practice with three of the modeling-process steps—behavioral event interviews (BEIs), transcript coding, and model drafting. The contents of the project overview are summarized below; the process steps will be described in sequence later in this chapter.

Project Overview

The overview outlined the expectations for the team's efforts by:

1. Stating the objective of the project

2. Explaining the steps of the modeling process

3. Defining terms

4. Identifying the future applications for the model data

1. Project Objective. The objective of the project was to enhance the overall capability and success of the organization through the assessment and development of competencies necessary for outstanding performance in the Account Manager role.

2. Steps of the Modeling Process. The modeling process included establishing an expert panel, collecting data, collating the data to build the model, and recommending specific interventions based on the model results.

3. Definition of Terms. To facilitate clear communications, a standard set of terms and definitions used in building this model was created (see Appendix A). Highlighted below are three of the most critical definitions needed to understand how the model was created.

- *Competencies:* Competencies are those characteristics and measurable patterns of behavior, knowledge, and skill that contribute to superior job performance.

- *Technical Competency:* A technical competency is a competency that is unique or specific to a role or function.

- *Business Competency:* A business competency is a competency that applies to many different positions in a company.

4. Future Applications for the Model. The training overview concluded with a description of how the model could be used. Each of the following applications will include the competencies defined in the model:

- Individual development plans

- Development of a training curriculum

- Staffing decisions such as hiring, transfers, and promotions

- Succession planning for promotions and job rotations

- Performance management for setting standards and performance expectations

- Job descriptions that include tasks, skills, and necessary knowledge

- Developing a common language for describing jobs and performance

The Expert Panel

After the team was trained in the modeling process, an expert panel was established. The seven-person panel included account managers and Global Staff members from different levels throughout the HR organization, as well as the team leader from the model-building team. The panel members were diverse in their job experiences and educational backgrounds. The composition of the panel was intended to maximize the number of different viewpoints reviewing the model as it progressed through the various stages of the building process, and to ensure acceptance of the model results in all areas of the HR organization.

The project was expected to take about 2.5% of the panel members' time.

The Framing Meeting

Meeting Agenda

The model-building team and expert panel met for most of a day to complete these tasks:

1. Review the overview of the project

2. Determine the *future* performance results/outcomes required from a successful account manager

3. Select the focus areas for the collection of data

4. Identify interviewees

5. Finalize the project schedule

1. Project Overview. The same project overview that was presented in the team's training session was reviewed and discussed by the team and panel at the start of the framing meeting. This enabled the panel to quickly reach a basic understanding of the project and allowed the team to interact with the panel before their working session began.

2. Future Performance Results. Given the role of Account Manager defined in the HR strategy, the team and panel brainstormed a list of outcomes that would be expected from account managers if they were to be successful in the future. Multiple flip charts were filled with performance results such as measurable customer satisfaction, cost-effective programs, innovative solutions to problems, and recognized leadership in HR.

After all ideas were recorded, the group began to cluster similar result areas into distinctly separate categories. The clusters lead to a discussion about focus areas for data collection.

3. Focus Areas. Each cluster of future performance results was given a title that summarized its contents and defined the areas that the team would focus on for collecting data.

These were the 12 focus areas:

- Business Professional
- Change Agent
- Communicator
- Consultant
- Customer Focus
- Educator
- Influential
- Integrator
- Problem Solver
- Process Facilitator
- Project Manager
- Trust

4. Identifying Interviewees. The team and panel studied the focus areas and brainstormed a list of individuals and companies that were recognized to be superior performers in at least one of the dozen focus areas. There were no restrictions placed on this list—companies could be from any industry, not just pharmaceuticals, and individuals could be in any profession, not limited to HR.

The group identified several superior performers for each of the focus areas. They selected at least one company or individual from each focus area to be interviewed during the data collection phase of the modeling project. In all, 16 interviewees made the final list, including individuals from a variety of different companies and professions. The original brainstormed list of superior performers was saved for selecting alternate interviewees in case someone was not available to be interviewed.

5. Project Schedule. A date for completion of the competency model was set by the HR Council at the time the project was sponsored. Prior experience with scheduling interviews and meetings suggested that the total time allowed to complete the process would greatly exceed the actual number of hours needed. Working backwards from the set completion date, the team and panel agreed on the following schedule:

Activity	Time Allowed
Interviewing and Transcript Coding — 16 interviews lasting from 1 to 3 hours — Coding 16 transcripts @ 2 to 4 hours per transcript	7 weeks
Building and Reviewing the Model — 16 to 24 hours	3 weeks
Defining Interventions Based on the Model — 12 hours	2 weeks
Finalize Presentation — 8 hours	1 week

Data Collection—Behavioral Event Interviews

In addition to the information about HR competencies collected in the literature search and during the framing meeting, the team collected a significant amount of behavioral data through the interviews with superior performers.

For its interview format, the team selected the behavioral event interview (BEI), which is similar to other structured-interview processes such as the critical incident (CI) interview and the critical behavior interview (CBI). The objective of a BEI is to obtain a detailed list of critical knowledge, skills, and behaviors required to perform in a position. Because BEIs collect information not only on observable behaviors but also on difficult-to-observe behaviors, their data constitute one of the best sources of information about competencies that predict superior job performance.

BEIs are often conducted by two interviewers, each leading part of the interview and asking clarifying questions (this two-person team is also responsible for coding the transcripts after the interview). The interviewers usually follow the nine step format defined below:

1. Overview

One interviewer describes the interview and how the data will be used; assures interviewee of the confidentiality of the interview and receives permission to use an audiotape for transcribing later.

2. Background

The interviewee is asked to give an overview of his or her current position—job title and reporting relationship, responsibilities, time in the position, and current challenges. If a new job is being modeled, questions about the responsibilities and challenges in the new position are also asked.

3. Tasks & Activities

Here the interview focuses on the tasks and activities performed in the job. The interviewee lists 6 to 10 major job tasks and the time required to perform them, and assesses which tasks are the most critical to the job.

4. Workflow

This step determines the sequence of tasks for performing work and requirements for initiating the work process; identifies the decision makers, the critical decision points, and any future changes that may have an impact on how the work is completed.

5. Knowledge & Skills

The skills and knowledge required to do tasks are identified. These are usually sorted into one of three categories: technical/professional, business/process, and relational/interpersonal. The interviewee may also comment on additional skills or areas of knowledge needed in the future, or current skills and knowledge that will no longer be needed, or both.

6. Learning

The interviewee is asked how the job was learned and what internal and external resources are available to facilitate the learning process. The interviewee is also asked for suggestions on how learning could be accelerated based on his or her experience.

7. Barriers

This step identifies any organizational and cultural barriers to superior performance and how the barriers are overcome.

8. Critical Incidents

Here the interview process looks at the job from a different perspective. It begins by asking the interviewee to list the abilities or personal characteristics that are important for doing the job. One of these characteristics is selected and the interviewee is asked to describe a situation in which this characteristic was demonstrated successfully. The situation is described with specific details of what was thought, said, and done. Next, the interviewee is asked to describe, in the same level of detail, a situation that was difficult or frustrating— one whose outcome may or may not have been entirely successful, but from which a great deal was learned. This situation may describe the same or a different characteristic from the list. Finally, the interviewee is asked for another example of when one of the important characteristics was demonstrated successfully.

9. Summary

The team concludes the interview by answering all of the interviewee's questions and explaining how the data will be combined to build the model. The interviewers offer to share the completed model and thank the interviewee for participating in the modeling process.

Interview Modifications

The team modified the BEI format for some of the interviews with superior performers. The second, third, and fourth steps—Background Information, Tasks and Activities, and Workflow—were omitted because many of the interviewees were not in Account Manager positions, and so their work tasks were not applicable to the new Account Manager role.

The other steps of the interview process were structured so that the interviewees were questioned specifically about their focus area of superior performance rather than about their overall abilities or characteristics. This provided deep insight into the behaviors causing superior performance in each of the focus areas, particularly through the three critical incidents that, in Step 8, each interviewee described.

Transcript Coding

The 16 BEIs yielded 320 single-spaced, typed transcript pages. The transcripts were coded in order to analyze the data in a more manageable form. Each interview team began by reading their interview transcripts and identifying examples of knowledge, skills, values, and behaviors demonstrated by the interviewees. If job incumbents had been interviewed, job tasks would also be coded in the transcripts.

When behavioral examples were found, the words or phrases were underlined on the transcript and coded in the left-hand margin with a descriptive word or two and one of the following letters:

B—Behavior
K—Knowledge
S—Skill
V—Value, Belief, Motive, or Trait

Definitions for these terms are provided in Appendix A.

When the interview teams had coded all of the transcripts, administrative support personnel transferred the information from the transcripts to Post-It notes, using one for each behavioral example identified. Here is an example of a typical Post-It note:

Behavior

Articulates Vision

Interview 5, Page 1, Paragraph 2

A shorthand version of the notes would replace the word *Behavior* with the letter *B* and abbreviate the third line to read "5, 1, 2."

Approximately 3,500 behaviors, skills, areas of knowledge, beliefs, motives, traits, and values were identified in the interview transcripts and represented on the Post-It notes.

Building the Competency Model

Model Overview

To understand the model and how it was built, it may be helpful to review the complete model first and use it as a reference as the model-building process is described in detail.

The model contains six different competencies that relate to superior performance. Five are business competencies that could apply to many different positions in the company and the sixth is a technical competency that is unique to the HR Account Manager position.

The six competencies include 23 skills, 12 knowledge areas, and 13 beliefs, motives, traits, and values. The team's picture of the competencies and related skills, knowledge, and values is shown in Figure 1.

The Building Process

Data Organization and Ordering

The team began to build the model by organizing and ordering the data from the interviews, framing meeting, and literature search. Managing the large volume of data was made easier through the use of the Post-It notes for sorting and grouping the coded behaviors.

Initially, the data were grouped into the four coded categories: Behaviors, Skills, Knowledge, and Values. Each category was assigned to a pair of team members who reviewed their coded Post-It notes and sorted them into groups of similar behaviors. The pairs referenced the original transcripts to make sure all of the notes in a group described the same behavior. A heading was given to each group and written on a flip chart. The flip charts for the four categories were presented to the entire team.

The team reviewed, discussed, and reached agreement on the behavior groups in each of the coded categories. When the same group heading was used in more than one of the categories, the team referred to the transcripts to determine if the behavior groups represented by the same heading were defining the same behaviors. If the groups included the same behaviors, the team decided which category was most appropriate and the groups were combined under that category. If the groups were describing different behaviors, a new heading was assigned to one of the groups and the groups remained in their appropriate categories.

For example, if the heading "Behavioral Science" was listed in the Knowledge and Skills categories, the team would read the transcript citings for each group to determine if they meant the same thing. If the descriptions were the same, the team would decide if the groups should be considered a knowledge

FIGURE 1: HR Account Manager Competency Model

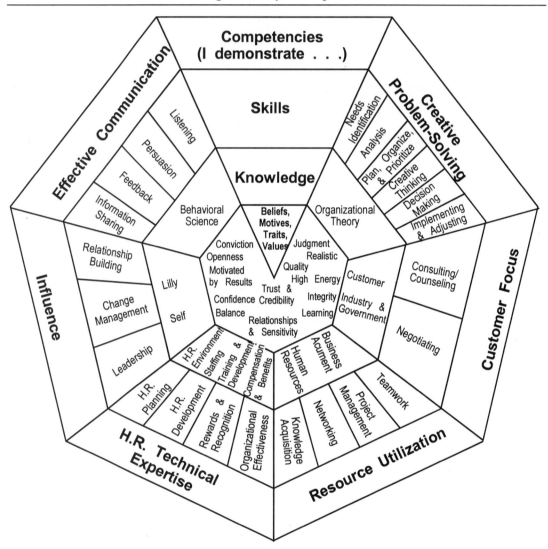

area or a skill and then combine both groups of data under the appropriate category. If, however, the transcript descriptions were different for the two groups, one of the groups would be renamed and they would each be placed in the appropriate category.

Cluster Identification and Interrelation

After all of the groups had been assigned to a category, the pairs worked with their original data to create clusters of groups that related to each other. For example, three of the clusters identified by the pair working with the Knowledge category are shown below.

Cluster	1	2	3
Knowledge of	• Organizational Theory	• Customer • Industry • Government	• Compensation and Benefits • Training and Development • Staffing • HR Environment

The entire team met again to review the clusters within each category and to decide which of the clusters related to one another across categories. The same three Knowledge clusters above are repeated below with their related Skills clusters.

Cluster	1	2	3
Skill	• Needs Identification • Analysis • Planning, Organizing, and Prioritizing • Creative Thinking • Decision Making • Implementing and Adjusting	• Consulting/Counseling • Negotiating	• Organizational Effectiveness • Rewards and Recognition • HR Development • HR Planning
Knowledge of	• Organizational Theory	• Customer • Industry • Government	• Compensation and Benefits • Training and Development • Staffing • HR Environment

As the team attempted to decide which of the values related to the other clusters, it became apparent that the values related to all of the other clusters and could not be separated from each other. Therefore, the beliefs, motives, traits, and values became the foundation for all of the clusters, as illustrated below.

Cluster	1	2	3
Skills	• Needs Identification • Analysis • Planning, Organizing, and Prioritizing • Creative Thinking • Decision Making • Implementing and Adjusting	• Consulting/Counseling • Negotiating	• Organizational Effectiveness • Rewards and Recognition • HR Development • HR Planning
Knowledge of	• Organizational Theory	• Customer • Industry • Government	• Compensation and Benefits • Training and Development • Staffing • HR Environment
Beliefs, Motives, Traits, and Values	• Balance • Openness • Conviction • Motivated by Results	• Confidence • Realistic • Relationships and Sensitivity • Quality	• Judgment • Learning • Trust and Credibility • High Energy • Quality Integrity

Naming the Competencies

The team concluded that each cluster represented a competency that was demonstrated by superior performers more often, in more situations, and with better results, than by average performers. After reviewing the six clusters, a name was selected for each competency that summarized the behaviors being demonstrated within the related skills and knowledge areas.

While comparing competencies, the team discovered that some of the skills and knowledge could apply to more than one competency. After some discussion, it was decided that the skills and knowledge areas would be assigned to the competency that the team determined was the most appropriate based on the data. For example, the skill "Listening" applies to several competencies, but the data suggested that the appropriate assignment was in the Effective Communications competency.

Model Definitions

Each of the competency headings in the model were behaviorally defined based on the interview transcripts. Pairs of team members worked together to draft definitions for the headings in an assigned portion of the model. The draft definitions were reviewed and refined by the entire team. Reviewing the definitions with the team was greatly enhanced through the use of a computer that projected images on a movie screen. Changes to the definitions were made and viewed simultaneously until agreement was reached that each definition was complete. Definitions for the model's headings are provided in Appendix B.

The Final Steps: Review, Applications, and Approval

Model Review

The expert panel met with the team to discuss the modeling process and to review the completed model. No changes were made to the model picture or any of the attached definitions. The panel and team also discussed how the model data could be applied to various HR processes. The recommended interventions are listed in the next section.

Model Interventions

The team identified five different model intervention categories:

- Model Implementation
- Rewards and Recognition
- Training and Development
- Assessment
- New Models and Updates

The interventions in each category are summarized in the following table.

Intervention	Purpose
Model Implementation	
Share model findings with the HR component, training roundtable, and interviewees.	Educate HR on the contents of the model, gain support, and begin application of model results.
Use model criteria in interviewing HR hires, transfers, and promotions.	Staff HR positions with the competencies needed now and in the future.
Use model criteria in performance management and development plans.	Enhance the competencies of existing HR personnel.
Training and Development	
Create an HR training curriculum and development plans based on skills and knowledge identified in the model.	Support development of competencies.
Update existing HR programs to include model content.	Explain performance expectations and standards.
New Models and Updates	
Build competency models for the areas of HR Technical Expertise—Organization Effectiveness, Rewards and Recognition, HR Development, and HR Planning—that validate the business competencies in the Account Manager model and expand the skill and knowledge definitions in the HR Technical Expertise competency.	Further validate the business competencies in the Account Manager model, identify capabilities required in the HR technical areas, and provide data to determine the *level* of HR technical expertise needed by account managers.
Update the HR Account Manager model by including the *level* of HR technical expertise required by account managers based on the technical area models.	Establish technical proficiency requirements for HR account managers.
Assessment	
(1) For each HR job/area, determine the proficiency level required in each competency to achieve the area's HR strategy. (2) Each individual/group assesses their capabilities against the model. (3) Determine the gap between job-required proficiency level and individual capability level.	Create staffing, training, and development plans.
Assess staffing needs for each HR line area to determine how many positions may be used for employee development and how many require experienced HR personnel.	Ensure balanced level of HR competencies to meet customer needs and enhance development opportunities. Serves as a foundation for the HR staffing strategy.

(continued)

Intervention	Purpose
Rewards and Recognition	
Develop a benchmark job description/profile for the HR Account Manager job based on the model.	Create standardized job description to support the competency model.
Create an HR technical ladder based on model data.	Reward and recognize HR technical and generalist positions.
Review compensation program to ensure competency-based rewards.	Reward and recognize competency maintenance and development.

An implementation plan was created by the team that assigned each intervention, and included a scheduled completion date. The responsibilities for each category were as follows:

Intervention Category	Responsibility
Model Implementation	HR Account Managers
Training and Development	HR Development
New Models and Updates	Each HR Technical Area
Assessment	HR Account Managers
Rewards and Recognition	Rewards and Recognition

Model Approval

The completed model, recommended interventions, and implementation plan were presented to the HR Council and approved without modification. The model was published as a part of the conference materials for the Linkage Incorporated Competency Conference (fall, 1995). Periodic evaluations of the model were planned to ensure that it would continue to reflect the current HR strategy.

Recent Developments

Since the Account Manager Competency Model was approved, some of the recommended interventions have been completed, others are currently being developed, and some have been incorporated into regular HR processes. The status of various interventions is described below.

Model Implementation

The model has been shared with all members of the HR component throughout the world. In some areas, the model criteria are being used to interview HR hires and to determine appropriate HR transfers and promotions. The criteria are also being used in performance management and development plans.

New Models and Updates

Competency models for each area of HR Technical Expertise—Organization Effectiveness, HR Planning, HR Development, and Rewards and Recognition—have also been developed. These models validated the five business competencies in the Account Manager model and expanded the skill and knowledge definitions within the HR Technical Expertise competency. The Account Manager model and four technical area models have been combined to form a single model—the HR Competency Model—which contains the five business competencies and one technical competency with sections for each technical area in HR.

Rewards and Recognition

A global HR career path has been designed to reward and recognize both HR technical and generalist positions and to allow for cross-functional moves. Each level of the path is defined by performance criteria that must be demonstrated *before* an individual can attain that job level. The HR Competency Model data was used to help define the path's performance criteria.

Assessment

The HR Competency Model was used to develop a computerized competency assessment tool that enables each area within HR to rate the level of proficiency in each competency that is *required* by each HR position to achieve the area's HR strategy. Once the assessment of the positions is completed, the tool is then used to rate the *observed capability* level in each competency for the individuals in the positions that were previously assessed for required proficiency levels. Differences between the two ratings identify performance gaps for development planning.

Along with the assessment tool, a resource guide containing interventions that relate to the model criteria was given to the assessment participants to create development plans to address their competency gaps.

Training and Development

The existing HR curriculum is being enhanced based on the HR Competency Model data and the gaps identified by the competency assessment.

APPENDIX A

Glossary

Advantage: The competitive edge to provide unique products and services chosen by customers—sourced in cost, differentiation, focus, or capability.

Behavior: An observable sequence of physical actions, verbalizations or nonverbal cues, i.e., *what people do or say* (Linkage Inc., 1994, p. 3).

Belief: An internal representation of experience embodied in a set of statements regarding the truth, validity, or relationship of the objects of the experience, i.e., *what people hold—with varying degrees of certainty—to be true* (Linkage Inc., 1994, p. 3).

Business Competency: A business competency is a competency that applies to many different positions in a company.

Competency: A characteristic and measurable pattern of behaviors, knowledge, and skills that contribute to superior job performance (Linkage Inc., 1994, p. 3).

Core Capability: An integrated set of processes, structures, systems, tools, or technologies that uniquely differentiate a company and provide competitive advantage with customers.

Core Competency: Those organizational competencies or capabilities that can be leveraged for increased competitiveness. *Core competency* is a term used to describe a corporation and not an individual (Linkage Inc., 1994, p. 3).

Cultural Context: The collection of guiding, organizing, and operating principles that represent both a summary of past collective learning within the company as well as guidelines for action, behavior, and learning in the future.

Knowledge: A consciously accessible body of information composed of data, facts, concepts, and relationships relevant to action in the job context, i.e., *what people comprehend and understand* (Linkage, Inc. 1994, p. 3).

Mission: A statement about the boundaries of the business, i.e., *the products, markets, customers, and technology* that define the core of the enterprise.

Motive: A consistent pattern of thought reflecting a recurring concern or desire for certain goal states or conditions, i.e., *what people are driven to think about, seek, or act upon* (Linkage Inc., 1994, p. 3).

Skill: A consistently demonstrated ability to perform certain physical or mental tasks or job responsibilities, i.e., *how people apply knowledge to behavior* (Linkage Inc., 1994, p. 3).

Strategy: A statement regarding how the business will compete within its industry to win customers from competitors.

Task: An assigned piece of work, i.e., *job duty.*

Technical Competency: A technical competency is a competency that is unique or specific to a role or function.

Trait: A physical quality of a person *or* an underlying behavioral tendency inferred from consistency in response to various tasks, people, or situations, i.e., *what people are predisposed to do* (Linkage Inc., 1994, p. 3).

Value: A set of internal evaluations and judgments regarding the relative worth, desirability, or importance of some object, entity, or action, i.e., *what people evaluate to be good, positive, useful, or important* (Linkage Inc., 1994, p. 3).

Vision: A simple but powerful image of the future of the business that defines and communicates the purpose, direction, and intention of the leadership team.

APPENDIX B

HR Account Manager Competency Model

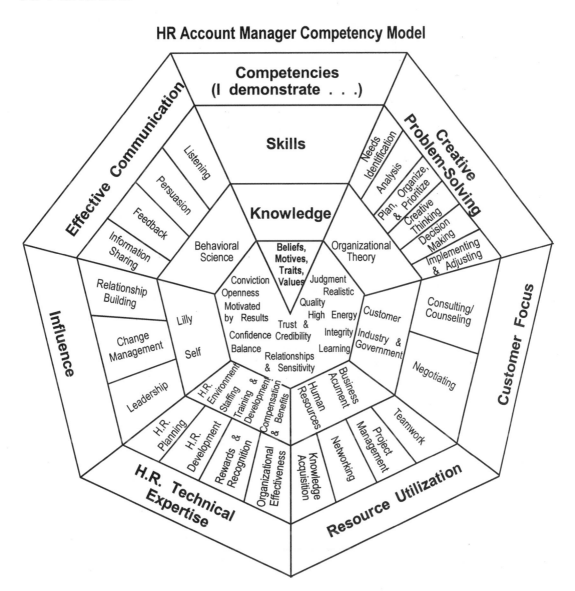

The definitions of the model's Competencies, including the Skills, Knowledge, and Values components, are presented on the following pages.

Creative Problem-Solving

Competency	Behavioral Definition
Creative Problem-Solving	Analyzes situations and identifies innovative solutions to address needs. Develops and implements plan of action.

Skills	Behavioral Definition
Needs Identification	Recognizes gaps between current situation and desired outcome.
Analysis	Gathers data regarding a situation or issue. Reviews data for understanding, trends, striking differences, or precedent. Evaluates the data from a variety of perspectives.
Planning, Organizing, and Prioritizing	Develops strategic and tactical plans and prepares others by identifying the actions necessary to accomplish the results. Arranges schedules of projects and activities based on importance. Systematically develops a method for accomplishing an objective.
Creative Thinking	Generates and assists others in the development of new ideas. Thinks beyond convention, i.e., "out of the box." Creates an environment where alternative thinking is rewarded.
Decision Making	Assesses risk associated with alternatives. Reaches conclusions based on available data and accepts responsibility for the resulting action.
Implementing and Adjusting	Puts into action solutions to problems and enhancements to processes. Changes course when situations, data, or customer input dictate that a change is necessary.

Knowledge of . . .	
Organizational Theory	Organizational design and implications of structural changes on business strategy, reporting relationships, and span of control.

Customer Focus

Competency	Behavioral Definition
Customer Focus	Consults with internal and external customers to assess needs and establish goals that benefit all parties. Partners in planning and prioritizing to achieve customer satisfaction.

Skills	Behavioral Definition
Consulting/ Counseling	Listens and gathers information non-judgmentally. Provides advice or expertise. Calls on other resources and experts, as appropriate. Advises others of trends, possibilities, and similarities to ensure replication, where relevant. Provides an objective viewpoint.
Negotiating	Facilitates a win-win agreement and establishes a contract.

Knowledge of . . .	
Customer	Customer's business, organization, culture, strategy, needs, strengths, and weaknesses, and critical success factors.
Industry and Government	Industry best practices, issues, risks, regulatory/legal requirements, and trends.

Resource Utilization

Competency	Behavioral Definition
Resource Utilization	Identifies and coordinates resources to achieve objectives. Works with others to establish networks. Fosters a learning environment.

Skills	Behavioral Definition
Teamwork	Respects the differences in people, values diversity of ideas, and works with others to achieve goals. Actively participates in meetings and shares opinions that differ from others without hindering progress. Places goals of team ahead of individual goals.
Project Management	Determines the business case, scope, and objectives of the project. Identifies how the project should be integrated with other initiatives. Prepares an implementation plan and finds resources to assist in the delivery of the project(s). Anticipates obstacles and plans contingencies. Reviews plans with decision-makers and project owners to ensure support. Delivers project according to the established schedule and within planned costs.
Networking	Identifies and employs the necessary resources and tools to accomplish objectives. Builds and sustains a strong network of professional contacts and resources both inside and outside the organization.
Knowledge Acquisition	Identifies gaps in understanding and actively seeks ways to obtain additional information.

Knowledge of . . .	
Business Acumen	Management theories, economic theories, and general business concepts.
Human Resources	HR organization, strategy, philosophy, culture, tools, services, technical competencies, and relationship to other components.

HR Technical Expertise

Competency	Behavioral Definition
HR Technical Expertise	Keeps current on the issues, practices, and procedures in HR technical skill areas. Assures delivery of HR services that achieve corporate and business-unit objectives.

Skills	Behavioral Definition
Organizational Effectiveness	Understands the client's situation, from their point of view. Analyzes the situation from relevant theory and practice. Understands root causes to include probing deeply to gain understanding of the relationship between different pieces of the problem. Seeks information to include non-obvious dimensions of the client situation. Obtains agreement on mutual project parameters, expectations, and outcomes. Establishes clarity of roles, project scope, deliverables, timeline, and methodology. Formulates a plan or an intervention that appropriately addresses a client's issue or problem. Constructs specific interventions, considering available tools, resources, potential constraints, and contingency plans. Obtains buy-in (influencing key decision-makers). Resolves conflict and identifies and procures resources. Communicates to the larger organization to keep people informed. Cares for the emotional well-being of the group. Clarifies roles and gains commitment. Utilizes appropriate criteria to analyze performance. Employs results in the continuous learning process. Communicates effectively through the use of formal presentations, written material, and verbal interchange. Chooses the optimum media mix to communicate the desired message. Creates effective, high-quality written products under short time constraints. Effectively and engagingly communicates ideas to various audiences. Creates written material that conveys a sense of value added. Presents a compelling case while "under fire."
Rewards and Recognition	Aligns customer's business objectives and corporate reward and recognition programs. Communicates linkages between the programs and the company's total compensation philosophy and objectives. Applies business skills with specific application to compensation and benefits (e.g., analysis and calculation of statistical measures; application of judgment to determine validity of data; synthesis and summarization of large volumes of data; use of computer skills to gather and analyze data; use of sources of economic data and application of economic concepts in analyzing and projecting data; and calculation of cost impact of compensation and benefit programs).

(continued)

HR Technical Expertise *(concluded)*

Skills	Behavioral Definition
Human Resource Development	Applies a systematic methodology to improve performance (e.g., analysis, design, development, implementation, and evaluation). Integrates instructional and learning systems, workplace design, performance support, incentive systems, organizational design and development, and selection and retention systems to enable achievement of business goals. Selects the most effective and economic means of achieving business goals. Champions Human Performance Technology as the major approach to achieve desired human performance results. Identifies human performance implications of business drivers (strategy, technology, stakeholder requirements, customer expectations, etc.). Creates HRD strategic plans that support and align with business goals and objectives. Integrates HRD planning into the business planning process. Partners with customers to identify and achieve valued outcomes. Builds customer capabilities. Obtains agreement on expectations and outcomes with customers.
Human Resource Planning	Creates staffing plans that are aligned with current and future needs of the business.

Knowledge of . . .	
Compensation and Benefits	Total compensation philosophy; strategy and policy; legal and regulatory factors affecting compensation and benefits; compensation program design and administration; job analysis and job evaluation; equity program design; employee-benefit program design and administration; current compensation and benefits practices and trends; and Lilly-specific compensation and benefit practices.
Training and Development	Performance technology, systems thinking, and partnerships and alliances.
Staffing	Equal Employment Opportunity laws, recruitment, selection, retention, job posting, redeployment, succession, and career planning.
HR Environment	Best HR practices, issues, risks, regulatory/legal requirements, trends, change, metrics, process, strategy, socio-technology, and systems thinking.

Influence

Competency	Behavioral Definition
Influence	Facilitates change and motivates others to action. Builds relationships by demonstrating behaviors that others view as honest and credible. Maintains a balanced perspective and focuses on results, not rewards.

Skills	Behavioral Definition
Leadership	Develops and articulates the vision, strategy, and plan. Translates the vision to others and gains commitment. Models the desired actions and behaviors and holds self and others to a high level of responsibility and accountability. Transfers credit for success and owns credit for failure. Creates an environment that is supportive of team formation and development. Facilitates group interactions by encouraging involvement and contribution of others. Admits when wrong or does not know the answer. Observes, evaluates, and learns from others.
Change Management	Creates an environment that accepts and encourages change. Demonstrates an understanding of the change process and the impact of change on people. Gains support by openly communicating and involving others in the change process. Manages the balance between urgency and patience in implementing change.
Relationship Building	Earns credibility and trust. Treats others with understanding, empathy, and respect. Follows through with commitments. Provides frequent and effective communications. Requests help when needed, admits own mistakes, and acknowledges when something is not known. Builds rapport with a variety of people, including senior management.

Knowledge of . . .	
Self	Personal strengths, weaknesses, past successes and failures, and goals.
Lilly	Corporate organization, culture, strategy, and interrelationship of components.

Effective Communications

Competency	Behavioral Definition
Effective Communication	Presents information openly, clearly, and with conviction. Listens to others and responds appropriately. Requests and provides feedback in a timely manner.

Skills	Behavioral Definition
Information Sharing	Assesses the audience and targets the message using relevant terms to meet its needs and ensure understanding. Explains complicated things in a simple manner. Reads audience reaction to the message and adjusts message accordingly. Communicates openly, honestly, and regularly. Establishes open lines of communication and presents information and decisions in a concise, balanced, and factual manner. Actively participates in meetings and expresses both supporting and opposing views constructively.
Feedback	Gathers relevant data and facts and prepares plan of action for giving feedback. Gives feedback while maintaining self-esteem, listening and responding with empathy, asking for help in solving the problem, and sharing feelings and rationale. Seeks advice/feedback from competent sources on own performance and actions. Asks questions to better understand areas for improvement and foster learning. Responds favorably to developmental feedback, makes improvements and changes relative to the feedback, and strives for continuous learning and self-improvement.
Persuasion	Sells ideas and convinces others to agree by explaining features, advantages, and benefits.
Listening	Listens to others' ideas, concerns, questions, and issues with interest, empathy, and objectivity. Asks clarifying questions to ensure understanding of the message. Listens by observing others' reactions to the message.

Knowledge of . . .	
Behavioral Science	Concepts of motivation, group dynamics, response to change, and behavioral psychology.

Beliefs, Motives, Traits, and Values

	Behavioral Definition
Balance	Achieves balance in all aspects of life—work and personal life, customer and business needs, employee and company needs—and uses humor to help keep things in perspective.
Confidence	Expects to succeed and has a positive impact on the organization, not threatened by past mistakes, accepts feedback without loss of self-esteem, accepts new challenges even when they contain an element of risk.
Conviction	Demonstrates a strong belief in issue, product, process, or team. Expends energy and resources to convince others based on individual feelings. Feels sense of urgency regarding convictions. Persistent.
High Energy	Demonstrates high enthusiasm and commitment, influences others to participate by showing excitement, initiative, drive, and purpose.
Integrity	Conducts self with the highest of ethics, honesty, forthrightness, justice, sincerity, and truth in all matters. Upholds values tenaciously and is unwilling to compromise Company values even for small issues. Perceived by others as having virtue.
Judgment	Translates past experiences and previous learnings into decisions relevant to the current situation. Reaches conclusions with an intuitive knowledge of the correct approach to addressing each issue.
Learning	Recognizes need for continuous learning from a diverse set of experiences both within an organization and from external resources. Uses history to predict future behaviors and continues to learn from past events. Strives to create a learning organization by replicating the successes of others appropriately.
Motivated by results, not rewards	Motivated by the results of the work rather than the reward, political ramifications, or credit received for participation.
Openness	Holds a fundamental philosophy that everything should be communicated with exceptions only for situations where legal or other confidentiality issues take precedence. Uses honesty, patience, sincerity, and self-disclosure when communicating with others and believes that the objective of communication is to create learning on both sides. Shares information to assist others in understanding concepts or visions.
Quality	Gives the best in all efforts, including work output, self-improvement, and relationships with others. Demonstrates patience and waits for a successful outcome even though a quick solution might satisfy short-term needs. Measures success in terms of client satisfaction and own quality standards.

(continued)

Beliefs, Motives, Traits, and Values *(concluded)*

Realistic	Recognizes that there are no magic solutions and that it is not possible to solve everything at once. Owns mistakes, and learns from them. Keeps things in perspective. Acknowledges that learning comes from successes and failures.
Relationships and Sensitivity	Considers establishment of relationships vital to success of all. Earns the right to give feedback to others. Demonstrates flexibility and teamwork and treats others as equals. Readily includes ideals from others and recognizes the value each individual brings to a group. Willingly gives appropriate credit to others. Shows respect for others in all interactions.
Trust and Credibility	Earns the respect of others by demonstrating credibility and truthfulness. Behavior matches all verbal communications. Used as a resource when help is needed, including advice regarding sensitive or confidential matters. Generates loyalty in others.

References

Linkage Incorporated. (1994). *Introduction to competency modeling workshop [workshop participant materials]*. Lexington, MA: Author.

About the Contributor

Debra L. McDaniel, SPHR, is a Senior HR Associate with Eli Lilly and Company. She is currently working in Global Training and Development supporting strategic training and development initiatives. A certified Senior Professional in Human Resources, she holds a bachelor's degree in psychology from Carthage College and a master's degree in industrial relations from the University of Wisconsin–Madison. Ms. McDaniel has had a variety of experiences within the HR profession, including former positions with Consumers Power Company and Exxon Chemical Company. She also holds active memberships in a number of HR and HR development organizations, such as the Society of Human Resource Management (SHRM) and the Institute for International Human Resources.

6.

A COMPETENCY-BASED INTERVENTION FOR SUPERVISORS IN A PUBLIC HUMAN SERVICES AGENCY

Marcia R. Sanderson, LMSW-ACP — Director, CPS Training Institute
Jason McCrory, M.S.S.W. — Project Coordinator, CPS Training Institute
Murray A. Neuman, Ph.D. — former Director, CPS Training Institute

Background

Client Agency Description

The client organization in this case study is the Texas Child Protective Services (CPS) program. CPS is the largest of three divisions within its public sector agency, the Texas Department of Protective and Regulatory Services. The organization's 5,100 CPS staff members investigate child abuse and neglect and provide in-home services to families, foster care and adoption services, and programs for runaway children. The staff are mainly college-educated, carry large caseloads, and are on the front lines fulfilling society's critical responsibility to protect children from harm. In 1995, the agency investigated 108,000 reports of child abuse or neglect.

CPS is a training-intensive business. It requires comprehensive expertise, detailed knowledge of policy and law, and a high level of professional judgment and skill. Even graduate-level social workers need extensive pre-service training before assuming a CPS caseload. All staff attend a variety of in-service trainings to advance their skill level and to learn about policy and practice changes as those changes emerge.

In the 1980s, the client agency's training programs across the state generally were somewhat disjointed. Although there was a strong investment in pre-service training for workers, the program was not implemented uniformly across the ten administrative regions. In-service training, delivered by a variety of internal and external providers, tended to be driven by ad hoc priorities rather than coordinated planning. Supervisors, a critical link in casework quality and liability issues, had limited training related specifically to their role.

Agency leaders agreed that CPS training should be better coordinated, more uniform across the state, and more carefully planned. In 1990, a strategic planning group examined resources and performance indicators across a variety of program functions. The group's final report recommended developing a new comprehensive training model. The report set a goal of more consistent and effective training, integrated with job expectations and performance, in order to provide quality services to clients.

The Purpose of This Case Study

One result of the planning group's recommendations was the creation of the CPS Training Institute in 1991. Funded by CPS, the Institute is a partnership of the agency with four graduate schools of social work in Texas. The consortium plans and implements new professional development initiatives for CPS. In the process, it strengthens the ties between social work education and child welfare practice. From its inception, the Institute has maintained a strong focus on flexibility and responsiveness and credibility, trust, and accountability for the quality and impact of its training.

This chapter will describe the Institute's application of a planning model similar to Dr. David Dubois' Strategic Systems Model (1993). The model allowed the Institute to effectively respond to the professional development needs of the client agency. The performance improvement intervention described focuses on CPS supervisors. As in most real-world scenarios—and especially in the public sector—some adaptations to the model were required.

Front-End Needs Analysis, Assessment, and Planning

Program-wide Philosophy Setting, Needs Identification, and Needs Analysis

As a result of the 1990 strategic planning effort, a comprehensive professional development planning project was launched in 1992. The CPS Training Institute was asked to facilitate the writing of a comprehensive professional development plan.

A ten-member task force of key players was convened, with representation from CPS field staff, trainers, and managers. The task force considered the current status of professional development for all levels of staff, established guiding principles and a broad model for professional development, broadly identified gaps and needs, and made specific recommendations for existing and new programs. The five-month process resulted in a lengthy master plan that was adopted by the program as its professional development model.

The task force began with the agency's new mission statement and developed professional development principles that supported and elaborated on the mission. This grounding in the agency's mission was reflected in the plan's opening section: "This document reflects our belief that a comprehensive and systematic approach to ongoing professional development coordination can make a significant impact on the efficiency of the organization, on the performance of individual staff, and ultimately on the effectiveness of [the program's] services to clients." (Texas Department of Protective and Regulatory Services, 1993, p. 2)

The planning document was organized under the broad principle of *Performance Support*. As described in the plan, the goal of strengthening performance, especially that of front-line staff, permeates the entire agency. The concept of performance support encompasses reward systems, human resource systems, performance feedback, the job performance environment, the organizational context, and professional development (education and professionalization).

The overarching principle of performance support, in combination with the agency's mission statement, was the foundation for further guiding principles related to performance enhancement (see Figure 1).

FIGURE 1: Guiding Principles from TDPRS Comprehensive Professional Development Plan for CPS

Guiding Principles for CPS Performance Support Interventions

- **The agency exists to deliver services that improve clients' lives.** The first commitment of the agency's mission statement relates to quality client service. The second and third commitments in the mission statement address the organizational culture and environment necessary to support the goals of service delivery. All performance support efforts are rooted in the agency's vital primary mission.

- **The agency achieves its mission by valuing and enhancing the performance of its employees.** The commitments in the mission statement can be fulfilled most effectively by integrating the agency's resources and processes toward the goal of supporting the performance of service delivery staff, which influences quality client outcomes most directly. This mission-oriented focus also requires that the performance of all employees be enhanced, including those who perform other vital agency tasks and functions. All employees are valued for their ultimate contribution to the performance of front-line staff as they provide services to clients.

- **The agency enhances performance by valuing its employees as *people*.** Just as the agency values the worth of the families and individuals it serves, it must clearly value its own people. Members of the organization are first of all *persons* who seek meaning and purpose in and through their work. The agency's explicit focus on supporting the performance of the staff charged with the organization's primary mission allows every member of the organization to understand the significant purpose and value of her or his own contribution. Each has an important stake and role in achieving the agency's mission.

- **The agency enhances performance by valuing its employees as *professionals*.** Each member of the organization performs best when valued as a competent, productive professional. Every employee brings a unique set of knowledge, skills, experience, values, and potential that, collectively, is the agency's most precious resource.

- **The agency enhances performance through individual and workgroup *empowerment*.** The agency expresses the value of its employees by establishing an environment, a culture, opportunities, and resources that enable and encourage their best work. To enhance individual, group, and organizational performance, the agency must provide its members with the tools they need to do their work effectively.

- **The agency enhances performance through *adaptation*.** Some of the factors that impede employee performance are not intrinsic to the individual, but instead are due to elements of the organization. Improving individual and organizational performance requires adequate performance feedback mechanisms, a close analysis of the systems within the agency that affect the employee's work, and careful, strategic re-tuning of those systems to optimize employees' capabilities.

- **The agency enhances performance through *integration*.** A corollary of the above principle is that training is not a panacea for every performance problem. Rather, all agency components must work together to facilitate effectiveness. This linkage of organization structure, process and functions must be *proactive* to prevent performance problems and *continuous* to respond to problems and to steadily improve effectiveness.

Source: Texas Department of Protective and Regulatory Services, *Comprehensive Professional Development Plan for CPS*, pp. 3–4.

The second section of the comprehensive report included a variety of recommendations related to competency-based training programs for new workers, tenured workers, supervisors, and specialized areas. All professional development efforts were to be performance-oriented and organized around a set of identified job competencies.

Response Plan

Once the agency approved and adopted the comprehensive planning document, it began to prioritize the report's recommendations in order to select a few for immediate action.

Across Texas, the 400 CPS supervisors reflect a diverse mix of tenure and educational levels and a variety of expertise related to the special functions of their respective units. These supervisors are a key link for agency mission, policy, and performance. They provide a professional level of administrative and policy-related supervision, casework supervision, and developmental supervision for their units. They guide and approve critical decisions that rescue children from harm and restructure families.

Supervisors are an important level of intervention for ensuring quality service to clients. Supervisors teach and reinforce new concepts and behaviors on a daily basis. They also have more staying power than workers—that is, since worker turnover is high, training given to supervisors has a longer-lasting impact on the agency. And because there are fewer supervisors compared to workers, statewide training can be delivered more efficiently.

The agency selected front-line supervisors as an immediate, high-impact, manageable focus for performance enhancement interventions. The CPS Training Institute was charged with responding to their professional development needs. The Institute's strategic approach included (1) identifying and validating competencies for the supervisor position, (2) conducting training needs assessments, (3) prioritizing training interventions, and (4) developing and delivering portions of supervisor professional development that blended with programs already in place.

Competency Modeling

Competency Development Process

The competency identification model chosen by the Institute was a customized generic method. Since extensive work had been done nationally to develop competency sets for CPS supervisors, the Institute's action plan used these competency sets as a starting point for developing a comprehensive list of knowledge, skills, and abilities for the work done by CPS supervisors in Texas.

A competency identification task force was formed that included representatives from all constituent groups who would be affected by the competency model. CPS administrators, supervisors, and trainers, as well as staff from the Institute (including faculty from the schools of social work), made up the committee.

The first task of this group was to gather data from a variety of sources that addressed competencies for supervisors in child protection settings. Data was drawn from job descriptions, performance appraisal systems, training curricula, and accreditation materials from national sources. These sources included, but were not limited to, the Child Welfare League of America Supervisor Training Institute, the National Registry of Accreditation in Child Protective Services, the American Public Welfare Association, the National Association of Social Workers Task Force on competencies for CPS, the National Resource Center on Child Abuse and Neglect, and several sources from within the agency, including the *Personnel Handbook* descriptions for CPS supervisors and the standard performance evaluation form.

A list of 51 distinct competency areas was compiled from this material. A grid that matched these 51 items with their 12 sources allowed the group to see which competency areas were acknowledged as important by what sources. Those that appeared to be the most relevant for practice in Texas were chosen and organized into five categories: Foundations of CPS Work, Casework Methods and Practice, Supervisor as Manager, Supervisor as Leader, and Supervisor as Developer of Staff. Examples of individual competency items are shown in Figure 2.

FIGURE 2: Texas CPS Supervisor Competencies

Competency Area	Competency Item Examples
Foundations of CPS Work	■ The supervisor can assess for risk, plan interventions, and make decisions. ■ The supervisor can recognize symptoms of chemical dependency. ■ The supervisor is familiar with agency policy and procedures.
Casework Methods and Practice	■ The supervisor is familiar with various stages of CPS service. ■ The supervisor is familiar with the family preservation practice approach. ■ The supervisor ensures that workers incorporate the child's permanency needs in case plans.
Supervisor as Manager	■ The supervisor can handle time demands and crisis situations in an efficient and effective manner. ■ The supervisor can identify positive and negative conflict and can respond appropriately. ■ The supervisor has knowledge of the community and its resources.
Supervisor as Leader	■ The supervisor knows styles and functions of leadership. ■ The supervisor effectively involves staff in decisions that affect them. ■ The supervisor knows the stages and roles of group process and development.
Supervisor as Developer of Staff	■ The supervisor promotes learning through modeling and reinforcement. ■ The supervisor knows and can use various kinds of supervision with staff to motivate, assist, and evaluate. ■ The supervisor deals fairly and promptly with performance problems.

Competencies were chosen and phrased to reflect satisfactory rather than exemplary practice. As promotion within the department is tied to a "meets requirements" rating rather than a "superior" or "exceeds expectations," the committee wanted these competencies to dovetail with that system. In addition, in anticipation of revamping the performance rating systems within the agency, these competencies could be of use in that process.

The initial list of competencies was presented for review to 52 supervisors in four different settings that included training sessions, regional supervisory meetings, and a statewide supervisor advisory group. Ten questions were asked in a structured format to solicit input from the groups. Examples of the questions include:

- Do you think the identified skills are sufficiently comprehensive to be representative of all the tasks which CPS supervisors need to know? Are some skills omitted in this list that should be included?

- Are there skills in this list that should be omitted?

- Are the competencies presented relevant to your work as a CPS supervisor?

- Are these competencies realistic expectations of CPS supervisors?

- If training were to be developed for specific competencies, what would be the top three on your "wish list"?

The task force used information from these surveys to make final revisions to the competency list before the material was forwarded for more in-depth validation.

Needs Assessment

Statewide Survey

The Institute developed a survey that collapsed the competencies into 40 discrete items, asking about the importance of each competency for the supervisory role, as well as the need for training in that competency. This survey was sent to all CPS supervisors, program directors, and regional directors, as well as to a sample of 20 workers from a statewide CPS worker advisory committee.

Several steps were taken to maximize the response to the questionnaire. The cover letter explaining the survey and its importance was signed by the director of the CPS program. The supervisors involved in the original review were asked to encourage peers in their regions to complete the survey. The regional directors were kept abreast of developments related to the survey through their monthly meetings. As a result of these efforts, 47% of those included responded to the survey, a high percentage for a mailed questionnaire of this type.

Based on survey results, 37 competency areas were rated as having high relevance for CPS supervisors in Texas. Three areas were ranked somewhat lower ("moderately important"): adoption, foster care, and independent living skills. These areas were viewed as more specialized and not applicable to many supervisors, particularly in urban regions where practice is more highly specialized at the unit level. Survey results substantiated that the competency set accurately represented the tasks and responsibilities of supervisors. No additional competencies were added to the list, but the small differences between rural and urban practice were noted.

The second part of the survey ranked training needs as they related to the competencies. A much broader range of responses was given in this section of the survey. Sixteen items fell within the "high" range for training need, 17 in the "moderate" range, and 7 in the "low to moderate" range. The highest areas of training need were (1) working with supervisee problem behaviors, (2) techniques of effective supervision, (3) styles of leadership, and (4) educational supervision.

Survey data was summarized on both a statewide and regional basis. While regional information was very similar to that obtained statewide, it provided targeted data that could be used for training planning at the regional level. A brief summary of the statewide results was mailed to all CPS supervisors, program directors, and regional directors.

Regional Focus Groups

Focus groups were held in each of the regions to gain more specific information about the training needs of supervisors related to the competencies. These groups served two purposes: to give a better understanding about the particular issues that should be addressed in curriculum development, and to provide additional opportunities for participation by as many people as possible in determining the training plan. Eighty supervisors participated. Several areas were explored in the day-long meetings:

- Training factors that make training useful, effective, and applicable to the job

- Assessments of specific trainings that supervisors had attended while with CPS

- Suggestions for improving CPS training

- Specific problem situations that supervisors encounter

- Specific problematic staff behaviors

- Information from the regional training coordinator on training needs of supervisors

Data from these ten focus groups was compiled into two types of reports:

- Training: a 4-page summary sent to all focus group participants and a 16-page synopsis for use by decision makers and curriculum writers.

- Organizational Issues: a separate report presented to CPS administrators in a private meeting related to systemic issues that have a direct impact on performance.

While issues such as organizational mandates, caseload size, and policy issues were outside the purview of the Institute to address, these factors can have significant negative influences on performance. The Institute saw a critical need to share these issues with agency administrators and to clarify what types of performance factors the Institute could address in training as opposed to what types would require a more systemic approach by the agency.

Plan of Action

The Institute and CPS decided to approach training in an incremental way, beginning immediately with training on the most-needed topics before developing a full supervisory training plan. Data from the focus group process indicated a need for developing supervisory skills in working with problem staff behaviors. Training was viewed as a viable format for improving those skills.

The extensive competency-based needs assessment process was the starting point for the curriculum development process. The detailed focus group information related to problem behaviors, and situations allowed content to be specifically tailored to the expressed needs of CPS supervisors. This was especially important because focus group members criticized previous trainings for being too generic and not focused on the realities of CPS practice.

Curriculum Planning

Goals were established for the curriculum based on the training needs assessment and the focus group input. To satisfy CPS staff, training has to be practice-oriented, experiential in nature, and use adult learning strategies to impart information. In addition, an emphasis was placed on methods of improving transfer of learning from the classroom to the practice arena.

Curriculum content was tied directly to the challenges and problem situations identified by supervisors. This ensured its relevance to everyday practice and provided immediate support to supervisors who had documented specific learning needs. Learning objectives were formulated from the examples given by supervisors in the focus groups.

Then, a brief outline of possible training topics that would be included in the final curriculum package to meet the established learning objectives was developed. Practice examples in the curriculum were drawn from the assessment process. Theoretical and application strategies were drawn from an extensive review of business and human-services literature and curricula.

Intervention Design, Development, and Implementation

The result of the initial planning process was the development of a two-day in-service training session for all CPS supervisors, titled "Supervising Individuals With Diverse Needs." Curriculum development included several steps. First, a curriculum development committee, composed of Institute staff and faculty and CPS supervisors from each region, reviewed the competency list, the focus group reports, the preliminary learning objectives, and the brief outline of possible training topics. In addition to approving these items, the committee participated in planning an extensive review and revision process for the curriculum.

Description of Training

The first step of this process was to script a first draft of the curriculum that would address the learning objectives approved by the curriculum committee. The curriculum had the following features:

- The objectives were written in terms of behaviors to be gained, changed, or reinforced. The objectives were divided into two categories—those that would help the supervisor understand self, worker, and situation; and those designed to teach the supervisor to apply action strategies to change problem behaviors. Examples of these objectives: Recognize the need to use positive reinforcement to build "emotional bank accounts"; Utilize techniques for overcoming negativity; Resolve conflicts with staff using a win-win approach; and Apply strategies for dealing with difficult people.

- Eleven learning objectives were established for the two-day curriculum.

- The curriculum, developed using the principle of 20-minute modules, was based on learning and retention theories emphasizing shorter and more dynamic presentations and activities.

- All content presented in a lecture format was accompanied by learning activities designed to reinforce the knowledge gained and to ensure that new skills are practiced. This format is firmly rooted in the philosophy that adults remember far more of what they do than of what they see or hear.

- As with all Institute training, the training was developed to be presented by a social work faculty member and a CPS practitioner in a team format. This model is effective as it combines both theoretical and practice-oriented approaches to learning. In addition, the presentation itself models productive team interaction in a way that parallels the supervisor-worker and worker-client relationship.

- Each concept or learning module was tied directly to CPS case examples and to situations that participants themselves brought to the training. Tailoring to the experiences of the participants has been one of the most highly valued aspects of Institute training. Generic management training, while appreciated by some, often had not met the needs of a majority of CPS staff, according to data from the focus group reports.

- Each participant used an "Action Ideas" page throughout the training to document specific ideas that were particularly relevant to his or her interests. These action ideas were used to finalize the "Participant Action Plan" at the end of the session. The Institute followed up with participants several months later to measure the success of implementation of planned changes in behavior from the action plan, as described below in the section on evaluation.

Testing and Revising the Curriculum

Once the curriculum was developed in draft form, a one-day walk-through was presented to the curriculum committee. Revisions were made according to their feedback. The next step was to offer the full two-day package in one region to a training-sized group of supervisors for additional feedback. As a result of this pilot, fine-tuning related to timing and activities was completed.

Preparing for Training Delivery

Once the curriculum was finalized, social work faculty trainers and CPS practitioner-trainers met to review the curriculum and to learn tips on visuals, activities, training styles, and experiences from the pilot training. In addition to this session, all trainers had previously received skill development in creative training techniques. The Institute's investment in trainers' presentation skills was highly beneficial and resulted in far more effective training sessions.

Flyers describing the training and its benefits were sent to all CPS supervisors, as well as to the program directors who supervise them. In addition, briefings on the content were presented in several advisory and executive forums to encourage attendance.

Implementation Concerns

Several issues were addressed regarding the presentation of the curriculum. First, as participation in the training was voluntary, special attention was given to educating supervisors about how this training session would meet their specific needs and be of direct benefit to them in their work. The course was also included in the training requirements for the voluntary CPS supervisor certification program.

Second, the Institute considered how to best present training to supervisors ranging in tenure from one month to 20 years or more. Although dividing the training groups by experience was an option, the Institute believed that optimal learning would occur by maintaining this broad range of experience in the classroom. The agency also wanted to ensure that tenured staff were provided with the opportunity to develop new skills for effective management.

Third, scheduling issues were of great importance. Each region scheduled the sessions at their convenience, rather than having a schedule determined by the Institute. Although this created additional logistical problems for the training teams, the flexibility was appreciated by region personnel, whose calendars were filled with local training and initiatives. This approach involved regional staff in the process, building ownership at that level. All sessions were scheduled in facilities away from the workplace to avoid distractions during the training. While this added to costs and required additional contracting with hotels and other facilities, separating training from work reduced the number of participants called away for phone calls or other business.

Finally, maintaining training consistency across the state was an important goal. Overall, the content delivered remained the same, even though social work faculty and CPS practitioners could draw on their own unique knowledge and experience. The two-day training allowed for some tailoring of the material by individual trainers while maintaining the overall integrity of the curriculum. Such an approach supports academic freedom along with training consistency.

Training Summary

Twenty-three two-day sessions of "Supervising Individuals With Diverse Needs" were presented across the state. A total of 365 supervisors (over 90%) attended. This was a high participation rate for voluntary training at a time when case loads were increasing and supervisors were dealing with other agency initiatives.

The Institute presented the same curriculum in special sessions to program directors so that knowledge and skills could be reinforced at all levels. These sessions were offered separately from the supervisor sessions to ensure that supervisors could participate fully. In addition, two regional directors chose to attend the sessions for program directors to take advantage of the skills training.

Evaluation

Choice of an Evaluation Model

Two evaluation training models were considered for assessing the effectiveness of "Supervising Individuals." The first, Kirkpatrick's model (1975, 1978), focuses on participants' reactions to the training, participants' learning achievements, changes in participants' behavior, and results regarding organizational impact. The second, the CIPP model (Stufflebeam et al., 1971), encompasses four types of evaluation: Context evaluation, Input evaluation, Process evaluation, and Product evaluation. In applying the CIPP model to a training intervention, evaluation is assigned a key role in each phase of development and implementation, from the front-end needs analysis through the evaluation of the training itself and its subsequent outcomes.

Because the CIPP model can be used to help make decisions throughout the lifetime of a training intervention, it was thought to be the best choice. The model also has the advantage of being suited to the promotion of transfer of learning, a key goal for the Institute. Context and input evaluation activities help identify and develop appropriate transfer interventions for a given training. Process evaluation activities help ensure that transfer considerations are integrated into all phases of the intervention through the development and monitoring of transfer objectives. Finally, product evaluation activities measure the extent of training transfer, as well as the outcomes and impact of the transfer.

Evaluation Questions

During the development and implementation of the supervisor training, several evaluation questions were raised for each phase of the Strategic Systems Model process. Information collected in response to these questions was used to help shape, refine, and revise the training materials. The information also provided an indication of the degree to which trainees transferred what they learned to their work setting.

The four types of evaluation in the CIPP model correspond to the four kinds of decisions made while developing and implementing this training: planning decisions (context evaluation), structuring decisions (input evaluation), implementation decisions (process evaluation), and recycling decisions (product evaluation).

The important evaluation questions raised during the project are shown in Table 1. These questions are organized by Strategic Systems Model phase (e.g., curriculum planning) and type of evaluation (e.g., context evaluation).

TABLE 1: CIPP Evaluation Questions Related to the Strategic Systems Model Phases

Strategic Systems Model Phase	Evaluation Component	Relevant Evaluation Questions
Front-End Needs Analysis, Assessment, and Planning	Context Evaluation	What is the agency's mission? What are the agency's strengths, weaknesses, and unmet needs? What are the major problems facing the agency? What is the nature of the job and work environment? What are the most pressing professional development needs of the staff? Do staff have the appropriate backgrounds, skills, and resources for their work? What principles should guide a system that supports the development of staff?
Competency Model Development	Input Evaluation	What competencies are needed to perform the job? What supervisor competency models have been developed by other states or organizations involved in similar work? What process should be used to arrive at appropriate competencies and who should be involved in the process?
Curriculum Planning	Input Evaluation	What are the overall goals and specific objectives of the curriculum? Will achievement of the goals and objectives have a positive effect on the identified problems? Do agency staff view the goals and objectives as relevant and important?
Learning Intervention Design and Development	Input Evaluation	Can existing materials be used or modified? How should the objectives and training activities be sequenced? For the training content and target group, what are the most appropriate media and training exercises? Does the intervention design promote transfer of learning from the classroom to the job? What follow-up activities would help sustain the desired trainee outcomes?

(continued)

TABLE 1: CIPP Evaluation Questions Related to the Strategic Systems Model Phases *(concluded)*

Strategic Systems Model Phase	Evaluation Component	Relevant Evaluation Questions
Learning Intervention Implementation	Process Evaluation	Was the training implemented as intended? What were the number and characteristics of the trainees? Were there problems with facilities, beginning/ending times, or the amount of time spent on each training segment? What observations, suggestions, and reactions did the trainers and trainees have to the training? Was the training judged by the trainees as having been relevant? What did the trainees find most/least useful about the training? Did the desired learning occur during the training? What improvements or corrections are needed?
	Product Evaluation	To what degree did transfer of learning take place? Do the trainees still apply what was learned 6–8 weeks after the training? Did managers, clients, or others observe any positive changes in those trained? How was the agency affected by the training intervention? Was the training cost-effective given the client impact and trainee outcomes? Did the training make a positive contribution to the agency culture? What information can be used from the product evaluation to improve subsequent versions of the training?

The following discussion provides a more complete picture of how the CIPP evaluation approach was used in the development and assessment of "Supervising Individuals With Diverse Needs." A sampling of the evaluation findings derived from the various assessment activities is provided in the process evaluation and product evaluation sections. The findings of context and input evaluation activities have been described earlier in the chapter.

Context Evaluation

Context evaluation provided information that helped shape the rationale for training goals and objectives. It examined and described things such as the characteristics of the workplace, relevant characteristics of the trainees (e.g., educational and attitudinal), competencies needed to perform the job, unmet needs, major problem areas, and needed changes in behavior that could be influenced by training.

Activities used to gather the context evaluation information included needs assessment surveys, examination of performance measures, focus groups, and literature reviews. In addition, past efforts (not described here) that produced the agency performance measures reviewed during our process included task analysis, direct observations in the work setting, interviews with the target trainees and their managers, employee exit interviews, and the critical incident method.

Input Evaluation

Input evaluation provided data for decisions about the use of resources to support the training's goals and objectives. Input evaluation involved identifying and analyzing instructional strategies for achieving the goals and objectives, assessing approaches to implementing the selected strategies, evaluating existing training materials for their adoption or modification, developing tailor-made training segments, selecting appropriate media, and deciding on follow-up activities.

Input evaluation activities included literature reviews, reviews of existing curricula, input from subject matter experts, input from instructional-design experts, interviews with potential trainees to determine instructional preferences, informal assessment of pretraining behaviors and attitudes, and interviews with staff development personnel knowledgeable about the target trainees.

Process Evaluation

Process evaluation provided feedback on the implementation of the training. Its purpose was to identify problems with the content and design of the training materials or problems with the implementation. It also involved keeping detailed records on all aspects of implementation, such as number of individuals trained, characteristics of the trainees, how trainees were scheduled for the training, trainee and trainer reactions to and satisfaction with the training, and assessment of the adequacy of the training facilities.

Examples of process evaluation activities were the curriculum pilot test, trainee assessments of the training content, facilities, and trainers; trainer assessment of the training content, facilities, and trainee performance and attitudes; basic record keeping of number of trainees, trainee characteristics, and implementation problems; and classroom observations by the Institute training manager.

Listed below are examples of responses given by the training participants immediately after the training session.

- Ninety-six percent of the trainees agreed/strongly agreed that the workshop was relevant to their work as CPS supervisors.

- Ninety-eight percent agreed/strongly agreed that the trainers were knowledgeable about the topic.

- Ninety-three percent agreed/strongly agreed that the workshop was presented in an interesting manner.

- Ninety-two percent agreed/strongly agreed that they had acquired strategies for coping with difficult people.

- Ninety-four percent agreed/strongly agreed that they had gained new insights into their own style of supervision.

Product Evaluation

Product evaluation focused on assessing the overall effectiveness of the intervention. This was facilitated by gathering information on trainee outcomes and agency impact as a result of the training. The main approach to product evaluation in this case was the Participant Action Plan Approach (U.S. Office of Personnel Management, 1980). The PAPA involves action planning and post-training follow-up to promote the transfer of what was learned in training to the job.

Participants were introduced to action planning at the beginning of the training and were asked to think about how they would use what they learned back on the job. At the end of the training, the participants developed action plans consisting of two to four things learned in the training that they intended to try once they returned to their jobs. Examples of action items were "Practice active listening with my employees" and "Use the win-win strategy when dealing with resistant, hostile, or unmotivated clients."

Two to four months after the training, participants were interviewed by telephone. Their responses were categorized to capture the types of behavior changes attempted, the degree of successful implementation, the impact of the behavior changes, the problems or barriers encountered, and suggestions for improvement of the training.

Examples of PAPA evaluation results follow:

- Ninety-one percent of those contacted had tried an average of two action items related to what had been learned in the training.

- The most frequently tried action items were "Providing positive feedback to employees," "Empathetic listening," "Adjusting my own style to better supervise employees," and "Asking for more staff input."

- Seventy-two percent of the trainees believed that they had been "fully" or "mostly" successful in implementing their action items.

- Eighty-nine percent of the trainees believed that implementing their action items had either a "a lot" or a "fair amount" of impact.

- Forty-seven percent of the trainees reported that their biggest barrier to implementing their action items related to their own self-management: that is, staying motivated in a demanding environment, remembering to use new skills, and changing old habits.

In general, the positive impressions trainees had immediately after the training were sustained at the time of follow-up months later.

Feedback Into Professional Development System and Further Developments

Feedback Into Institute Programs

To build on the success of the first intervention, the CPS Training Institute was asked to develop a second two-day supervisor training module. This curriculum was titled "Leadership: Empowering Yourself and Others." The content was based on the second cluster of competency-based training needs identified in the original needs assessment. The new module incorporated the same instructional approach and the same built-in transfer of training and evaluation components as "Supervising Individuals."

This second module met with similar success. As a result, the same model of needs assessment, instructional design and delivery, and evaluation has been continued by the Institute in further interventions for supervisors and workers. The Institute is committed to assessing emerging needs within the agency and responding quickly and effectively.

Feedback Into Agency Professional Development Planning

The positive process evaluation for "Supervising Individuals," and more importantly, the impressive transfer-of-training evaluation, demonstrated the effectiveness of a competency-based, needs-driven, thoughtfully planned collaborative approach to professional development interventions. As a result, the agency made "Supervising Individuals" and "Leadership" mandatory for all new CPS supervisors, acknowledging the strength of modules.

This chapter has focused on the Institute's role in supervisor professional development. The client agency has continued to develop a variety of professional development pieces based on its original comprehensive professional development plan. To date, the major initiatives have included:

- Identification of a professional development coordinator within the CPS program, whose responsibilities range from training coordination to serving as a liaison with related functions within the agency such as performance evaluation and personnel policy.

- Creation of an ongoing professional development coordination team to implement the original performance support plan and provide further direction to professional development.

- Implementation of a competency-based CPS supervisor certification program through the CPS Training Institute.

- Development and implementation of a comprehensive supervisor professional development plan. The plan includes mandatory "survival skills" training immediately after promotion, a year-long mentoring program, sequential and integrated competency-based training during the first two years, and ongoing professional development requirements.

- Design and implementation of a comprehensive worker professional development plan similar to the one for supervisors.

The agency continues to develop and implement recommendations from the original performance support plan, guided by its core principles. Future efforts will include changes in the performance evaluation system to reflect new requirements and understandings about performance, and major investments in computer-based performance support interventions. For example, the Internet will be used as a tool to deliver "remind and refresh" follow-ups to classroom training and modules on worker safety and other performance or policy topics that staff can access when they need the information.

Conclusions

Lessons Learned

Several key points emerge as important to the successful implementation of a training intervention that crosses institutional boundaries.

1. Giving Time to the Process

One of the most critical issues in establishing complex systems across multiple organizations is giving adequate time for the process to occur. This process time is required to establish trust and to understand and appreciate the strengths of different organizational cultures. It is necessary to become aware of the controls and constraints that the various systems must exercise in fulfilling their missions. Finally, time is required to ensure that careful planning occurs, given the highly visible nature of a new training venture such as the CPS Training Institute.

The issue of trust was particularly important in Texas because past efforts in a large-scale partnership were less than successful. The contract between the universities and the agency that established the Institute was the first major statewide effort to bridge these systems since that difficult time. It was important that leaders in the partnership be comfortable with the process and allow initial conflict to occur.

2. Responsiveness

Willingness of the Institute to be responsive to the short-term needs of CPS was a critical piece in building trust. A typical university strategy might have been to take two to three years to carefully research and plan for an entire training program and intervention process. Instead, the development of the "Supervising Individuals" curriculum was a "reactive" approach related to current needs, rather than the "proactive" approach that later grew out of this project. See Rothwell and Kazanas (1988) as cited in Dubois (1993, p. 119) for further discussion of this concept.

Demonstrating the capacity to address the needs of CPS staff through this short-term training intervention provided a concrete product and the assurance that the Institute was a valuable partner. This encouraged the agency to consider involving the Institute in long-range planning and to utilize the resources provided by the universities when developing ongoing training efforts for supervisors.

3. High-Quality Products

The extensive process time dedicated to the development of quality products demonstrated the capacity of the collaborative model to meet the needs of the agency and the universities. The benefit of involving the faculty at the universities in training is the state-of-the-art information and research they bring that can be incorporated into the curriculum. Packaging information from academic settings into practice-oriented training maintained the relevance for the target audience, as did the use of CPS practitioner trainers who could share practice wisdom and skills. Finally, the emphasis on providing trainers with extensive training in presentation skills ensured that the material was delivered effectively.

4. Accountability

From planning the training through the delivery and follow-up, extensive work went into the development of the Institute evaluation model, including individual evaluation tools for training sessions. Demonstrating the success of the training from both process and outcome standpoints lent substantial credibility to the work of the Institute. Since accountability is extremely important in a legislatively funded agency with tight fiscal constraints, demonstrating that funds were well spent was mandatory. In addition, choosing a responsive approach to training for this initial effort and giving extra attention to accountability issues helped build trust among organizations, demonstrate the capacity for effectiveness, and test developmental strategies and procedures. This, in turn, laid the foundation for further and more comprehensive work between the universities and the agency.

5. Inclusiveness

Involving as many players as possible in needs assessment, conceptualization, design, and implementation reinforced the idea that this training is shaped by and for the staff to whom it is offered. The Institute paid careful attention to keeping staff at all levels informed about results of surveys, training, special workshops, and so forth through memos, reports, newsletter articles, and phone conversations. Reports were offered to all governing and advisory committees of the Institute and the agency throughout the process. This attention to inclusiveness added to the comfort level of all who participated.

6. Relationships

Maintaining open and responsive relationships with key decision-makers, organizational units, and state and regional contacts was essential in fostering trust and information exchange. These relationships formed the basis for discussing those things that did not go as planned, as well as for celebrating successes.

7. The Town/Gown Syndrome

Embedded in issues of trust are organizational differences between the academic and practice arenas. Academics tend to prefer long-range planning, deliberation of all viewpoints, comprehensive assessments, and theoretical approaches that guide decision making. CPS practice tends to be crisis-oriented, requires quick response time, needs practical tools and techniques for accomplishing complex interventions, and is under constant public scrutiny. When the partnership includes giving time to process, relationship building, inclusiveness, and accountability, these factors can be addressed. Such a process allows the strengths of each organization to be effectively utilized on behalf of professional development of staff.

8. Adaptation to the Real World

When this process began, there was a vacuum in supervisor training within CPS. Long-range planning to lay out the entire supervisory training program could have taken place before the development of "Supervising Individuals." Nonetheless, concentrating on the initial course allowed us to address real problems and build a track record of success.

The success of the first course and the subsequent related "Leadership" course led to the development of a long-range proactive plan that integrated both CPS and Institute training efforts. As noted in the previous section, this comprehensive supervisor professional development plan is now mandatory for all new supervisors and builds skills in a sequential fashion for the work, rather than filling in gaps as they become evident during the course of a supervisor's career.

Conclusion

Evaluation results clearly documented the success of the training. It promoted intended changes in behavior in ways that were meaningful to those trained. From identifying training needs to evaluating the impact of the intervention addressing those needs, the Strategic Systems Model planning process provided a flexible framework for building a product that was relevant and useful to the intended audience. The experiences reported throughout this chapter provide strong support for application of the model to professional development in public human service agencies. In addition, they provide important insights about interagency training partnerships.

Acknowledgments

The work described in this chapter would not have been possible without the participation of many key people. We would like to acknowledge the support of Carol Martin, CPS Program Specialist for Performance Support and liaison to the CPS Training Institute. She has been with the Institute since its inception and was on the original team that laid the groundwork for the Institute's development. Charlene Urwin, Institute special projects staff, managed the focus group process conducted around the state and assisted with the editing of this chapter. Joan Richardson, Institute training manager, developed the curriculum and trained the trainers for this training effort.

Finally, none of this would have been possible or relevant without the input from so many supervisors and other CPS staff throughout the process. Providing meaningful, effective programs that help them in their jobs is the reason for our existence.

References

Dubois, D. D. (1993). *Competency-based performance improvement: A strategy for organizational change.* Amherst, MA: HRD Press.

Kirkpatrick, D. L. (1975). *Evaluating training programs.* Madison, WI: American Society for Training and Development.

Kirkpatrick, D. L. (1978). Evaluation of training. In R.L. Craig (Ed.), *The training and development handbook.* New York: McGraw-Hill.

Rothwell, W., & Kazanas, H. C. (1988). Curriculum planning for training: The state of the art. *Performance Improvement Quarterly, 1*(3), 2–16.

Stufflebeam, D. L., Foley, W. J., Gephart, W. R., Guba, E. G., Hammond, R. L., Merriman, H. O., & Provus, M. M. (1971). *Educational evaluation and decision making.* Itasca, IL: Peacock.

Texas Department of Protective and Regulatory Services. (1993). *Comprehensive professional development plan for Child Protective Services* [agency document]. Austin, TX: Author.

U.S. Office of Personnel Management. (1980). *Assessing changes in job behavior due to training: A guide to the Participant Action Plan Approach.* Washington, DC: Author.

About the Contributors

Marcia R. Sanderson, LMSW-ACP, is currently Director of the Children's Protective Services Training Institute at The University of Texas at Austin and Director of the Office of Community Projects at the University of Houston Graduate School of Social Work.

Jason McCrory, M.S.S.W., is currently Project Coordinator for the Austin office of the CPS Training Institute.

Murray A. Newman, Ph.D., is currently a researcher for child welfare projects in the Office of Community Projects at the University of Houston Graduate School of Social Work. He is a former director of the CPS Training Institute.

7.
A NEW MODEL OF LEADERSHIP
Developing and Implementing a Competency Model and an Integrated Human Resources System for First-Line Leaders at Motorola Semiconductor Products Sector

Jeremie Hill Grey, Ph.D. — former LATG/East Valley Group Training Manager
Sarabeth Simpson — former CPSTG Group Training Manager

ADDITIONAL CONTRIBUTORS:

Christine Florez — LATG/East Valley Compensation and Benefits Manager
Ann Igoe, Ph.D. — former LATG/East Valley Training Design Manager
Jennifer Fox Kennedy, M.S. — LATG/East Valley Senior Instructional Designer

This chapter documents the design and development of a competency model for the new role of supervisors within the Motorola Semiconductor Products Sector. A first-line leadership model based on data and projected needs was developed and approved, training resources were developed or adapted, and a new compensation system and promotional matrix, including job descriptions, was developed to support the implementation of the new model.

Background and Strategic Organizational Profile

Based in Schaumburg, Illinois, Motorola is one of the largest and oldest of America's high-technology corporations, supporting a workforce of approximately 150,000 employees worldwide. Founded in Chicago in the 1920s by Paul Galvin, the company first manufactured radios and radio equipment and over the years has expanded this initial role to include products such as computers, cellular phones, and pagers, as well as a host of technologies. Central to all the products are the "computer chips" manufactured by the Semiconductor Products Sector (SPS) headquartered in Phoenix, Arizona. SPS itself employs 50,000 engineers, technicians, and manufacturing and support personnel worldwide, among them hundreds of manufacturing supervisors. It has large-scale operations in the United States—in Arizona, Texas, California, and North Carolina—and in many locations abroad.

Motorola has experienced tremendous growth in the past few years, yet the Galvin family, still actively involved in the company's management, have succeeded in retaining the company's commitment to its people, to long-term employment, and to family values. In turn, employee loyalty is exceptionally strong, and long length of service is typical of the employee population. The need for career and skill development is crucial in such a case, assuming major importance within the human resources function. Every Motorolan is therefore required to complete at least 40 hours of training annually. In meeting this requirement, SPS employs approximately 300 training personnel worldwide in addition to the corporate services of Motorola University (MU). Many of these training specialists are involved at various levels in educational counseling and production of curricular roadmaps and guidelines, as well as scheduling and offering training programs and keeping necessary records. (For more information about Motorola, see Chapter 2.)

Key Issues and Events

In the latter half of the 1980s, major changes occurred in the role that supervisors played in the company, and the new roles required changes in human resource (HR) systems and training for the supervisory population. (Supervisory training was a major focus of the training specialists reporting through the Human Resources Department.) Traditionally, supervisors within Motorola had been junior management, and had typically risen through the ranks after years of meritorious service. Approximately 80% of supervisors at Motorola worked in manufacturing areas, with each supervisor responsible for between six and (in some extreme cases) 60 line workers. The attainment of a supervisory position was until recently, the culmination of a career for many workers. The position traditionally carried with it substantial authority, and assignment to the position was considered recognition for work well done over a period of many years. Supervisors were responsible for attendance, hiring, discipline, and dismissal; they exercised considerable control over the work lives of their subordinates and were generally older employees with many years of factory experience.

The roles and responsibilities of supervisors had changed radically as a result of two major trends in manufacturing areas. The first, the movement within the factories toward work teams, had made "supervision" an anachronism. "Supervisors" were no longer required in the classic sense; what was needed was leadership and a willingness to share authority and to lead in a collaborative environment. The second trend involved the constant increase in technical and business skills required of the leader. Years of experience on a factory floor were no longer sufficient for the demands of the business. Requirements for formal education and constant training and retraining were resulting in the recruitment and hiring of college graduates for positions formerly occupied by those who had before risen through the ranks over a period of years. New college graduates with degrees in operations management were rapidly displacing the traditional supervisor. These trends not only required increased training and education, but also signaled a major cultural shift within the factories.

The Crucial Need for Action

By 1991, the management teams of the factories within Motorola were clamoring for HR attention to this growing issue. Although Motorola Semiconductor had long had training and promotional matrices for supervisors, established years before, these were obsolete and incomplete; they had been designed for the older model of supervisor. Career counseling was a major concern of Motorola management, and the career path and development guidelines for those in supervisory/leadership positions were increasingly unclear. Managers of supervisors had inaccurate and incomplete information, and could not adequately counsel their employees. The supervisory ranks were now split between the traditional, homegrown supervisor and the young operations-management graduates. The experienced supervisors had reasonable technical knowledge of the manufacturing area, but they were reluctant to share authority and had never been trained to understand the actual business. The young operations-management graduates, on the other hand, tended to learn the business rapidly and were receptive to change, but they lacked practical experience and technical knowledge in the factories.

At the time we conceived this project, the numbers were about equally divided between the two types of supervisors. It was clear that both groups faced considerable development challenges to take the factories into the 21st century. The future would require first-line leaders who

— could provide leadership to teams, and teams with far more diversity than ever before

— could develop the people within their areas to take more responsibility

— understood the business

— understood manufacturing processes and procedures

— could operate at a higher level of performance and initiative

— could manage their own learning and skill development, as well as that of their subordinates

— had the potential to grow into higher levels of manufacturing leadership

Motorola's fast-paced environment and rapid growth (30% in three years), coupled with rapid organizational change and the placement of supervisors on all shifts in multiple locations, added to the complexity of the situation.

An increased emphasis on performance management and career counseling created pressure from managers of supervisors to begin the project. Given the rate of change and formidable cultural aspects of the situation, we knew that a systems approach would be required. We had to build a model of what an ideal first-line leader would be and do, and had to create compensation, performance management, and employee relations tools to implement the program and support the changes that were required.

Initial Project Phase: Semiconductor Products Sector

Within SPS, we began the project in 1992 as a joint venture between two major training groups: CPSTG and LATG. In selecting our management review board, we turned to the Technician Council, which had been formed for another competency-based effort, the Technician Project (see Chapter 2 for an extensive discussion of this project and the Council). Our target audience consisted of the hundreds of supervisors within SPS in Phoenix, with a secondary customer group consisting of managers of supervisors within the manufacturing area.

Initial Data Collection and Analysis

The method we used was similar to that of the Technician Project. Our first step was to assess the numbers, locations, and levels of the supervisors within our target population. The resultant data yielded that over 80% of those classified as supervisors were located within the manufacturing area, which indicated to us that we had to develop the key model for manufacturing supervisors, with slight variations for the relatively few supervisors located within other areas.

Once we had assessed the demographic information, we collected all relevant documentation, including job descriptions at all levels, and other existing compensation documentation. Immediately we encountered the same problem that had confronted us during the Technician Project: compensation documentation was focused on minimal skills and an old model of performance, and so lacked the detail and best-performer information that would be required to train supervisors to a model for improved performance.

Although the existing supervisor matrices were now clearly obsolete, we decided to use a similar format, one with which our customers were already familiar and comfortable. After providing criteria for selection, we asked our council to identify for us those supervisors who were considered "best experts," essentially possessing skills that resulted in their being viewed as the best in their field. To engineer a new model of supervisor/leader, we needed to understand the current best practice for supervisors, to identify what they did well and differently from other supervisors who were not considered excellent performers;

then we would establish requirements and training programs to help other supervisors attain the experts' level of performance. We asked the organizational representatives on the Council to identify for us expert supervisor performers at various levels within each organization, and conducted information interviews to identify precisely what the experts did, how they did it, and organizational issues that would have to be resolved to enable other people to learn and apply those skills.

Information Interviews

We arranged to interview the expert supervisors for two- to four-hour periods. Selection criteria for these subject matter experts (SMEs) appears below.

Selection Profile for Subject Matter Experts (SMEs)

- Top 10% of ranking and rating group in each level of supervisor

- Reputation by supervisor and peers (and employees, if applicable)

- Between 3 and 20 years' experience with the company.

Ideally we would have selected a total of 36 supervisors. Reality intervened, however, in terms of availability, and we actually interviewed around 24. Manufacturing was divided into two areas:

- Front-end: wafer fabrication areas

- Back-end: assembly and test areas

Our sample had to reflect both, because specific tasks and duties varied between those two types of areas. A grid was used to identify the individuals who needed to be interviewed, as shown in Figure 1.

We developed a semistructured interviewing questionnaire/protocol similar to that developed for the Technician Project. Questions took a funneling approach, moving from a generic level of information on general roles/responsibilities, and becoming increasingly specific about duties, expert and nonexpert performance,

FIGURE 1: Supervisory Interview Grid

Grade / Operation	Level 1			Level 2			Level 3			Level 4			Level 5			Level 6		
Front-End	1	2	3	1	2	3	1	2	3	1	2	3	1	2	3	1	2	3
Back-End	1	2	3	1	2	3	1	2	3	1	2	3	1	2	3	1	2	3

training methods, critical incidents, and barriers to performance. A similar protocol is provided in Appendix A, with questions added to illustrate the process. Instructional designer Mary Jane Thome conducted the interviews.

Data Analysis and Results

Following the information interviews, data was sorted and analyzed using naturalistic technique (e.g., we clustered and prioritized like information). A data summary was presented to our sponsoring management group for review. A number of issues that had surfaced during the interviews were referred to appropriate departments for resolution. Data confirmed what we had learned from the managers requesting our assistance and analysis. The supervisory role was shifting from an autocratic position that essentially drove production into a leadership role. Old-style supervisors concentrated on getting product out the door and focused on control issues and technical skills, and most reward systems continued to support those priorities. Data showed, however, that the supervisors who were viewed as most valuable by their bosses and peers were those who had developed keen interpersonal, leadership, and teaming skills. This profile constituted a major change.

The information that resulted from the interviews, when added to the job data we had collected in the earlier phase of the project, gave us a solid understanding of not only current status but the great changes taking place, with implications for needed change. We also knew that job descriptions, promotional matrices, and the reward system would have to be consistently updated if that change was to be implemented. At this point, however, events in Motorola combined to change the scope of the project.

Second Project Phase: The First-Line Leader Project

Introduction of Competency-Based Curriculum Methodology

In 1992, Motorola University had formed a team of training specialists representing most of the major groups and sectors across the corporation, and had chartered it to define a common training design and development methodology for these various groups. MU Design Manager Ken Hansen and Project Leader Bob Aron introduced the team to competency-based curriculum, and the team set about adapting the methodology to meet Motorola's needs. One output of the Competency-Based Curricular Team was a standard set of definitions (also cited in Chapter 2). These definitions were based on the concept of organizational outputs, or accomplishments, and the competencies required to execute these. Our definitions included:

Accomplishment/Output	A discernible output of a business operation, initiative, technology, or organizational role that requires specific competencies.
Competency	The ability to perform to a defined criteria. The organizing principle is structured around knowledge, skills (or skill clusters), and values determined through analysis that support *functions* within a business. Competencies usually occur at two levels: novice or expert.
Curriculum	A listing of competencies required to attain a business objective or accomplishment, the knowledges and skills required to execute them, and the resources available to learn them—NOT a list of courses, although these may be attached to the curriculum as part of the available resources for learning

Up to this point, Motorola had never sought to identify corporate-wide supervisory or management competencies; courseware for this function was usually handled by Sector management training groups, rather than by

Corporate. However, in the course of working on the Competency-Based Curricular Team, nearly all of us received the same request from management: to build curricula for the new model of supervisor/leader. When the Competency-Based Curricular Team ended, those of us with these similar needs decided to continue our association and to test the theories generated by undertaking a corporate-wide supervisory model.

Mission and Focus

Coordinated by Scott Hayes, MU Management Development Manager, our group recruited several additional members to ensure representation from key areas across SPS (in size, over a third of Motorola) and the corporation. These areas may be noted in the list below, which includes the individuals who were major players in the development of the overall supervisor/leader model.

— Pam Bossert, Training Manager, Microcontroller and Memories Technologies Group, SPS, Austin

— Julie Forbes, Leadership Development Manager, SPS, Phoenix

— Jeremie Hill Grey, LATG/East Valley Group Training Manager, Mesa

— Scott Hayes, representing Motorola University, and Ken Hansen, MU Design Manager

— Jennifer Fox Kennedy, Motorola University West and later LATG/East Valley Senior Instructional Designer, Mesa

— Todd Nalodka, Testing/Assessment Manager, SPS, Phoenix

— Patricia Patterson, Senior Consultant, Communications, Power, Signal Technologies Group, SPS, Phoenix

— Eric Paul, Training Manager, Microprocessor and Memories Technologies Group, SPS, Austin

— Mahbod Seraji, Instructional Design and Development Manager, Land Mobil Products Sector

We were now a team—later to be known as the First-Line Leader Project Team—and we took as our mission the development of a corporate-wide model of the new supervisor/leader and the development of training programs to support the implementation of that model.

To avoid "reinventing of the wheel," team members resolved to use the data generated by the interviews within SPS. The Sector, after all, represented 30% of Motorola's workforce. We reckoned that we could use the SPS data as a straw man and validate its accuracy within other major groups. We first did a demographic study of supervisors across the corporation, and learned that approximately 80% of them, as in SPS, were involved in manufacturing, with the remaining 20% (like SPS) scattered across many functional areas. Manufacturing, therefore, became our focus.

Data Collection, Analysis, and Results

To validate the accuracy of our findings in SPS, and the applicability of our conclusions to others within the corporate supervisory population, we used a series of surveys. Some were sent to key managers, and others to selected supervisors. In many cases, to obtain the best possible data, we actually scheduled appointments with managers and supervisors and walked them through the surveys, noting their responses. We reasoned that doing so would improve our response rate and allow us to capture more detail.

Each team member was responsible for data for his or her individual organization. As part of our data gathering, we asked key managers to rank for us by importance the various tasks of the supervisor/leader. In response to our information that the vast majority of training for new and continuing supervisors took place as one-to-one on-the-job training, we asked key supervisors to identify the importance of training for the various areas of responsibility, tasks, and duties. A sample survey, reduced in size, appears in Figure 2. We have not included the entire survey because it represents actual data, but the survey itself comprised five detailed pages.

FIGURE 2: Sample Manager/Supervisor Survey

Training Value Rating Survey
Front-End Manufacturing Supervisor

What is the value of training to your performance of this task?

n/a	—	Not applicable to my job
1	—	Of little importance to my job
4	—	Of some importance to my job
7	—	Of critical importance to my job

Circle the appropriate answer; the "n/a" (not applicable) rating should be circled if you are not currently performing this task.

A. Provide safe working environment

1.	Educate operators on safety procedures	n/a	1	2	3	4	5	6	7
2.	Provide safety equipment	n/a	1	2	3	4	5	6	7
3.	Monitor environment	n/a	1	2	3	4	5	6	7
4.	Provide timely response to unsafe situations	n/a	1	2	3	4	5	6	7
5.	Support safety teams	n/a	1	2	3	4	5	6	7

Additional Tasks

_____	1	2	3	4	5	6	7
_____	1	2	3	4	5	6	7
_____	1	2	3	4	5	6	7

B. Achieve manufacturing goals

1.	Analyze past performance	n/a	1	2	3	4	5	6	7
2.	Analyze monthly forecast	n/a	1	2	3	4	5	6	7
3.	Set daily goals	n/a	1	2	3	4	5	6	7
4.	Determine production needs	n/a	1	2	3	4	5	6	7
5.	Establish production plan	n/a	1	2	3	4	5	6	7
6.	Solicit commitment	n/a	1	2	3	4	5	6	7
7.	Coordinate manufacturing efforts	n/a	1	2	3	4	5	6	7
8.	Execute production plan	n/a	1	2	3	4	5	6	7
9.	Monitor current performance	n/a	1	2	3	4	5	6	7
10.	Communicate current performance	n/a	1	2	3	4	5	6	7
11.	Establish contingency plan	n/a	1	2	3	4	5	6	7
12.	Resolve problems	n/a	1	2	3	4	5	6	7

Additional Tasks

_____	1	2	3	4	5	6	7
_____	1	2	3	4	5	6	7
_____	1	2	3	4	5	6	7

When data was complete, we met as a group to sort, analyze, and summarize the data, and then sent out copies of the summaries for review by those we had interviewed. The results showed clearly the direction that was required: supervisors had to become business-savvy leaders and to work through teams. This finding gave us clear priorities, but what precisely does a "business-savvy leader" do, and what does he or she have to know to do it? Our next step was to use these data to generate detailed competency models.

Competency Modeling

As we described in our chapter on the Technician Project, within SPS we had further adapted the Motorola University competency team methods, incorporating tools and techniques that we had used in our specific areas. Our modifications were largely based upon the work done by Geary Rummler within SPS in preceding years, and involved the use of the Rummler competency model format. Again, we selected this tool for the following reasons:

1. The format lends itself well to group process and would provide a mechanism to create consensus on a function that was, after all, not yet existing and, therefore, not a model in the truest sense.

2. The information elicited in the completion of this model would include action, criteria, and enough detail to build performance objectives and subsequent curriculum. We needed to develop both, as well as to create new job descriptions and promotional hierarchies and to obtain management approval for them.

3. The SPS technical community had previous experience with this modeling method and was comfortable with it.

A sample annotated competency form is shown in Figure 3.

Using the data gathered from interviews, surveys, and our subsequent analysis, and working closely with our management review group, we created a new model, which we called the First-Line Leader. The "supervisor" title carried

FIGURE 3: Sample Annotated Competency Form

TARGET POPULATION: First-Line Leaders　　　　**LEVEL: Generic for All Levels**
SMEs/Focus Group Members: (names of those from whom we took data and their groups)

OUTPUT/ACCOMPLISHMENT:

Tasks (prioritized)	Measures	Standards	K/S/A	Resources
1. Data from previous collection	1. Necessary to write perform-ance objectives and to know how the project affects the bottom line and performance management	1. Necessary to write perform-ance objectives, and for eval-uation and performance management	1. Prioritized knowledge, skills, attributes, etc.	1. Know documents or training mater-ials or programs currently in use, generated by the job, or important in some way to the outputs and tasks
2. 3. 4. . . .				

When these models are complete, detailed analysis enables designers to:

- write performance objectives
- match objectives to existing programs
- set up program evaluation
- nail down the gaps

- create specific job aids
- engineer current performance based on current best practices and use scenario/futures planning to determine change required

a connotation associated with the old model—the autocratic head of a manufacturing unit whose main responsibility was driving product. We wanted to convey the significant change in role required, and the substantially different skill inventory required to accomplish that change. At MU's urging, we made the model as generic as possible so that it could be used after validation in many organizations. We retained the detail for our particular areas, however, to enable us to do appropriate technical training within the semiconductor areas.

The new model stressed vision, leadership, team development, and forward-thinking human resource management skills. Technical skills were still important, with an increased emphasis on business knowledge. Stress was no longer placed only on product output; human resources outputs were a higher priority. A sample of the model is shown in Figure 4. A simplified version, produced for management review, appears in Figure 5.

FIGURE 4: Sample of First-Line Leader Model

1.0 Providing Focus

Accomplishment: Creation of an environment where the work of team members supports and reflects the team's mutually arrived at vision, mission, objective, and goals.

Competencies	Key Measures	Standards	Knowledge/Skills	Existing Resources
1.1 The ability to **define a vision, mission, objectives, and strategies** in order to set a direction for the group's work[1]	1.1 • Documented team vision, mission, objectives, and strategies • Cascade Company vision, mission, objectives, and strategies • Management support	1.1 • Follows established Company format • Company vision, mission, objectives, and strategies	1.0 a) Know Company vision, etc.[1,4] b) Know general direction of the team[1] c) Communication skills[1,2,3,4,5] d) Know canned presentations available[1] e) Presentation skills[1,3] f) Meeting facilitator skills[1] g) Knowledge of different meeting formats[1] h) Recording skills[1] i) Writing effective goals[1] j) Word processing skills[1,3] k) Writing skills[1,3,4,5] l) Listening skills[1,2,5] m) Recognize communication styles of others[1,2,5] n) Effective influence skills[1,2,5] o) Clarifying individual team member responsibility[1] p) Negotiating skills[2,5]	1.0 a) Leadership Institute — Leadership — Effective Mfg. Supervision — Technical Leadership — Emp. Lead (MGT 345) b) Leadership Challenge Workshop — Leadership — Effective Mfg. Supervision — Creative Mgr. (EXE 601) c) Performance Management — SOS I (Communication Skills) — Interaction Management — Listening Skills d) [Further research needed] e) Effective Presentations f) Effective Meetings for Managers g) Effective Meetings for Managers i) Performance Mgt. — Effective Mfg. Supervision j) (See Computer Skills Training)
1.2 The ability to **gain commitment from the workgroup** in order to achieve the vision, mission, objectives, and goals[2]	1.2 • Signed: — Goal statement — Performance statement	1.2 • Within 2 days of 1.1 being documented • Company Performance Plan Procedure		

(continued)

FIGURE 4: Sample of First-Line Leader Model *(concluded)*

2.0 Manage Interpersonal Relationships

Accomplishment: Creation of an environment in which team members solve problems, assign work and communicate with minimal supervision or work interruption, recognize opportunities to work together and do so, resolve conflicts without intervention, operate within legal parameters, and foster ideas sharing and cooperation in completing tasks.

Competencies	Key Measures	Standards	Knowledge/Skills	Existing Resources
2.1 The ability to **share daily direction of work activities.**[6]	2.1 • Daily direction is set and acted upon by all team members	2.1 • Daily, monthly performance goals are met	2.0 a) Leadership skills[6,7,8,10] b) Knowledge of program status[6,7] c) Knowledge of overall program[6,7,8,11]	2.0 a) Leadership Institute — Leadership — Effective Mfg. Supervision — Technical Leadership b) Effective Mfg. Super. — SOS II — Mgt. Dev./Div. (EEO 105) — Mgt. Cont. Imp. (ENG 335) c) Effective Mfg. Super. — SOS I & II — Helping Others Succeed (MGT 937) — Mgt. Personal Growth (MPG 135) — Maximizing Perform. (MGT 946)
2.2 The ability to **suggest alternative solutions** in order to coach teams in problem solving[7]	2.2 • Acceptance of and commitment to the selected alternative	2.2 • Viable, selected actions	d) Communication skills[6,7,8,9,10] e) Recognize communication skills of others[6,10,11]	d) SOS I (Comm. Skills) — Dealing w/people (PDE 518) — Bld. High Perf. Teams (MGT 821) — Listening skills e) Influence — Interaction — Interaction Mgt. — Effective Interaction w/Employees

FIGURE 5: Simplified Version of Model

Job Model for the First-Time/First-Line Leader

Based on an extensive data collection effort, the following job model for the transitional First-Time/First-Line Leader (FTFLL) was derived. Essentially, a FTFLL is any individual who occupies the lowest-level leadership positions—including, but not limited to, the formal supervisor. Furthermore, this model is for the "transitional" FTFLL. Thus, it refers *not* to the job as it currently stands, but to the intermediate step in the transition to how it is expected to be in the future.

Provide Focus

The FTFLL will lead the work group or team in developing the vision, mission, objectives, and goals they work toward. They will ensure that work group or team members identify with the vision, mission, objectives, and goals, and will motivate team members in achieving them. They will provide a positive role model to work group or team members on how to approach work. They will encourage the work group or team by providing support, encouragement, and timely feedback.

Major Accomplishment:
Daily individual work supports and reflects the teams' mutually arrived at vision, mission, objectives, and goals.

Competencies:

- The ability to define with team members a vision, mission, objectives, and goals in order to set a direction for the group's work.

- The ability to gain commitment from the work group in order to achieve the vision, mission, objectives, and goals.

- The ability to provide praise or recognition to employees in order to encourage and motivate them to achieve the vision, mission, objectives, and goals.

- The ability to demonstrate specific role behaviors and values consistent with the company's key beliefs in order to model appropriate style in accomplishing work.

- The ability to focus and prioritize the work group's efforts in order to ensure that the vision, mission, objectives, and goals are met.

Manage Interpersonal Relationships

The FTFLL will promote cooperation and cohesiveness among work group members. They will use a team approach to accomplish work whenever appropriate. They will be familiar with legal parameters regarding the use of teams and will follow such parameters in the application of teams. They will create a work environment to

(continued)

FIGURE 5: Simplified Version of Model *(concluded)*

encourage individual participation in problem solving and decision making. They will delegate authority and responsibility to work group or team members. Furthermore, they will encourage work group or team members to allow each other to participate in problem solving and decision making when working in a self-directed manner. They will build rapport between themselves and work group or team members as well as direct the members of the work group or team in developing rapport among themselves. They will direct work group or team members in resolving differences among themselves only when necessary.

Major Accomplishments:
Team (work group) members problem-solve, assign work, and communicate with minimal supervision or work interruption.

Team (work group) members recognize opportunities to work together and do so.

Teams operate within legal parameters.

Team (work group) is flexible and fosters idea sharing and cooperation in completing tasks.

Competencies:

- The ability to delegate work to the lowest competent level in order to minimize daily direction.

- The ability to suggest alternative solutions in order to coach teams in problem solving.

- The ability to identify when and when not to intervene in a decision-making issue.

- The ability to communicate information, formally and informally, to both individuals and groups, using various communication devices and methods.

- The ability to effectively interact with others in order to build rapport and trust.

- The ability to manage conflict within a group and to train the group to manage conflict in order to maintain productive working relationships.

- In order to create a cooperative and participatory work environment, the FTFLL must have the ability to
  — create expectations for appropriate behavior
  — reward appropriate behavior

- In order to use teams appropriately, they must have the ability to
  — recognize situations where creation of a team is appropriate
  — coach members in how to implement teams
  — reward appropriate behavior
  — apply current Motorola policies to teams

Selecting a Curriculum

To execute a curriculum in support of the new competency model, we translated the model into performance objectives. We were aware from the first that there were many courses available within Motorola that might be available for adoption or adaptation. Our goal was to have to design and develop as little courseware as possible for purposes of cost control. Detailed target-population descriptions and performance objectives allowed us to make realistic matches with courseware already in existence. It also allowed us to articulate those skills for which there was not yet any training. We summarized these at the end of the project and scheduled them for design and development. A sample of the performance objectives is provided in Figure 6.

FIGURE 6: Sample of Performance Objectives

Performance Objectives: First-Line Leader

1.1.0 Provide Focus

Creation of an environment where the work of team members supports and reflects the team's mutually arrived at vision, mission, objectives, and goals.

Common skills and knowledge used in all leadership tasks 1.1.1 through 1.1.5

  1.1.0.a Know Company vision, etc.

   1.1.0.a1 As a training exercise, the First-Line Leader will locate and collect into a single file the Company's vision, mission, objectives, and strategies.

   1.1.0.a2 The First-Line Leader will present a 15-minute training session to other First-Line Leaders explaining how one assigned aspect of the Company's vision statement relates to his/her group.

  1.1.0.b Know general direction of the team

   1.1.0.b1 The First-Line Leader will prepare a one-page report defining the general direction of the group and present it to his/her manager (or training mentor if not one and the same) for feedback, as a training exercise.

(continued)

FIGURE 6: Sample of Performance Objectives *(concluded)*

1.1.0.c   Communication skills (Also See 1.2.0.d.)

    1.1.0.c1   After observing role play of a team meeting, the First-Line Leader will identify three methods of active listening utilized by the team leader.

    1.1.0.c2   After observing role play of a team meeting, the First-Line Leader will formulate correct responses to objections intentionally mishandled by the team leader.

1.2.0   Manage Interpersonal Relationships

Creation of an environment in which team members solve problems, assign work and communicate with minimal supervision or work interruption, recognize opportunities to work together and do so, resolve conflicts without intervention, operate within legal parameters, and foster ideas sharing and cooperation to complete tasks.

Common skills and knowledge used in all Manage Interpersonal Relationship tasks 1.2.1 through 1.2.8

1.2.0.a   Leadership skills (Refer to 1.1.0.a through 1.1.5.)

1.2.0.b   As a training exercise, the First-Line Leader will collect weekly <u>status reports</u> from each member of a team he/she is currently participating in. He/she will develop a composite weekly status report for distribution to the team.

1.2.0.c   Same as 1.1.0.b. The First-Line Leader will prepare a one-page report <u>defining the general direction of the group</u> and present it to his/her manager (or training mentor if not one and the same) for feedback, as a training exercise.

1.2.0.d   Communication skills. (Also See 1.1.0.c.) The First-Line Leader will conduct a phone survey of three team members and document follow-up on assigned action items, as a training exercise.

1.2.0.e   Having observed a staged meeting, the First-Line Leader will <u>identify the communication style</u> of each individual as one of the types included on a list provided with the course. (Same as 1.1.0.m.)

1.2.0.f   As a training exercise, the First-Line Leader will schedule 30-minute informal meetings with three members of a team or training group whom he/she doesn't know very well. The First-Line Leader will document two new personal items he/she learned about each individual and one work-related expertise for each individual.

1.2.0.g   Listening skills (Refer to 1.1.0.c1 Communication Skills.)

1.2.0.h   Effective influence of others (Refer to 1.1.0.n.)

For the first release of the model for First-Line Leader, we decided to simplify the competency forms, reasoning that the simpler format would be more user-friendly (see Figure 7). However, further experience suggested that even this modified format may have been too dense in terms of print. We eventually published a version using only two columns: competencies, and available resources.

We were fortunate to discover existing good-quality courseware for many of the key leadership training needs, and adopted an entirely new curriculum for first-line leaders. In addition, three members (Pat Patterson of CPSTG, Eric Paul of MMTG, and SPS Assessment Manager Todd Nalodka) worked together to create a competency-based self-assessment tool designed to be used by existing supervisors to identify those areas where retraining was most necessary. Once training needs were met and courses scheduled, we turned our attention to compensation and implementation issues.

Dealing With Compensation and Implementation Issues

To carry out this stage of the project most effectively, team members decided to handle compensation and implementation issues separately, or group by group. Different super-groups had different job descriptions and compensation guidelines, and local training groups handled these issues after our initial publication of the completed competency model and the resource guide.

The SPS Approach

Within SPS, we rallied forces, receiving outstanding compensation and employee relations support from Compensation Manager Christine Florez, Murlene Jefferson, and Jane Maxson. After a series of informational presentations (given over a ten-month period by Jeremie Hill Grey and later Christine Florez), the Sector Compensation Group agreed to pilot the First-Line Leader Project as an experiment in competency modeling linked to promotion and rewards. The Compensation professionals on our team completely rewrote all job descriptions for the first-line leadership function, simplifying them and

FIGURE 7: Sample of Simplified Competency Form

1.0 Providing Focus

Accomplishment: Creation of an environment where the work of team members supports and reflects the team's mutually arrived at vision, mission, objectives, and goals.

Competencies	Objectives	Training Resources
1.1 The ability to define a vision, mission, objectives, and strategies in order to set a direction for the group's work.	1.1 The First-Line Leader will write a vision, mission, objectives, and strategies with team. He/she will obtain appropriate management approval.	Leadership Institute (MGT 910) Leadership (HRD 113) Effective Mfg. Supervision (MFG 240) Technical Leadership (TCH 400) Leadership Challenge Workshop (MGT 222)
1.2 The ability to gain commitment from the work group in order to achieve the vision, mission, objectives, and strategies.	1.2 The First-Line Leader will document in a brief memo how he/she gained the commitment of the team and will be able to show how individual performers' objectives and strategies combine to meet the team's objectives.	Performance Management Skill Training (PMS 100) SOS I (Communication Skills) (HRD 315) Interaction Management (MGT 303) Effective Presentations (MGT 201) Leading Effective Meetings (MGT 202)
1.3 The ability to provide praise or recognition to employees in order to encourage and motivate them to achieve the vision, mission, objectives, and strategies.	1.3 The First-Line Leader will for the period of three months, maintain a log and document a summary of incidents where he/she recognized the achievements of others with various levels of praise and recognition (both formal and informal). He/she will include copies of formal reward request forms, recognition memos, thank you notes, phone messages, etc. The log will be reviewed by his/her training mentor, who will evaluate for appropriate actions. The First-Line Leader will continue to demonstrate the use of appropriate levels of praise and recognition on an ongoing basis.	Effective Listening (HRD 108) Understanding People (HRD 104) Maximizing Joint Productivity and Innovation (MGT 169) Influence (MGT 111) SOS II (Coaching and Counseling) (HRD 136) Effective Interactions With Employees (MGT 106)

linking them directly to the attainment of competencies. An implementation team (led by Christine Florez, Donna Horowitz of CPSTG, Sarabeth Simpson, and Pat Witkiewicz) worked for nearly a year in conjunction with the Compensation representatives to work out promotional matrices, cultural change mechanisms, and other systemic issues to ensure acceptance and success of the project. Promotions would now be based on measurable competency attainment.

Communication packages, created by East Valley Training Design Manager Ann Igoe and Christine Florez, alerted managers of supervisors to the coming changes. Ann also created a series of tools, including an organizational assessment, and automated the supervisor self-assessment tool created earlier. The automated tool was very clever, consisting of a camouflaged Excel worksheet that automatically totaled scores as supervisors answered the competency-based questions. The worksheet was also linked to a resource guide; when the assessment was complete, the supervisor was provided with a detailed resource list suggesting those areas of study that had been identified during the self-assessment exercise.

The implementation task force designed and developed a workshop to train managers of supervisors in the new system. The workshop was developed according to instructional design principles, including an instructor's guide with text, answers to frequently asked questions, and training materials to be used for the instructors rolling out the project to the manufacturing areas. A sample of the instructor's guide (somewhat modified in style) appears in Appendix B.

Response to the workshop was generally very positive, and implementation occurred smoothly. Because expected performance was clearly defined at each level, supervisors liked the competency-based approach. Helen Marvin, an area HR manager, likened the process to stepping stones just under the surface of a body of water. Helen commented that superb performers always appear to be walking on water, but in fact merely know where the stepping stones (skills, abilities, and resources) are placed. Spelling out requirements using a competency-based approach makes those stepping stones visible or available to all employees in a function, and greatly increases the probability of developing larger numbers of employees who are able to "walk on water."

Conclusions

Implementation of both the training package and competency-based compensation guidelines and tools has been too recent to make an adequate assessment of the success of the First Line Leader Project. Level 1 (reaction) data, however, suggests that the project was very well received and easily understood, and that learning from the training materials is satisfactory. Level 2 (learning) instruments in the workshop also indicate success. Another year or two must pass before the organization can evaluate using Level 3 (changed behavior on the job) and Level 4 (accomplishment of business objectives) measures.

The entire project required the contribution of several dozen people in three different environments over a period of years. Already, however, the project has significantly altered the performance expectations for Motorola SPS's first-line leadership, and has paved the way for competency-based approaches in other major functions, including those for engineers, software professionals, and technicians.

APPENDIX A

Information Interview Protocol—SME

This semistructured information-interview format is designed to be used during a two- to four-hour information session with subject matter experts. The questions are intended to elicit information on a variety of key training/skill issues for performance improvement. Interviewers should refrain from adding interpretative comments, and should check frequently for accuracy of information by repeating responses and asking clarifying/probing questions to attain maximum data. Careful notes should be kept and confidentiality assured. Respondents should be told that they will never be quoted as individuals, and that all data will be presented in summary format. Explain the protocol to respondents before beginning the interview.

Please remember that we are interested in function rather than job description. Job descriptions may be very inaccurate. Note any discrepancies that become obvious during the course of the interview so that we may resolve any issues.

Demographic Data

Name:

Grade:

Title:

Date:

Location:

Shift:

Date of Hire:

Roles and Responsibilities

1. What do you view as the role of a supervisor? If there are several roles, which is the most important? Which take up the most time? How do you know which role is expected of you?

2. What do you consider to be the major duties and tasks of a supervisor? Begin with those that occupy the majority of your time. About what percentage of the average day do you spend on that?
    — What makes you start doing that?
    — What makes you stop?
    — What types of people do you interact with?
    — Is there any documentation that you use while you're doing that? If so, can I have a copy?

3. What do you see as the supervisor's career path?

Critical Incidents

4. Please name three to five specific examples that you think represent effective or successful types of supervisor behavior.

5. Can you think of three to five specific examples that you think characterize ineffective or unsuccessful supervisors?

Training Priorities

6. If you can remember when you first started, what were some of the major problems you had to deal with as you settled into your job? Start with the most difficult.
    — Did someone help you with that?
    — What do you think might have made a difference?

7. Can you tell me what kinds of training you have had?
    — What was the most valuable?
    — What was the least valuable?

8. What skills or knowledge are essential to a new supervisor?
    — Just entering the field?
    — Just entering the job level?

Interfaces/Communication Skills

9. What groups of people do you spend the most working time dealing with?
   — Can you give me three examples of effective or successful interactions with these folks?
   — Three examples of ineffective or unsuccessful interactions?

10. What is your reporting structure?
    — From whom do you receive the most direction?
    — Can you tell me for what supervisors are most often rewarded? How do you know that?

11. Can you tell me what characterizes an effective operator? An ineffective operator?

12. Can you tell me what characterizes an effective technician? An ineffective technician?

13. What is your relationship with manufacturing specialists? With high-performance work teams? What constitutes effective supervision with a high-performance work team? Ineffective supervision with a team?

APPENDIX B

Manufacturing Leader Workshop—Sample Contents

This sample contains Module 1 and the beginning of Module 2. The table of contents for the entire workshop is included to illustrate the full dimension of this tool.

Table of Contents

Instructor Guidelines

Module 1: Introduction

Module 2: Description of First-Line and Manufacturing Leader Projects

Module 3: Organizational Readiness

Module 4: Performance Expectations

Module 5: Assessment, Transition, and Development

Module 6: Selection of New First-Line and Manufacturing Leaders

Module 7: Conclusion

Student Guide

Extra Materials

Instructor Guidelines

Proposed Audience:	Manufacturing Managers, Section Managers, and Human Resources Managers as intact teams
Workshop Goal:	Participants will leave the workshop with the commitment, skills, knowledge, and enthusiasm to implement and sustain the Manufacturing Leader process in their organizations.
Materials:	• Instructor Guide
	• Instructor Foils
	• Student Materials

- Notes pages
- Development Guide
- Grade-Level Parameters Matrix
- First-Line/Manufacturing Leader Competency Expectations
- Transition Plan Flowchart

MODULE 1—Introduction

INSTRUCTOR SUGGESTIONS

Overview:	This module introduces the workshop, explains the beginnings of the project, and sets the stage for change.
Objective:	Participants will understand the goals and objectives of the First-Line/ Manufacturing Leader Implementation Workshop.
Assessment of Objective:	Address any questions or concerns before you move on to Module 2.
Materials:	Instructional Foils 1 through 7
Time:	5 to 7 minutes (If you have participants introduce themselves, add more time.)

LESSON PLAN

Instructional Foils

Instructor Notes

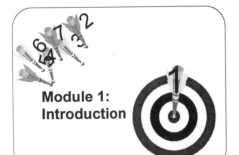

Manufacturing
Leader
Workshop

The First-Line and Manufacturing Leader Implementation Workshop

Hand participants their materials as they enter the room, or have the materials at each participant's seat.

Module 1:
Introduction

Good morning. I'm _____ , your instructor.

Introduce anyone else facilitating with you; then introduce topic at hand: First-Line/Manufacturing Leader Implementation Workshop, Module 1.

Introduce the participants or have them introduce themselves. You will probably have three diverse groups in each class.

Instructional Foils	Instructor Notes

Introduction

Objective:

➟ Participants will understand the goals and objectives of the Manufacturing Leader workshop.

Objective

Participants will meet this goal:

- Understand the goals and objectives of the First-Line/Manufacturing Leader Implementation Workshop

MOTOROLA is undergoing unprecedented changes. Our products, processes, and marketplace have changed. Perhaps less evident are changes in how we manage and lead people. MOTOROLA needs leaders who can successfully transition to a more facilitating, coaching role.

Motorola is undergoing unprecedented changes. Our products, processes, and marketplace have changed. Perhaps less evident are changes in how we coordinate manufacturing resources and lead people. Motorola needs leaders who can successfully transition to a more facilitating, coaching role.

THE PROJECT

➟ **The Team:**
  ➟ Operations
  ➟ Compensation
  ➟ Training
  ➟ Human Resources
  ➟ Career Management Center
➟ **The Result:**
  ➟ Manufacturing Leader Performance System

In September 1994, an Operations-driven task force from East Valley and Phoenix began looking at the role of the supervisory employees and the promotional system which supported supervisors. This team also included representatives from Compensation, Training, Human Resources, and the Career Management Center.

Its charter was to assess how well supervisory employees were supporting business goals, leading change, and supporting the employees in their organizations. The result of the team's work is the First-Line/Manufacturing Leader performance system we will be discussing today.

Instructional Foils

This workshop has been developed to give you:

➤ an understanding of the Manufacturing Leader job function

➤ the changes expected for the supervisory role

➤ the importance of your support of this new role

Workshop Goals:

➤ understand and support the Manufacturing Leader system

➤ assess your organization's readiness to implement the system

➤ prepare organization specific performance metrics

➤ integrate IDP, performance management, and IDE

➤ understand how to assess current employees create a timeline for Manufacturing Leader implementation

Instructor Notes

This workshop has been developed to give you, the managers of First-Line/Manufacturing Leaders, an understanding of the definition of the First-Line/Manufacturing Leader job function, the changes expected for the supervisory role, and the importance of your support of this new role. Your management teams' demonstrated support will be critical to the success of the program and your employees.

Our goals for this workshop are for you to:

• Understand and support the First-Line/Manufacturing Leader system

• Assess your organization's readiness to implement and sustain the First-Line/Manufacturing Leader performance system

• Begin to prepare organization specific metrics to assess First-Line/Manufacturing Leader performance

• Understand how to integrate the First-Line/Manufacturing Leader system with Individual Development Plans, and performance management

• Understand how to assess current employees' skill levels and develop transition plans for them, and

• Create a timeline for implementing the First-Line and Manufacturing Leader system in your organization

MODULE 2—Description of First-Line and Manufacturing Leader Projects

INSTRUCTOR SUGGESTIONS

Overview: This module discusses the history of the First-Line/Manufacturing Leader projects, the competency models developed to support the projects, the expected benefits of the performance system, the new job description and performance expectations, and promotional requirements for First-Line/Manufacturing Leaders.

Objective: Participants will meet these goals
- Know the history of the First-Line/Manufacturing Leader project and its expected result
- Understand the First-Line/Manufacturing Leader competency-based approach to performance models
- Understand the need for transition planning in order to implement the First-Line/Manufacturing Leader performance and reward system

Assessment of Objective: Address any questions or concerns about the content before you continue to Module 3.

Materials: Instructional Foils ___
First-Line/Manufacturing Leader Development Guide
Grade-Level Parameters Matrix
First-Line/Manufacturing Leader Competency Expectations
Transition Plan Flow Chart

References

Aron, R. (Ed.). (1993). *Motorola University Competency-Based Curriculum Team, Summary report and presentation*. Phoenix, AZ: Motorola University.

Rummler, G. A., & Brache, A. P. (1990). *Improving performance: How to manage the white space on the organization chart*. San Francisco, CA: Jossey-Bass.

About the Contributors

Jeremie Hill Grey, Ph.D., former Group Training Manager for the Logic and Analog Technologies Group, Motorola Semiconductor Products Sector, received her doctorate in educational media from the University of Arizona. Dr. Grey has 20 years of professional experience in training and development for high technology companies, including curriculum design and development (especially competency-based curriculum), instructional design and development, training administration, and documentation/publications. She previously managed training or publications groups for Intel Corporation, The Singer Company (Software and Aerospace), and served Motorola for six years as Development Manager and later Group Training Manager of a major technology group in the Phoenix area. Still a Phoenix resident, she is now a senior consultant for the Learning Consortium.

Sarabeth Simpson, former Group Training Manager for the Communications, Power, and Signal Technologies Group, Motorola Semiconductor Products Sector, received her undergraduate degree from Arizona State University. Ms. Simpson has served Motorola for 27 years in a variety of HR management positions, including Training and Development, where she became interested in learning labs and competency-based curriculum. She is currently the Director of Human Resources for Sector Support Operations in the Semiconductor Products Sector.

Christine Florez, LATG/East Valley Compensation and Benefits Manager, Semiconductor Products Sector, received her undergraduate degree from Arizona State University. Ms. Florez has served Motorola for 15 years in a variety of HR positions. She became involved in competency-based curricula while providing employee relations support for the SPS Technician Project, and brought that orientation with her when she was appointed Compensation and Benefits Manager. Her enthusiasm for the competency-based approach and innovative development of compensation support have contributed immensely to the success of the competency projects.

Ann Reid Igoe, Ph.D., former LATG/East Valley Training Design Manager, Semiconductor Products Sector, received her doctorate in instructional design from Arizona State University in Tempe, and was a student of Howard Sullivan. As East Valley Design Manager, she supported competency modeling for engineering and detailed design support for the implementation of the Manufacturing First-Line Leader Project. Dr. Igoe is currently a faculty member at Grand Canyon University.

Jennifer Fox Kennedy, currently Senior Instructional Designer for Motorola Semiconductor Product Sector Training (LATG), received her M.S. in instructional systems at Florida State University, where she was a student of Walter Dick and Roger Kauffman. Ms. Kennedy has authored competency-based curricula for a variety of functions, including technicians, leadership, occupational health, human resources, and engineering, and was a major contributor in SPS's development of the competency-based methodology.

8.
A COMPETENCY-BASED APPROACH TO TRAINING DELIVERY
The American Express Experience

Carmen Hegge-Kleiser — Vice President, Center for Learning Effectiveness

Background

In 1995, American Express dramatically reengineered its training function to increase its business impact while achieving best-in-class economics. Prior to reengineering, training was highly decentralized, with each business unit having its own stand-alone training function. Ninety percent of the training was delivered in a traditional three-day classroom format by professional internal trainers or external educational consulting firms. Course design and trainer certification for "soft-skill" training was largely delegated to external vendors without a consistent set of American Express standards. As a result, there was extensive duplication of course content (up to 60%) at great expense to the company. Moreover, line management was not an active partner in the learning process.

A New Approach to Training Delivery

The Center for Learning Effectiveness (CLE) was created in 1995 to provide a more cost-effective, consistent approach to curriculum design, trainer certification, vendor management, and training measurement for American Express employees around the world. At the same time the Center was created, the number of internal professional trainers was reduced by 40%. Consequently, the Center created and implemented a plan for the increased use of line managers, external contracters, and other internal human resource professionals as trainers.

Line instructors at the VP level were paired with Human Resources staff and used to deliver leadership training to directors and managers. In addition, sales executives were used to teach customer-focused selling skills in Japan and Asia, and customer service managers taught the course "Achieving Exceptional Customer Relations" to their associate staff in Latin America.

The Center discovered that such an approach conferred a number of benefits. The use of line executives lent credibility and clout to the courses. Line instructors generally achieved high ratings on level I evaluations. They also were able to draw on their own experience in American Express to make the course even more relevant.

Another benefit was content mastery by the line instructors, for, as noted by CEO Harvey Golub (who has taught the leadership course), in order to teach a course, a person had to master the content. Teaching also improved the coaching capability of line managers. For example, according to Craig DeWald, Senior Director of Quality and Customer Service Education, "we have found that line managers who teach customer service skills are more likely to work with their staff to transfer the learning back into the workplace and successfully reinforce the learning on the job. When line managers are not actively involved, there are more likely to be disconnects between what people learn and what managers reinforce."

To supplement the use of line instructors, CLE partnered with the Forum corporation to establish an American Express global-sales rules contract trainer network. By using Forum's expertise and contacts, CLE was able to build its own global contract trainer network in eight months. Other benchmarked companies had taken years to achieve a high-quality global contract trainer network. The objective was to obtain instructors at a level of quality equivalent to the best educational firms the company had used in the past, but at one-third the cost. By using external contract trainers instead of internal instructors, CLE was able to shift the cost of instruction from a fixed expense to a variable one. Contract trainers were especially effective for topics where industry experience and exposure to other companies enhanced the course content. This was especially true for the sales curriculum and had potential for other training areas like quality, team, and leadership training.

Still, even with contract trainers, a structured method to ensure selection quality was required. While Forum provided a valuable behavioral checklist to use in the selection process, it was not grouped by competency clusters with behavioral scales to indicate a level of proficiency to serve as a basis of comparison between candidates. Moreover, it was not tailored specifically to the American Express culture. Since it was designed for selecting professional trainers, it was less effective in the selection of line instructors. It was clear with the company's new training delivery strategy that CLE needed to rethink how it selected and certified internal and external instructors to ensure a consistent level of high-quality instruction.

Building a Training Delivery Competency Model

To better understand the competencies that distinguish superior trainers, from effective trainers, as well as the baseline skills required for CLE curriculums, American Express decided to build its own competency model for the role of Training Delivery. To do this, CLE partnered with the internal Competency Model Development Group, headed by Melanie Stopeck.

The team used the classic definition of competencies—characteristics/ behaviors based on knowledge, skill, ability, motivation, and other personal characteristics that lead to successful performance in a particular role. A competency model is a behavioral profile for success in a particular job or role. In this case, the model's design reflected not only specific role requirements but also the strategic direction of the company, major business challenges, corporate culture, and organizational dynamics.

Assumptions and Role Definitions

In constructing the competency model, the team assumed that training delivery by American Express staff was not someone's full-time job, but rather an assignment he or she might receive in addition to regular job responsibilities. For external contract trainers, the assumption was that this was their primary role. The role definition was limited to pure training delivery (with consulting not considered part of the role) and consisted of the following:

I. Preparation

- Review course materials
- Prepare flip charts and other supporting media
- Rehearse delivery
- Prepare examples, metaphors, and so forth
- Set up room
- Notify trainees
- Create materials
- Organize supplies
- Plan logistics of training

II. Delivery

- Convey course content accurately and appropriately to audience
- Use appropriate delivery style (platform and/or facilitation)

III. Evaluation Administration

- Administer level I evaluations
- Administer level II evaluation
- Collect and review evaluations and course feedback

IV. Develop plans to address issues

V. Follow-Up (optional)

- Contact participants to assess application of learning

To develop the competency model, the team needed data that would help them determine the competencies critical to the Training Delivery role. The following section explains the methodology that was used.

Methodology

Data for model development were collected via subject matter expert (SME) interviews and behavioral event interviews (BEIs) of job incumbents. A review of relevant external literature was also conducted to supplement data collection.

The SME interviews enabled the team to:

- Identify the key roles and responsibilities to be modeled

- Define the performance requirements and success indicators of trainers

- Identify the minimal skills required for successful performance (current state)

- Identify if and how the training delivery role may change in the future, and the corresponding competencies required to ensure optimal performance

- Derive a list of characteristics that differentiate superior performers from average performers

- Explore the issues and environmental factors that may make it difficult for trainers to achieve optimal results

The BEIs provided the team with different, but no less important, kinds of data. The goal of a BEI is to find out the drivers of effective incumbent behavior through what the interviewee has done on the job in the past. The BEI is a structured interview that focuses on what the interviewee does, thinks, says, and feels as it relates to behaviors that define job success. The interview uncovers personal characteristics and interpersonal abilities as well as technical skills for job performance, and it produces behaviorally specific performance data that allow managers to make solid selection and development decisions.

Survey Participants

Level I evaluations were used to identify effective and superior performers in the Training Delivery role. Average and superior performers as well as subject matter experts were identified for each curriculum from three groups: internal training experts, external training experts, and line instructors.

Of the 21 interviews conducted, 9 were New York-based staff. Other domestic locations that were represented included Phoenix, Arizona, and Ft. Lauderdale, Florida. Forty-three percent of the interviews were with International American Express employees or contract trainers, with representation from Europe, Latin America, and Asia. All CLE curriculum areas were represented in the sample, as was Operations Training.

Data Analysis and Competency Identification

Once the data were collected, they were content-analyzed and competencies were identified. These competencies are what top performers use more often, in more situations, and with better results. The formation of a competency model required the examination of all available data for convergence of competencies. Competencies that emerged most frequently were deemed critical to the role and were clustered to reflect the principal responsibilities of training delivery. It took four weeks to conduct the interviews and complete the content analysis to develop the model. Cycle time in developing the model was greatly reduced through careful planning and the use of level I training evaluation data to identify the most appropriate participants for the interviews.

The Training Delivery Competency Model

The model comprises ten competencies, as can be seen in Figure 1: American Express Training Delivery Role—Competency Clusters. It was designed to be used for all curriculums, line as well as external contract trainers, and both U.S. and international candidates. The competencies are grouped into five different clusters: Personal Effectiveness, Knowing the Customer, Technical/Functional

Expertise, Facilitation Skills, and Platform Skills. Demonstration of these competencies will result in superior performance in the Training Delivery role. The competencies are briefly described in the following section.

FIGURE 1: American Express Training Delivery Role—Competency Clusters

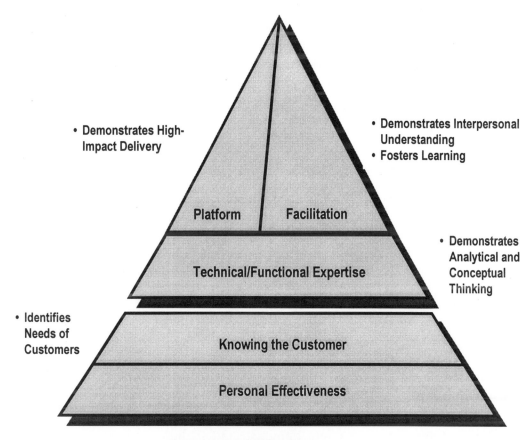

• Demonstrates High-Impact Delivery

• Demonstrates Interpersonal Understanding
• Fosters Learning

Platform   Facilitation

• Demonstrates Analytical and Conceptual Thinking

Technical/Functional Expertise

• Identifies Needs of Customers

Knowing the Customer

Personal Effectiveness

• Demonstrates Self-Confidence
• Demonstrates Adaptability
• Displays Concern for Order and Quality
• Pursues Learning and Self-Development

Cluster 1: Personal Effectiveness

Demonstrates Self-Confidence. The competency is believing in one's own ability to conduct training or facilitate learning even in challenging situations. It includes behaviors such as acting independently, seeking challenges, and managing extremely challenging situations.

Demonstrates Adaptability. This is defined as the individual's ability to adapt and perform effectively within a variety of training situations and with various individuals or groups, including co-facilitators, sponsors, and participants. The effective/superior training deliverer also adapts his or her approach as the requirements of a situation change, including unforeseen events. Specific behaviors include working effectively in ambiguous situations and working constructively under stress and pressure.

Displays Concern for Order and Quality. Individuals who possess this competency demonstrate an underlying drive to reduce uncertainty by being prepared to deliver a quality product. In addition, they monitor work or information for accuracy (self and others) and deliver above and beyond customer expectations. Not only do these individuals prepare for training, they also anticipate the unexpected.

Pursues Learning and Self-Development. Possession of this competency indicates a genuine desire and intent to foster learning and development of self and others. An individual with this competency is committed to continual growth and skill enhancement.

Cluster 2: Knowing the Customer

Identifies the Needs of Customers. This competency is defined as understanding and considering the requirements of customers (training participants, training sponsor, external customers, etc.) before making decisions and taking actions. The behaviors demonstrated include managing expectations of the primary client and anticipating customer needs.

Demonstrates Analytical and Conceptual Thinking. A training deliverer who possesses this competency is able to bring perspectives and approaches together, and to combine or condense them in creative and useful ways.

Cluster 3: Technical/Functional Expertise

"Technical/Functional Expertise" covers three main areas: content knowledge, instructional technique knowledge, and organizational knowledge. Competence is assessed by a matrix that examines the three main content areas against training factors such as course content, audience, and other critical dimensions (e.g., credibility and developmental considerations) at one of three levels of knowledge (basic, competent, mastery).

In assessing content knowledge, it is important to determine at what level the trainer needs to understand the course content for a given audience. For example, for a sales training course with sales team directors, would a trainer be required to have basic knowledge of the content area, a moderate level of knowledge, or a mastery of the content area? Figure 2 provides a description of the knowledge levels.

FIGURE 2: Competency Description

The Knowledge Levels	
Basic knowledge	understands the fundamental components of this area
Competent knowledge	demonstrates a working knowledge of this area
Mastery knowledge	indicates the individual has a sophisticated understanding of the area and is able to expand on the fundamentals by integrating other knowledge areas

Cluster 4: Facilitation Skills

Fosters Learning. Trainers who possess this competency create an environment that is conducive to learning. They use a variety of instructional techniques and facilitation tools to promote self-discovery by learners. This competency includes behaviors such as providing instruction and demonstrating advanced facilitation skills.

Demonstrates Interpersonal Understanding. Possession of this competency indicates that one is willing and able to understand the unspoken or partly expressed thoughts, feelings, and concerns of others. The competency takes into account the varying levels in understanding others, which may include motivation, attitudes, and behavior. Some behaviors include speaking effectively and projecting credibility.

Cluster 5: Platform Skills

Demonstrates High-Impact Delivery. One who possesses this competency is able to provide clear, well-organized presentations. This individual effectively listens and responds to the audience, engages the audience, projects credibility, and is able to think on his or her feet.

Behavioral Levels

Each competency is defined by five levels of behaviors, in order of increasing behavioral sophistication. The Training Delivery Competency Model assumes the level of competency demonstration necessary to be effective will vary depending on the nature of the course taught, the type of trainer and the level of expertise (i.e., whether it is a line professional, a human resource professional, or an external training vendor), and the audience. "Personal Effectiveness" and "Knowing the Customer" are considered essential competency clusters, ones that every effective trainer must possess. These competencies should be part of the required selection criteria. The relative importance of the other competency clusters—"Technical/Functional Expertise," "Facilitation Skills," and "Platform Skills"—may vary depending on the nature of the course content, the type of trainer (i.e., line professional, human resource professional, external training vendor), and the audience. These three clusters are more easily developed than the other two clusters.

Because the model is applicable to a variety of training situations, it is highly versatile. As Melanie Stopeck has pointed out, "built into the model is the flexibility to adjust decision-making criteria for both selection and development purposes depending on the course content, the preferred training delivery method, and the expertise of the trainer. Not all training situations warrant the same requisite skills in a trainer. The model we have developed recognizes that."

Real-life behavioral examples were included for each level in the scale. The examples were adapted from the BEI data collected from training incumbents. An illustration of a competency scale is presented in Figure 3, on the following page.

Use of the Model in Selection and Trainer Certification

A team of American Express training professionals with cross-business unit representation from around the world was chartered to utilize this new competency model. The team was redesigning the trainer selection, certification, and evaluation processes as illustrated below:

Selection	Certification	Ongoing Support
Outcome: High-level profile of competencies of participants	Outcome: Assessment (initial) of content and non-content competencies for each participant.	Outcome: Assessment and suggested development of content and non-content competencies for each participant.

FIGURE 3: Competency Scale

Displays Concern for Order and Quality

Definition:

Demonstrated an underlying drive to reduce uncertainty by being prepared to deliver a quality product. In addition these individuals monitor work or information for accuracy (self and others) and deliver above and beyond customer expectations.

1. **Delivers all Key Aspects of Training Content:** Follow leader's guide to ensure accurate delivery of content.

   "I knew what I was doing. I was comfortable with the leader's guide."

2. **Prepares for Training:** Organizes thoughts and materials before training; is able to answer questions regarding content; generates relevant American Express examples wherever possible.

   "I went into this one absolutely knowing the material inside and out."

3. **Manages Agenda:** Monitors progress of training program against program timeline and agenda and makes adjustments as necessary to ensure complete delivery of content.

   "I constantly assess where the group is and where I need to be to make sure I complete the training."

4. **Anticipates the Unexpected:** Has prepared answers to potential participant questions; has contingency plans in place if agenda does not go as planned; follows up with others to make sure things are in order (e.g., makes sure materials are ready).

   "The night before the training, I thought about what questions the audience might have and how I could answer them."

5. **Demonstrates Discretionary Effort:** Goes above and beyond what the program outline describes in order to better facilitate learning; does more than is required or expected in the job and/or does things that no one has requested which will improve or enhance the training experience; follows up with participants and/or sponsor after training session to assess if learning has occurred; double-checks logistical preparations (e.g., double-checks ahead of time that all logistics are handled, including necessary materials, classroom set-up, etc.).

   "I did a lot of research about this group and their business issues so I would be able to deliver a relevant training program."

The group used the following guiding principles in applying the model and redesigning the associated processes:

- Don't reinvent the wheel. Find the best that American Express has to offer and use it or improve on it.

- Create a process that is flexible enough to be applied in all trainer certification situations.

- Incorporate the guidelines of the American Express Optimal Learning Formula:

  Right person—right time—right skilling—effective knowledge transfer—coaching and reinforcement.

- Incorporate the Trainer Delivery Competency model wherever appropriate.

The Trainer Selection Process

For the trainer selection process, the team developed three instruments based on the Training Delivery Competency Model: the Behavioral Event Interview Guide, the Facilitator Competencies Feedback Form, and the Facilitator Skill Self-Assessment. In those cases when a formal selection process is being used to identify trainers (primarily external contract trainers), candidates go through a behavioral event interview and give a "teach-back" of a segment of a course they have previously taught.

The Behavioral Event Interview Guide provides a structured interview format as illustrated in Figure 4: Training Selection Behavioral Interview Checklist. The candidate is asked an open-ended question to elicit examples of past behavior that the interviewer uses in determining the degree to which a particular competency has been demonstrated. The Facilitator Competencies Feedback Form is used to identify the competencies demonstrated in the "teach-back" section of the selection process (see Figure 5: Facilitator Competencies Feedback Form). The BEI is most effective in assessing competencies such as pursuing

FIGURE 4: Trainer Selection Behavioral Interview Checklist

Interview Question(s)	1.	Think of a time when you were under pressure. How did you maintain composure?
	2.	Think of a time when your environment changed and priorities shifted. How did you handle this?

Competency Cluster Assessment

Demonstrates Self-Confidence

- ☐ 0. Not shown
- ☐ 1. Presents self confidently
- ☐ 2. Acts independently
- ☐ 3. Demonstrates confidence in own ability
- ☐ 4. Seeks challenges
- ☐ 5. Manages extremely challenging situations

Demonstrates Adaptability

- ☐ 0. Not shown
- ☐ 1. Accepts change
- ☐ 2. Adapts to change
- ☐ 3. Works effectively in ambiguous situations
- ☐ 4. Works constructively under stress and pressure
- ☐ 5. Effectively manages changing priorities in a changing environment

Displays Concern for Order & Quality

- ☐ 0. Not shown
- ☐ 1. Delivers all key aspects of training content
- ☐ 2. Prepares for training
- ☐ 3. Manages agenda
- ☐ 4. Anticipates the unexpected
- ☐ 5. Demonstrates discretionary effort

Pursues Learning & Self-Development

- ☐ 0. Not shown
- ☐ 1. Reflects on self
- ☐ 2. Makes behavior changes
- ☐ 3. Actively solicits performance-related feedback
- ☐ 4. Demonstrates passion for learning
- ☐ 5. Inspires others to learn

FIGURE 5: Facilitator Competencies Feedback Form

Facilitator Competencies Feedback Form

Name:_____ Program Name:_____

Module Presented: _____

(Place check marks if observable)

❖ *Develops Rapport* **Observations/Recommendations**

— Maintains eye contact _____

— Uses open, inviting hand gestures _____

— Varies voice tone, volume, and tempo
appropriately _____

— Smiles _____

❖ *Speaks Effectively*

— Is clear and concise _____

— Uses easily understandable language _____

— Uses proper grammar _____

— Uses appropriate language (non-sexist,
non-racist) _____

— Gives clear instructions _____

❖ *Projects Credibility*

— Models concepts _____

— Demonstrates knowledge of the content of
the course _____

— Clearly explains complex concepts and/or
tools _____

— Receives feedback non-defensively _____

— Presents relevant examples _____

learning and self-development, identifying the needs of the customer, demonstrating adaptability, and fostering learning. A teach-back provides a live demonstration of platform skills. Both sources of data result in a more informed selection decision.

When internal staff are being used in a training delivery role, a formal selection process often is not appropriate. In this case, the competency model can provide criteria for nominating potential trainers and the Facilitator Skill Self-Assessment can identify "developmental priorities" that will need to be addressed before the individual can be certified. This approach also positions the teaching assignment as a developmental opportunity for internal staff. A partial example of the Self-Assessment is shown in Figure 6: Facilitator Skill Self-Assessment. External trainers that have been selected by American Express would also complete the Self-Assessment prior to the certification process.

The Certification Process

The certification process is illustrated below.

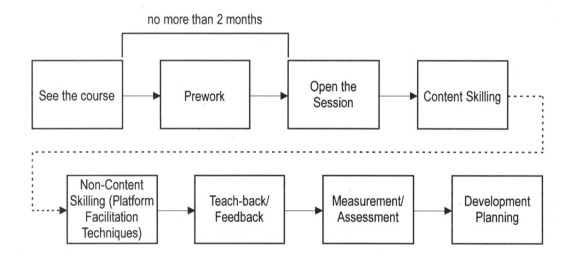

Figure 6: Facilitator Skill Self-Assessment

Facilitator Skill Self-Assessment				

Name: _____

Certification for Which Course? _____

The purpose of this self-assessment is to provide you with a snapshot of your strengths and areas for improvement as a facilitator. We will also use this information to create a trainer certification program that will best suit the needs of the individuals participating.

Please check the appropriate box in the form below.

Skill	Have you done it?	My skills need:		
		Some help	A little help	No help
Active listening				
Restating				
Paraphrasing				
Summarizing				
Questioning				
Use of open-ended questions				
Use of high-impact questions				
Refocusing/redirecting questions				
Using questions to check meaning/check for deeper understanding				
Answering questions and/or knowing where to get answers				
Leading a discussion				
Leading brainstorming sessions				
Getting participation/involvement from all participants				
Managing a discussion to bring out key points				
Managing disagreements with respectful resolution of different views				
Leverage agreements to build/reach consensus				
Bringing a discussion to a close/ summarizing a discussion				
Platform Skills				
Confident working with groups				
Effective use of flip charts				
Effective use of videotapes				
Effective use of overhead transparencies				
Effective use of handouts				
Effective use of other *(specify)*				

At most, the certification process should take five days of class time, including a walk-through of the class. While there is a generic process consisting of eight steps, the process design provides flexibility based on the initial competency assessment of the participants and the nature of the course they are being certified to teach. For example, in the first step, "See the Course," the options range from being an actual participant in the course facilitated by the master trainer to observing the course to viewing a videotape of the course. Likewise, the "Prework" step could consist of any or all of the following:

- Completing a reading assignment on adult learning

- Completing the preparation required in the course to be taught

- Completing a special written assignment on the content

- Non-content preparation (e.g., reading an article on facilitation techniques)

In the "Content Skilling" step, the master trainer provides exercises and/or other assessments to ensure required proficiency. In the "Non-Content Skilling" segment, participants demonstrate their acquisition of skill and content knowledge through mini-modules tailored to the course and the participants' skill gaps.

Standardized mini-modules have been created on the following topics:

- Using energizers and ice breakers

- Effective questions

- Classroom management

- Using visual training aids

- Handling resistance

- Linkages

- Learning about the audience

In structuring the session, the master trainer has the flexibility of using some or none of the mini-modules and makes these decisions based on the competency-based selection data captured earlier. An example of a commonly used module would be a discussion-facilitation exercise that requires the participant to handle questions of moderate to high levels of difficulty in a variety of facilitation situations he or she will likely encounter in teaching the course.

During teach-backs, the participants receive feedback from peers and the master trainer using the Facilitator Competencies Feedback Form. The master trainer then uses the data collected through the process to determine certification status (full, partial, none) and communicates this to the participant. They then jointly create a development plan.

The Ongoing Support Process

The ongoing support process varies depending on whether the individual is fully or partially certified, as illustrated in Figure 7: Ongoing Support Process. Data on every trainer (competencies, certification status, utilization and level I evaluation scores) are entered and tracked in the American Express Global Training Management System.

FIGURE 7: Ongoing Support Process

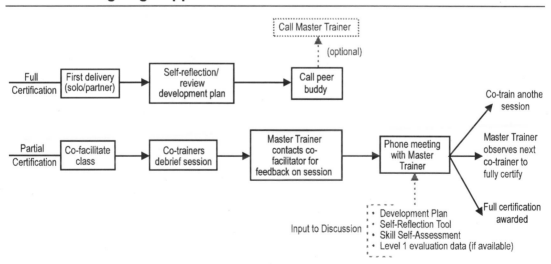

Conclusion

As Robin Lindbeck, the American Express Learning Design Consultant who led the training certification process improvement team, concluded: "While deployment of the model and all its applications are still in the early stages, we are excited about the potential impact of the model in creating a cost-effective yet high-quality training delivery capability and enabling a more strategic and planful approach." In the leadership course, where the certification model and training certification process have been used extensively, trainers give the process high marks. Line managers feel more confident about both the course content and their facilitation skills. As one line executive noted, "This is the first time I've been trained in effective facilitation skills. These skills will be as valuable to me on the job as in the classroom." Human resources professionals report that the process is "the most effective trainer certification process" they've been through inside or outside the company. Most importantly, the class participants are giving the trainers high ratings and content mastery scores have markedly increased.

About the Contributor

Carmen Hegge-Kleiser is Vice President of the Center for Learning Effectiveness of American Express' Department of Human Resources. She is a human resource executive with over 15 years of combined generalist and specialist experience in financial services and telecommunications. Ms. Hegge-Kleiser has reengineered domestic and international training programs for American Express employees in Leadership, Team, Quality, Customer Service, Change Management, and Sales Training.

9.
COMPETENCY-BASED CULTURE CHANGE

Mindy Hall — former Director of Professional Development, Rhône-Poulenc Rorer, Inc.

Background

I think it is fair to say that most organizational development practitioners, at one point or another in their careers, have a dream of truly facilitating the shaping of a culture. My opportunity to do just that came with a company known as Rhône-Poulenc Rorer, and my position there as head of Professional Development for North America. This chapter reflects that journey and explains key initiatives that were utilized to begin the process of re-shaping the culture across six different business units in the North America zone.

Rhône-Poulenc Rorer (RPR) is a multibillion-dollar global pharmaceutical corporation based in suburban Philadelphia; the company is devoted to the improvement of human health around the globe. It operates in more than 150 countries and is supported by 23,000 employees worldwide. It focuses its discovery, development, manufacturing, and marketing of human pharmaceutical products in select therapeutic categories: Oncology, Anti-Infectives, Plasma Proteins, Respiratory, and Thrombosis.

The company is divided into seven zones of responsibility: Worldwide Research and Development, Worldwide Industrial Operations, Worldwide Strategic Marketing, the Americas (North and Latin), Asia/Pacific, Europe, and Emerging Markets. The effort described in this chapter was undertaken in our Americas zone and began in April 1994 with an eight-word charge: *to build a development culture across North America*. This charge came jointly from the top line and human resource executives responsible for the Americas zone—a significant point, for it illustrates a strong partnership of senior-level endorsement, an endorsement that has been critical to the success of affecting and sustaining the organizational shifts that were envisioned from the start.

Building this development culture was an adventure similar to building an actual structure: a strong foundation was laid, key pillars of support were assembled, a "roof" to hold the structure together was provided in the form of a competency profile for our North American management, and different doors for entry were provided in re-creating the culture and involving as many people as possible in the effort. To take this metaphor one step further, we might say that the blueprints for our structure were based on five "architectural principles": the core components of culture change.

The Core Components of Culture Change

Culture change in a corporate environment typically involves these five components:

1. Creating a compelling vision

2. Generating energy and enthusiasm for the vision

3. Building both senior sponsorship and a critical mass of individuals who believe and are committed to the effort

4. Providing a common purpose, direction, and language for the new culture

5. Aligning human resource systems (i.e., recruitment, performance measurement, reward programs, and so forth) to support and reinforce the desired culture

Each of these components was essential to the success of the RPR adventure. Let's take a closer look.

Creating a Compelling Vision

While culture often functions at a level of assumptions, beliefs, and attitudes that largely go unnoticed and are simply accepted, there existed very distinct areas in the culture across North America where shifts in operating style would be critical. The most fundamental of these involved making people believe that they could, in fact, make a difference in the organization. Sparking that level of passion produced much-needed momentum for the efforts of creating this developmental culture.

It is important to recognize that cultural assumptions often guide managerial thinking about how to function within the company, with customers, and with one another, and that until the assumptions are unearthed, the way a company, a division, a department, or even an individual operates cannot be shifted. When building a new culture, it is important to weave together what employees and the organization want and need and to allow each to play a role in its creation; this is a key way in which cultures thrive and become internalized. Without such personal involvement on the part of the individual, the new culture may be complied with but not truly "take hold."

The North America zone of RPR began its journey with the conviction that creating a development culture was absolutely strategic to the long-term success of the business. This is not a new or revolutionary idea; in fact, in popular business magazines today, article after article report that the competitive advantages of yesterday, such as price and speed-to-market, are fast becoming competitive prerequisites, and that the differentiating features of successful companies in the future will rest not so much with their product line, but rather with their talent pool, leadership, and culture. However, what was revolutionary for the North American zone of RPR was the alignment of line executives, employees, and development professionals in terms of their commitment to taking this reality seriously and making it a key priority for long-term growth of the business.

The development culture across North America in 1994 had five distinct areas of weakness; the culture could be described in the following way:

1. As having a **"quick-fix" mentality**

2. As being **inconsistent** and **"siloed"**

3. As **lacking in "resource leveraging" across the zone**

4. As being **event-driven**

5. As being **full of historical gaps** between the message of embracing development and the reality of what was, in fact, being practiced.

Each area required its own strategy for change.

The **"quick-fix" mentality** that was evident across the zone could best be described through the words of an engineering manager from Ford who was quoted in the famous Peter Senge (1990) book, *The Fifth Discipline*. She stated the following:

> *I am beginning to "get" what this systems thinking and mental-models stuff is all about. It reminds me of when I first studied calculus. At first, I was totally lost. Calculus was a totally new way of thinking for me. But then I started to "get it." Within a year I had mastered the basics. Within five years, it was a core part of my professional capabilities.*

She then added:

> *If calculus were invented today, none of our corporations could learn it. We'd send everyone off to the three-day course. We'd then give them three months to try it out and see if "it worked." After it had failed, we'd conclude that it was of little value and move on to something else.*

Across North America, we were infamous for introducing a "flavor-of-the-month" development initiative, and much like the corporations projected in the example above, we would determine it unsuccessful if it didn't "take hold" immediately.

The **inconsistency in approach** occurred primarily because development initiatives were oriented solely toward the concerns of the business unit in which they were occurring. This, in effect, created **silos of development** with no shared purpose or direction; the development in one business unit could be substantially different from that in another unit. Consequently, **resources were not being leveraged across the zone** either in learning from one another or in creating economies of scale in the design and/or delivery of key development initiatives. Because there were no common threads linking the zone together, the business units within the North American zone operated more as independent components than as part of a greater whole.

Additionally, **development existed as an event**, rather than a process. The classic pattern of sending people away for development without any surety of the return on that investment of time, energy, and money was alive and well in the zone. Research from the book *The Lessons of Experience* (McCall, Lombardo, & Morrison, 1988) and from the publications of Lominger Limited, Inc. (see Eichinger & Lombardo, 1992) suggests that organizations will realize a greater return on investment for their development dollars by having a blended portfolio of experiences heavily weighted to development-in-place assignments augmented by coursework and learning from others. It appears that a large majority of American businesses do not culturally support development-in-place assignments, and thus could be missing golden opportunities to get more for less in terms of investment in people. The key for the North American zone, therefore, was to figure out the key levers needed to create this type of culture.

Finally, we had to overcome **a large gap between message and reality—** what was historically stated in terms of supporting and endorsing a development culture and what was practiced in achieving that culture. The challenge was to provide visible signs of endorsement for the "development message"; the signs had to reinforce the fact that creating a development culture meant going far beyond the process of simply training individuals. It had to become about a philosophy, a system, a way of being.

Development, in and of itself, provides both a valuable compass and catalyst for shaping an organization, and its effectiveness rests part and parcel with the climate it operates in, the quality and caliber of the development efforts, and the accountabilities built into its implementation and endorsement. It was therefore important to establish some baseline measurements about where RPR stood with respect to the climate of the organization. This was done by conducting both a third-party survey and several focus groups to identify not just the symptoms but also the root causes of the aforementioned cultural issues. One of the most significant findings from these methodologies was that although people had a high level of frustration in the midst of all the upheaval of the pharmaceutical industry, in general they were strongly committed to RPR and to bringing about positive change. This was a powerful hook on which to build a development strategy.

Generating Energy and Enthusiasm for the Vision

We leveraged this "hook" and utilized responses from the climate survey and focus group data to model an event after General Electric's WORK-OUT process. Originally sponsored by Jack Welch, WORK-OUT was designed as a five-day process to improve productivity and to "remove the more egregious manifestations of bureaucracy: multiple approvals, unnecessary paperwork, excessive reports, routines, rituals" (Tichy & Sherman, 1993, p. 430); in other words, essentially to take "work out" of the system. We customized the WORK-OUT process according to our distinctive needs and intentions: to drive energy into the system, to increase the level of employee involvement, and to provide a powerful and visible example that we were embarking on a quest "to do business differently." This was a significant event in the process of building our culture. It provided a platform for employee involvement while sending the message that each individual had a responsibility and opportunity to bring about the changes he or she wanted.

First, using broad themes from the climate survey and focus group data, we created five improvement teams; then the teams brought multileveled, cross-functional groups of employees together for three days. Each team tackled one key theme, such as communications, professional development, and compensation, and worked with a skilled facilitator for two days to develop five to seven key recommendations. On the third day, each team presented its recommendations to a panel of senior executives from across North America. After a brief caucus, the executive panel made one of four decisions:

- "Yes" to implementation with a target date; or

- "No" to implementation with the reasons why; or

- "In need of further study" with a date for feedback; or

- "Tabled" until the end of the day when one of the three decisions listed above would be taken.

This process encouraged a high level of employee involvement and generated momentum for the vision of creating an involved, vibrant climate; it also created a safe environment for people to take both risk and responsibility for shaping the culture in which they worked.

Although the event did not directly address the issue of implementing competency-based improvement, it was a critical step for us, infusing the system with energy and ideas, showing that everyone's input, from the senior-most executive's to the entry-level secretary's, mattered and had value. In *Team Zebra*, a book about the resurgence of Kodak's Black & White Division, Stephen Frangos (1993) states:

> *If you create an environment that motivates people to creatively solve problems and take an active part in their work, you'll realize tremendous gains in productivity, efficiency, and performance whether it's undergoing a major turnaround or a minor tune-up. We worked hard. We played hard. We brought about some important change. And that made it all worthwhile.* (p. xxiii)

Orienting this zone around the possibility of bringing about important change and being part of that effort was a critical milestone for us to reach before moving forward.

Building Senior Sponsorship and Critical Mass

The results of our WORK-OUT event were staggering. Twenty-six recommendations were adopted by the panel, four required further study, and only five were declined. Moreover, the open dialogue and interactive format so impressed the senior panel that they added two improvement suggestions of their own! To continue the work of building the new culture, three new organizational teams were formed: the Learning Organization Team, the Career-Pathing Project Team, and an internal Panel of Employees. All had different charters and a newly formed level of enthusiasm. Clearly, people were engaged and excited, both interested in and involved in creating change.

The bottom line truly is that the success of any system—be it development or performance measurement or any number of other systems that operate inside a corporation—is dependent on utilization, and utilization is dependent on people being engaged. The results of WORK-OUT showed strong signs of such engagement—of personal involvement and commitment.

Providing a Common Purpose, Direction, and Language

While WORK-OUT gave us the fuel to move the organization forward, the engine had yet to be widely communicated. Strategically, we had decided to orient our development culture toward providing competency-based development; it therefore was critical to educate the organization about what competency-based development would mean to them personally and how it would be used as the core, shared strategy across North America. Additionally, a common language of competencies had to be provided for employees to function effectively within the new culture.

With the above in mind, we built a management competency profile utilizing multilevel, multifunction input from entry-level managers up to and including senior managers; Eichinger and Lombardo's (1992) "The Career Architect" served as a building tool. The result was the creation of the North America Managers' Competency Profile. The final version of the profile includes 11 competencies, which make up the umbrella for the management population and by which we can orient and link our competency-based recruitment, development, and measurement systems.

In parallel with the effort of building the competency profile, a new project—the Leadership/Management Development Benchmark Study—was conducted. The main purpose of this project was to learn from "best practice" companies how they developed their human resource talent. The scope of the study included companies in the United States, Canada, and Mexico. It provided us with valuable information for directing our efforts from a design perspective, and caught the attention of senior management in seeing how other organizations were capitalizing on their human assets. The main themes, across the companies studied, on best practices for leadership/management development were the following:

- Ensure and leverage top management support and active involvement

- Regard employee development as a cultural value of the company

- Base development on a competency-driven system in which the competencies are aligned with the strategic imperatives of the business

- Build "brand recognition" for development efforts in order to market key successes

- Involve employees in the planning, designing, and evaluation of their learning

Many of these best practices were incorporated into the design of our Management Development Academy.

Aligning Human Resource Systems

The Management Development Academy was designed to provide a high-impact learning experience for developing our management talent at all levels, functions, geographies, and divisions across North America. It is targeted to our good/high-potential managers and is structured as a prestigious "school" to be accepted into, complete with an entry-application and screening process by an executive steering committee. The core philosophy of this academy is to provide competency-based development in line with the North America Managers'

Competency Profile through a variety of mediums. Some of those include pre-work assignments, customized 360-degree assessments/feedback, interaction with senior executives on strategic business issues, computer-based simulations, and individual development planning. The academy utilizes internal and external resources as faculty resources and partners with academic and business institutions to augment course content.

Another key initiative, planned for but not yet implemented, incorporates the southern hemisphere of the Americas' zone. This initiative is known as the Americas' Leadership Consortium. It will provide a forum two times per year for the leadership group (mid-level managers to vice-presidents) across both North and Latin America to convene for large-scale development opportunities and strategic business planning. The intended design includes partnering with experts in the field of leadership development, be they well-known business speakers or academicians, to provide some focused and high-caliber development to this group. The primary goal is to build a stronger sense of ownership and responsibility for shaping the company's current and future successes in this target audience; and although leadership can occur at any level in an organization, only the best leaders have the ability to leave powerful legacies. The key take-away objective, therefore, is to stimulate these leaders to consider what organizational legacy they would like to have an impact on, and then to teach them how to do that.

Essentially, both the Management Development Academy and the Leadership Consortium are examples of venues for growth and development where one size does not fit all; in the coming years, additional venues will need to be designed and implemented to offer the non-management populations the same opportunities for growth.

While the above are effective examples of how organizational improvement has been driven through the use of competencies, there is still much work to do in aligning other key human resource systems to reinforce more deeply the shift to a competency-based development culture. Our recruiting efforts are just now beginning to focus on competency-based interviewing in order to test for certain competencies during the course of an interview. "Seeding" the organization with new hires that mirror the competency profile toward which RPR is orienting the culture will be critical to its survival. Additionally, once those recruits are in the organizations, the development experiences to which they are exposed will determine their long-term success. This marks a critical link between one human resource system and another.

Finally, basic behavioral psychology suggests that what gets rewarded in American culture is often what gets done. Performance measurement systems must, therefore, be built to support the competency-based approach and also be linked to both recruitment and development to encourage the pull-through of these critical systems. Imagine a succession pool of people in your organization with the necessary core competencies to drive the future of your business; your only hard decision is where you want to place them in the organization at any given time. What a wonderful dilemma for an organization to be in!

Measuring Results

Measuring culture seems somewhat counterintuitive because it suggests the ability to quantify fairly unquantifiable elements, such as the way an individual feels about coming to work; the quality of the interactions that take place up, down, across, and through the organization; the level of belief, passion, and commitment that individuals carry with them to the job; and so forth. However, systematically measuring progress in the evolution of a culture provides valuable data on where to devote attention and what areas to further leverage. The North American zone has plans to measure progress via biannual climate surveys; the primary goals of this survey will be to assess how people perceive the culture, what level of enthusiasm they have for the changes, and what additional suggestions they have for ensuring the continued growth of a strong development culture. Depending on the data received in those surveys, interventions such as the aforementioned WORK-OUT-based event will be considered on an as-needed basis. Additionally, the effectiveness of the new culture will be measured, albeit in the longer term, via the pipeline of talented future leaders the organization is able to create.

As a result of the initiatives that were begun in 1994, the North American zone of RPR now has a competency-based system and language by which to operate. The move to competencies encourages a playing field that feels more level to all employees by focusing on skill "what-you-bring-to-the-party" portfolios, rather than on interpersonal "who-you-know" ways of operating. The use of competency language provides a common approach for individuals to relate to and understand. This shift to competency-based language has produced tangible results, such as richer performance discussions, improved interviewing skills, and more effective interpersonal interactions. These results have been documented primarily via anecdotal data; the biannual climate survey will provide an interesting analysis on whether the anecdotal information is either validated or discounted.

RPR continues to learn many lessons along the road to building this culture, and numerous parallel efforts engaging many different voices have been involved in the effort. While certainly senior sponsorship has been and will continue to be important, it alone does not make change happen; ultimately, all change is self-change and happens from the inside out. People make choices about whether and how they will change, and people change when they feel that the benefit of the change outweighs the price not to. Two years into creating this culture, many have been convinced that change is worth the investment.

RPR began with a commitment that the value of learning for the individual, the organization, and the bottom line equaled the value of making sales and profit targets. While the passion for this commitment continues to grow over time, the seed is firmly planted and the shift has occurred where professional development is now seen as an expectation for success rather than as a weakness to be noted, as an investment rather than as an expense. What RPR has done across the North American zone is best summed up through the words of Noel Tichy and Stratford Sherman (1993):

It takes an enormous number and range of ideas to transform an organization; ideas about values and strategies, ideas for practical improvement, ideas about how to do small things a little more efficiently, and ideas for sweeping change. Ideas get people excited and people moving.

The tremendous energy of many motivated and focused people is what it takes to creatively destroy and rebuild an institution. (p. 325)

The RPR adventure, thus far, has been challenging, frustrating, and wonderful; and every indication suggests that it will continue to be for the foreseeable future.

References

Eichinger, B., & Lombardo, M. (1992). The career architect. In *The leadership architect suite of integrated tools*. Lominger Limited, Inc.

Frangos, S., with Bennett, S.J. (1993). *Team Zebra*. Essex Junction, VT: Oliver Wight Publications.

McCall, M. W., Lombardo, M. M., & Morrison, A. M. (1988). *The lessons of experience: How successful executives develop on the job*. Lexington, MA: Lexington Books.

Senge, P. (1990). *The fifth discipline*. New York, NY: Doubleday.

Tichy, N., & Sherman, S. (1993). *Control your destiny or someone else will*. New York, NY: Doubleday.

About the Contributor

Mindy Hall, Principal of Peak Development, brings ten years of management and organization development experience to her own consulting practice, focusing on high-potential development, culture development, and team development. In her previous position as the Director of Professional Development for Rhône-Poulenc Rorer, she was responsible for all organizational and management development initiatives, team assimilations, and professional development strategy for business units in the United States, Canada, and Mexico. Ms. Hall holds a master's degree in human resource management and is currently pursuing her Ph.D. in human and organizational development.

10.
APPLYING COMPETENCY-BASED SELECTION AND TRAINING TO REENGINEERING

Carmen Hegge-Kleiser — Vice President, Center for Learning Effectiveness

> *Companies don't reengineer processes; people do . . . How companies select and organize the people who actually do the reengineering is key to the success of the endeavor.*
>
> —Michael Hammer and James Champy
> *Reengineering the Corporation*

Background

In the last few years, many corporations have undertaken massive reengineering initiatives, giving rise to expanded consulting practices in the area of reengineering. As Hammer and Champy (1993) have observed, "outsiders" from consulting firms were often ideal when the company had no prior reengineering experience and required a fresh perspective that was not heavily invested in the way things had traditionally been done.

This was descriptive of the situation facing American Express in 1993. American Express had just established a reenergized corporate quality function and was engaged in process improvement throughout the company. While it was achieving modest gains with a multitude of process improvement initiatives, the company lacked a coherent approach to reengineering and a systematic means for capturing organizational learning in this area. More immediate, dramatic reengineering gains were clearly called for in order for the company to achieve its net savings target of $1 billion for the year. Consequently, a number of external consultants were enlisted to provide the fresh perspective and reengineering expertise American Express lacked while it built up its own internal expertise.

Eighty employees were trained to become internal process improvement consultants. The role of Process Improvement Consultant carried with it four major responsibilities:

(1) assessing the training needs of process team members,

(2) conducting training or facilitation sessions to transfer process improvement methodology and general quality knowledge to teams and upper management as necessary,

(3) facilitating ongoing process improvement team efforts, and

(4) acting as a liaison with upper management concerning the process team's needs and progress.

Initially, process improvement consultants were selected without the use of a structured competency-based interview process. Functional expertise and familiarity with the process under review were the primary selection criteria at that time. Availability was another complicating factor in the selection process. Competing business demands often precluded optimal candidates from assuming the role. The developmental value of such an assignment was also unclear, which caused some candidates to question the value of such a move. As a result, most of the initial process improvement consultants came from the quality assurance function in operations, since they were viewed as having many of the requisite skills and it seemed to be a more logical career move for them.

Performance Gap Assessment

Training for these initial process improvement consultants focused almost exclusively on quality concepts, process improvement methodology, and group problem-solving skills. Team-building skills, change management techniques and process-consulting skills were not initially seen as core competencies that required a structured training approach. However, skill deficits in these areas emerged as barriers to overall effectiveness in the Process Improvement Consultant role. As Craig DeWald, Senior Director of Quality Education, explained, "a good grasp of quality and process improvement techniques was not enough. Cross-functional teams that had never worked together before and had no reengineering experience often required accelerated team-building and process consultation interventions. Moreover, the more dramatic reengineering required by the business was accompanied by significant change management issues." Expanding training alone was not a complete answer to closing this gap. The selection process needed to factor in personal traits that could not be taught, but were essential to effective performance (see Figure 1: Optimal Competency Utilization Strategy).

FIGURE 1: Optimal Competency Utilization Strategy

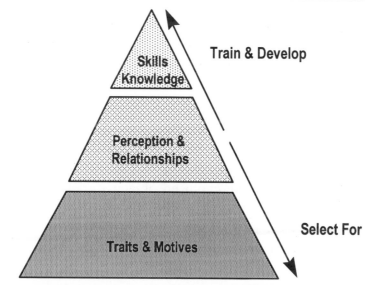

Personal Characteristics that Superior Performers
- **Demonstrate in more situations**
- **Apply with better results**

To address this issue, the Worldwide Quality Education group, with the sponsorship of the SVP Quality and Reengineering, partnered with Hay Consultants to develop a validated Process Improvement Consultant competency model that could be used in selection, training, and development. The team working on this project had three business objectives:

1. Reduce the consultant development cycle time.

2. Increase the effectiveness of current and future consultants.

3. Build internal capability to achieve the $1 billion reengineering target, and sustain those savings.

In developing the competency model, the team used the following:

-   Behavioral event interviews (BEIs)

-   A task analysis survey

-   Expert interviews

-   Expert panels

This approach was based on the belief that the best way to model outstanding performance is to study the top performers and understand what they do differently.

From the initial 80 process improvement consultants, the top six performers were selected for behavioral event interviews, based on the results they had achieved and feedback from the teams they had supported and the teams' executive sponsors. The BEI technique captured objective, detailed information about past behavior that formed patterns differentiating effective performers. This procedure focuses on what people have actually done in real situations, rather than on hypothetical statements about what they might do in a given situation. The interviewers assumed the role of detectives, probing for detailed descriptions of actual behavior. This approach elicits more objective data and produces a more detailed delineation between the behaviors and attitudes associated with success and failure.

Expert panels were also formed, and interviews were conducted with external consultants who had demonstrated success with reengineering projects in American Express and other major global companies. A limited number of internal experts who had recently been hired into American Express for their quality and process improvement expertise were also interviewed.

Current process improvement consultants, as well as team members, each completed a task analysis survey. This data along with the job descriptions provided a more detailed understanding of the role of Process Improvement Consultant in both theory and practice. It also provided a framework for analyzing the other data.

Process Improvement and Consultant Model

The model that emerged from this data had three primary competency clusters— "Quality and Integrity," "Cognitive Flexibility," and "Teamwork and People"— with two to three competencies per cluster (see the following page, Figure 2: Process Improvement Consultant Competency Model).

Cluster 1: Quality and Integrity

The "Quality and Integrity" cluster was the foundation of the model. The competencies in this cluster were the distinguishing points between effective and highly effective performers. It also was the most difficult set of competencies to develop. Consequently, it must be a major consideration in the selection process for process improvement consultants. The competencies in this cluster are (1) Being Accountable and (2) Pursuing Learning and Self-Development. Being Accountable captures the commitment to support process improvement activities in the organization. The most effective consultants show strong levels of ownership for the effort's results. The Pursuing Learning and Self-Development competency highlights the focus on the consultant as an instrument for improvement. The most effective consultants internalize continuous improvement

FIGURE 2: Process Improvement Consultant Competency Model

- Comprehending Issues
- Thinking Strategically and Conceptually

- Creating and Maintaining Effective Work Teams
- Coaching and Developing Others
- Orchestrating Change

Cognitive Flexibility

Teamwork and People

Quality and Integrity

- Being Accountable
- Pursuing Learning and Self-Development

FIGURE 3: Distinguishing Competency Matrix

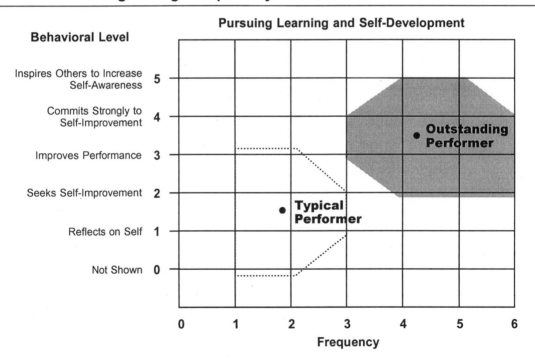

Pursuing Learning and Self-Development

Behavioral Level

Inspires Others to Increase Self-Awareness	5
Commits Strongly to Self-Improvement	4
Improves Performance	3
Seeks Self-Improvement	2
Reflects on Self	1
Not Shown	0

• **Outstanding Performer**

• **Typical Performer**

Frequency

and applicable learnings. The Distinguishing Competency Matrix (shown in Figure 3) illustrates the behavioral continuum for Pursuing Learning and Self-Development, and plots the gap between a typical performer and an outstanding one based on the American Express data.

Cluster 2: Cognitive Flexibility

The "Cognitive Flexibility" cluster reflects the manner in which information is processed by the consultant. Although this cluster of competencies is difficult to develop at higher levels on the behavioral continuum, it is considered a baseline competency set. While required for the role, baseline or essential competencies do not clearly differentiate the highly effective performers. Within this cluster are two competencies: Comprehending Issues, and Thinking Strategically and Conceptually. Comprehending Issues highlights the ability to understand individuals and groups in order to determine the best means of making an impact on them. At the lowest end of proficiency in the Comprehending Issues continuum, a consultant would be capable of focusing on emotional or literal content, and at the highest end, the consultant would understand complex underlying issues. Thinking Strategically and Conceptually emphasizes the use of information and concepts to overcome organizational hurdles and make a case for process improvement from a business perspective. The range of competency behavior in this instance moves from recognizing patterns in the process improvement effort to visualizing the future. The continuum is useful in plotting the proficiency level required for the task. For example, strategic reengineering would demand a higher level of competency in these two cases than a more limited process improvement effort.

Cluster 3: Teamwork and People

Teamwork and people competencies are the least difficult to develop. As in the case of the "Cognitive Flexibility" cluster, they are considered baseline or essential competencies. As you can see in the Essential Competency Matrix (Figure 4, on the following page), there is more overlap in the frequency of behavior between effective and high performers than was shown in Figure 3.

FIGURE 4: Essential Competency Matrix

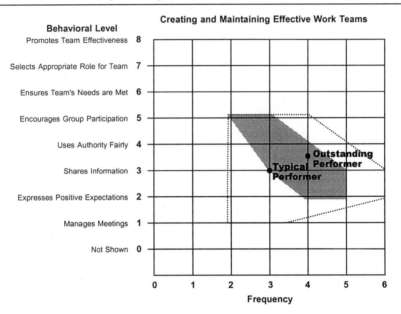

This cluster consists of three competencies: Creating and Maintaining Effective Work Teams, Coaching and Developing Others, and Orchestrating Change. The first competency, Creating and Maintaining Effective Work Teams, provides a foundation for collaborating effectively and eliciting maximum participation from team members. An effective consultant leads team members away from working in "silos" and helps them recognize and overcome barriers. The second competency, Coaching and Developing Others, emphasizes the ability to enhance understanding about process improvement and mobilize the team to a higher level of performance. The third, Orchestrating Change, reflects the importance of overcoming personal and organizational skepticism that inhibits time and effort allocated for process improvement activities.

Applying the Competency Model

One of the first uses of the data collected in developing the competency model was to refine the process improvement consultants' responsibilities and baseline qualifications as illustrated by the following role description.

PROCESS IMPROVEMENT CONSULTANT ROLE DESCRIPTION

Responsibilities:

- Assess training needs of process improvement team members.
    - Conduct assessments with process owner, team leaders, and team members through meetings or ongoing facilitation.
    - Analyze team progress, project scope, and educational needs.

- Transfer process improvement methodology and general quality knowledge to teams and senior management, as necessary. Act as liaison with senior management concerning team needs and progress.
    - Educate teams through facilitated sessions.
    - Provide periodic updates of team progress with sponsors.

- Facilitate team progress through ongoing meetings with teams, subteams, or individuals.
    - Apply quality tools and techniques.
    - Provide coaching and feedback to ensure optimal team performance.

Basic Qualifications:

- This assignment requires familiarity with AEQL concepts and TQM practices. Candidate should have prior experience working with a team. Proven ability to coach, motivate, and lead team members is a significant advantage.

- Proficiency in the use of basic math applications is essential. Ability to apply statistical analysis to spot trends and recommend action steps is preferred.

- Additionally, the individual must have strong presentation skills and a demonstrated ability to state complex theories in a cogent, simple, and effective manner.

Next, the model was incorporated in the selection process. First, an interview guide was designed based on the three competency clusters that formed the model. The questions were tested with a sample group to determine which ones yielded the most useful information. The general approach was a competency-based behavior event interview. For each competency area, a broad question was asked about a particular type of experience and followed up with probes to determine the extent to which a competency was displayed (see Figure 5: Sample BEI Questions). To determine skill and knowledge, the interviewer focused on what the person actually did or said in the situation. Probes regarding what the person actually thought and felt in the situation provided evidence of motivation and approach. An evaluation form was designed to capture the demonstrated competency level against company requirements (see Figure 6: Selection/ Evaluation Score Sheet). Based on the competency assessment study, minimum thresholds were established for each competency. An aggregate score of at least 7 points was required for baseline competencies, and a minimum aggregate score of 4 was required for the distinguishing competencies.

FIGURE 5: Sample BEI Questions

CLUSTER 1: Quality and Integrity

Question:
Tell me about a time you put yourself on the line.

Follow-Up Probes
- What led up to the situation?
- What did you say or do?
- What did you think or feel?
- What was the outcome?

CLUSTER 2: Cognitive Flexibility

Question:
Tell me about a decision you made that had a significant impact in your organization.

Follow-Up Probes
- What did you say or do?
- What did you think or feel?
- How did it turn out?

CLUSTER 3: Teamwork and People

Question:
Tell me about a time you made an important contribution to a group.

Follow-Up Probes
- Who was involved?
- What did you say or do?
- What did you think or feel?
- How did it turn out?

FIGURE 6: Selection/Evaluation Score Sheet

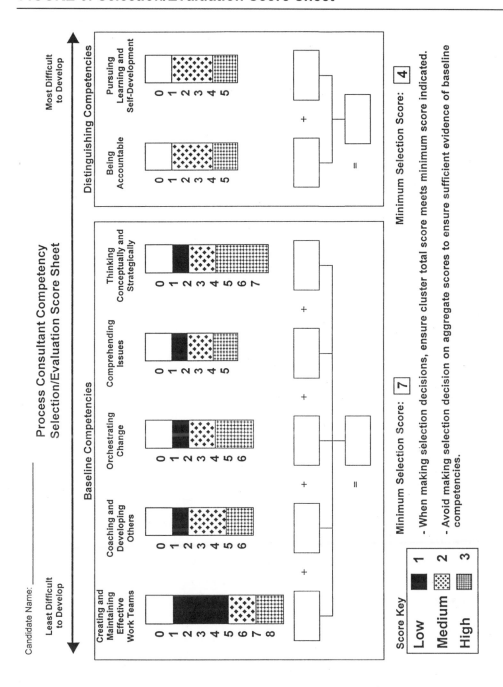

Process Consultant Competency
Selection/Evaluation Score Sheet

Training

Once these selection and evaluation tools were in place, the individuals conducting the interviews and making the selection decisions had to be trained in their use. Consequently, a training session was held for American Express quality advisors, the staff from Worldwide Quality, and the Quality Education team. After being briefed on the model and instructed in the use of the BEI methodology and tools, each participant went through a simulated interview and received feedback on his or her performance. Once certified in the BEI methodology, participants were responsible for screening potential process improvement consultants in the selection process, and were expected to serve as coaches of existing process improvement consultants.

The BEI process had three objectives:

1. To select new consultants

2. To provide developmental feedback

3. To assess strengths and training needs

In recent years, as the Process Improvement Consultant became less than a full-time responsibility, a self-assessment was designed based on the competency model. This instrument is more developmentally oriented and is now a requirement prior to attending training in process improvement consulting; it is also used as a coaching tool throughout the training process.

The training process for process improvement consultants has also been revised to capitalize on what was learned from the competency model development process. Process Improvement/Reengineering training provides an approach to process analysis, redesign, and management that builds skills in process-specific areas and brings direction to the application of established skills and experience in process improvement efforts. Prospective consultants receive training in the 12-step process management methodology and "tool box," along with project management practices that will enable them to build project plans. The training consists of three levels of consulting:

1. Structuring and managing the engagement

    - Understanding the context of the effort

    - Working effectively with the executive owner

2. Structuring and managing the project

    - Project planning, evaluation, and resourcing

3. Structuring and managing meetings

    - Creating session agendas

    - Facilitating through session agendas

The last part of the training focuses on participants developing and conducting facilitated sessions around a case study that incorporates the quality/process improvement tools/methodology. In these facilitated sessions, prospective process improvement consultants have an opportunity to conduct sessions that enable them to focus on areas where they were weakest in the self-assessment and to receive feedback on the degree of improvement they exhibit.

The initial training takes five days. Additional training in benchmarking, team-based problem solving, project management, and change management is available on a just-in-time, just-as-needed basis. This training provides a more in-depth look at the "how to" aspect of these topics. All this training has been designed in a modular fashion so that the consultant can provide it in a "just enough, just-in-time fashion" to accelerate the work of the process improvement team.

This effort contributed to American Express' success in achieving its $1 billion reengineering target. "More importantly," according to Doug MacKenzie, a former consultant to the company who now heads American Express Worldwide Quality, "the Quality Education team and the Center for Learning Effectiveness team, through this coordinated effort, have captured the key organizational learnings and institutionalized a consulting practice that will enable us to sustain the progress we've made."

References

Hammer, M., & Champy, J. (1993). *Reengineering the corporation.* New York, NY: HarperBusiness.

About the Contributor

Carmen Hegge-Kleiser is Vice President of the Center for Learning Effectiveness at American Express. She is a human resource executive with over 15 years of combined generalist and specialist experience in financial services and telecommunications. Ms. Hegge-Kleiser has reengineered domestic and international training programs for American Express employees in Leadership, Team, Quality, Customer Service, Change Management, and Sales Training. In 1993, she formed a cross-disciplinary team which created quality, CPI/reengineering and change management tools to support a company-wide reengineering/CPI effort. As Vice President of Human Resources for the American Express Traveler's Cheque Group, she was part of the executive team leading the TQM efforts that resulted in the business unit being selected as a 1992 service industry finalist for the Baldrige Award.

11.
A USEFUL APPROACH TO FACILITATING INDIVIDUAL ADJUSTMENT TO ORGANIZATIONAL CHANGE

Kenneth L. Pierce, M.A., R.T.C. — Consultant/Trainer, Corporate Training and Consulting Services, Holland College, Prince Edward Island, Canada

Much good literature has been written about assisting organizations, teams, and groups in moving to a performance focus within a competency-based organization. However, little attention has been paid to assisting individuals in this progress, and thus few strategies for individual adjustment are available. This chapter, which is intended to help fill that gap, describes a strategy that has been used successfully to assist faculty and learners in a community college in making the transition from a traditional learning environment to a competency-based one. It is hoped that the efforts recounted herein have value for organizations of all types who wish to enhance the adjustment of individuals to change.

Background

Since its inception over 25 years ago, Holland College has achieved both national and international stature as an innovator in both the technical and services industries. One mark of the institution has been its adoption and use of a performance-based, or competency-based, learning model. As a learning manager on the faculty for 19 years, I have had frequent discussions with colleagues about the difficulties encountered by faculty and learners alike in moving from a traditional model of learning to a performance-based one. Until recently, the strategies in place were clearly short of successful.

Despite programs offered over the years—such as Holland's survival-skills training program for faculty and an orientation program for new students—faculty and students could still take several days to several months to make the transition. As is often the case with those who find change a struggle, these individuals came to be described in less than complimentary terms: rigid, out of control, immature, irresponsible, lazy, naive, and shortsighted. However, at some level there was the suspicion that they were just acting as anyone might in a new, unusual, and scary situation, and that perhaps with the "right" approach and tools, we could minimize the trauma of this transition and accelerate everyone's adjustment to the new kind of learning organization.

It is generally conceded that each person has individual needs and brings those needs to any situation. Several models of human needs have been developed over the course of time, including models from Maslow and Erickson. In general, these needs are said to be filtered through a belief system about "self" and "personal competence" that can hamper a person's adjustment to change. With further advances in this area—especially in Choice Theory psychology, Neuro-Linguistic psychology, and Whole Brain Learning—there evolved a number of valuable concepts and tools for facilitating individual adjustment to change. Choice Theory, above all, offered Holland College the basis for an effective course of action.

Choice Theory, and how it was used in the learning organization to assist individual change, is thus the focus of our discussion in this chapter. Included are specific references that can help decision makers facilitate individual change in a positive way.

Choice Theory Psychology

- *What if we will always need to be able to change?*

- *What if change is one of life's guarantees?*

- *What if adaptability to change is one of the hallmarks of successful people?*

The questions above, though not surprising to many people, are usually far from the standard thinking of individuals or organizations wishing to move toward performance-based, or competency-based, management systems. Yet it is precisely these kinds of questions, along with the assumptions and knowledge behind them, that we must address if we are to approach change in a productive manner; if our thinking is limited, we will be, too.

A person's assumptions and knowledge regarding self and others, as well as his or her skill in dealing with stressful situations, are crucial elements in change management. All too often five "fatal flaws" come into play, impeding successful adaptation. Those flaws are introduced, and their analysis begun, in the following organizational "fairy tale" (presented with full apologies to Walt Disney).

The Five Fatal Flaws

ONCE UPON A TIME, there was a young entrepreneur named Snow White who, finding her world dangerously out of control and changing quickly, left her previous employment situation—managing a kingdom—and sought her fortune in the great unknown beyond the kingdom's gate.

She traveled until she stumbled upon a promising-looking opportunity in the mining industry; a small diamond mine with only seven employees. These employees were dedicated and hardworking but seemed to lack organizational skills. It looked like they needed the leadership and expertise of a smart entrepreneur who could take control of the operation and make it more viable.

The seven employees were impressed by Snow White's credentials. She was pleasant, attractive, cared about them, and appeared to have a good sense of what their organization needed. Soon she became a valuable part of the operation, focusing her attention on reorganizing the business. Time passed, and everyone seemed to be settling in, when something happened.

One day, one of Snow White's old competitors arrived in disguise at her door, and made her an offer. Snow White found herself in the position of having to make a quick decision, a common occurrence in the business world. Unfortunately, she was unprepared to make the *right* quick decision, for there were some serious flaws in her knowledge and belief system.

Snow White had not really learned yet why she was working at all, nor had she learned how to manage change and to adjust to it. She believed that managing a diamond mine was just another business in a new place—that the old rules of the game, her old knowledge and beliefs, would still work. She neglected to account for the fact that time and change are major constants in everyone's life.

Consequently, Snow White took a big bite into an attractive-looking opportunity and suddenly ended up out of business; what looked like short-term gain turned out to be long-term pain.

However, Snow White got lucky, as often happens in fairy tales, and eventually was rescued by another, more flexible entrepreneur also seeking to build a future. We are not likely to be so fortunate. But perhaps this explains our fascination with fairy tales.

What Snow White hadn't learned was that changing times can be a liability or an asset; she was not prepared for the realities of the times in which she lived. Five flaws in her belief system and skill repertoire made managing change virtually impossible for her.

1. Snow White **believed** that everyone viewed the world as she did.

2. Snow White **believed** that she did not have to adjust to the changing times.

3. Snow White **believed** that she did not have to prepare for the future by learning from her past.

4. Snow White **did not know** what really motivates people.

5. Snow White **did not know** how to maintain self-control in a stressful situation.

Had Snow White known and practiced Choice Theory, she would probably have had a much better chance to deal effectively with the challenges of her new organization.

Choice Theory and the Principles of Competency-Based Organizations

Choice Theory offers a simple and practical paradigm for managing change. Its effectiveness in a competency-based organization is understandable when one considers the underlying principles of competency-based or performance-based organizations. Foremost among them are the following:

1. Everyone can learn if they choose to learn.

2. Focus on the individual learner's needs.

3. Focus on learners' future potential, rather than their past history.

4. Give learners responsibility for their own learning.

5. Focus on giving learners choices.

6. Focus on learner's behavior or performance, in addition to thinking or knowledge.

7. Give control of progress to the learners.

8. Give accountability for the learning environment to the learning manager or supervisor.

These principles reflect the fundamental underpinnings of Choice Theory, as well. And it is these same principles that are reflected in Edward Deming's work on "quality" conducted in Japan many years ago.

For an individual with a background in a traditional workplace or learning environment—which tends to foster dependence, direction, and external control—this list of principles could generate strong feelings of fear and insecurity. If an individual has little awareness of why he or she is at work or school, the feeling can be magnified.

Most people have not had an opportunity to learn much about their own needs, what motivates them, or how to communicate with others. As a result, they come to organizations without the basic knowledge and skills required to participate fully in a constantly changing organization, and managers are often left with the task of helping them acquire those necessities as part of an ongoing, larger change process. Snow White is representative of such individuals, ones who resist change because they lack the insight into their own needs and the organization's needs.

The Choice Theory Model

William Glasser, M.D., an internationally known psychiatrist, writer, and educational consultant, developed a model to explain not only what motivates people but also why they come to work each day. His model, Choice Theory (formerly known as Control Theory), suggests that each individual is striving to get specific needs met and thereby achieve a measure of self-control and control over his or her world.

These needs are metaphorically represented as pictures that the individual collects over time. Every individual has a "photo album" in his or her mind, its contents derived from bits and pieces of experiences that felt good; the "pictures" are a personal collection of idealizations, representing those need-fulfilling pieces of the past that the individual feels will be need-fulfilling again. In the effort to recapture the good feelings associated with these pictures, the individual behaves as effectively as possible to maintain self-control while moving toward the pictures. Thus, each picture is tied in some way to one or more of the individual's needs.

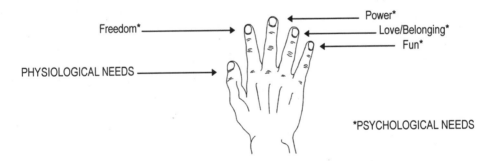

There are five of these needs, which can be represented by the thumb and fingers of one's hand.

Physiological Needs

The thumb represents the individual's physiological needs, which are genetically coded in the body and essential for survival. These include the need for safety, shelter, food, water, rest, air, and reproduction. Organizations have historically believed, and many still do, that employees go to work and students attend classes primarily to fulfill (in the short term or the long term) their physiological needs via a paycheck. Not so, suggests Glasser. While a wage is important to uphold our responsibilities and maintain our lifestyle, it is usually far down on the list of the reasons why people work or learn.

Psychological Needs

The four fingers represent the individual's psychological needs, those of the mind, which have evolved over time and are essential to personal well-being. Generally, an individual works or learns primarily to meet one or more of these needs.

Freedom. The first finger (pointing finger) represents the need for freedom, the need to believe that we are making significant choices in our lives. The need for freedom can be subdivided into

(a)   Freedom from the control of others

(b)   Freedom to be the person we want to be

Glasser indicates that the more employees or learners are bossed around with little freedom from the control of others, the less productive they tend to be and the poorer the quality of their products or services.

Power. The second finger (middle finger) represents the need for power, the need to be valued, to exert influence, and to be recognized. This need can be found in three distinct manifestations:

(a)   Power to be in control of our own body

(b)   Power to control objects around us

(c)   Power to exert influence on others

Glasser distinguishes power from authority. Authority is bestowed on an individual by an organization—for example, through a specific job title. Power, on the other hand, is given to individuals by themselves or other individuals. Employees and learners come to work with a need to be healthy, to be valued for their skills and their ability to exert influence, and to be heard.

Love/Belonging. The third finger (the ring finger) represents the need for love or belonging, the need to love or care for others and to have it returned and experience a sense of belonging. Individuals need to feel part of a team or an organization, to belong to something important and to be able to express their caring back in appropriate ways.

Fun. The fourth finger (the baby finger) represents the need for fun, the need to see that we are progressing, moving forward in significant ways. Individual staff and learners need to believe they are somehow better off now than they were at an earlier time, that they are improving themselves in important ways, that they are learning and laughing as they move forward.

According to Glasser, these are the needs that people bring to organizations and that they perceive as threatened by change. All the needs—the psychological as well as the physiological—are genetically encoded, he argues, and must be met regularly if individuals are to feel satisfied with their lives. Glasser supports his claim that psychological needs have a genetic base by pointing out that they, too, have been essential to our survival on the planet. For instance, if we had not learned to create a choice-laden, free environment, wherein we feel empowered, influential, and able to work with others in cooperative, caring units while experiencing the enjoyment of progress, we would not have survived.

Each of us, at any point in time, will have a "dominant" need—one need that overshadows the others. This need's satisfaction takes precedence over the rest and becomes reflected in our behavior. Most individuals will, over time, develop self-control—ways to get such needs met—and any significant environmental or organizational change is likely to instill the fear of losing that control. Moreover, if an individual has used a learning environment or a job as the primary vehicle for getting a dominant need met, then he or she will experience even greater stress during a change process.

Choice Theory's Assumptions

Choice Theory's approach to change, communication, and learning is based on the following ten assumptions about people and their behavior.

1. **Everyone knows what they want.** Each individual knows what is personally need-fulfilling or what personally feels good, even though he or she may not be able to put it into words.

2. **Every behavior has a purpose.** At any given time, each individual is behaving in ways that get personal needs met.

3. **All people are basically good; no one sets out to be bad.** Labels such as "Good Employee" or "Bad Employee" refer to the person rather than his or her behavior. We cannot change being a person with needs, but we can change our behavior. Behaviors are bad insofar as they prevent us (and sometimes others) from getting needs met.

4. **All people share genetically encoded needs that are essential to survive.** The individual defines the hierarchy of how these needs will be met. In contrast to Maslow's model, the hierarchy is constantly being changed by the individual as he or she interacts with the world.

5. **A person will always need to be able to make choices, even in settings in which freedom is limited.**

6. **Each person is responsible for meeting his or her own needs and can learn a better way to do so.**

7. **Every behavior is the person's best attempt at that time to get needs met.** An individual's current behavior is based on the extent of his or her awareness of options and perception of what may work to get needs met at the moment.

8. **An environment that encourages positive behaviors facilitates change more than one that focuses on negative behaviors.**

9. **A person will not change if there is no clear benefit—that is, if it is not need-fulfilling in some way.**

10. **Every behavior is a total behavior having four interconnected parts: a doing state, a thinking state, a feeling state, and a physiological state. By initiating changes in what we do and think, we can change the feelings and the physiology of the body.**

Dominating Needs: Two Examples

To better understand dominating needs and how such needs in a person might appear to others, let's take a look at two examples, the first from the education arena. Here the perceiver of those needs would be a learning manager or supervisor.

Suppose four new students enter a business administration program at a community college such as Holland (a competency-based, or performance-based, institution). Each student is unique in his or her own way—a learner who brings personal history, beliefs, and needs to the competency-based environment.

Dick is a 19-year-old high school dropout who has worked for six years as a waiter in a local upscale restaurant. He has returned to school to meet his "freedom" need so that he will have more career choices in the future. He is hardworking but seems to lack self-confidence.

Anne is a 35-year-old mother of two who dropped out of a university because costs were too high and her experience there didn't seem to be leading anywhere. Because her controlling need for "power" is very compelling, she wants to work with people in a business setting. She believes she has something to offer and learns quickly.

Mike is a 45-year-old former service-station operator who only finished elementary school. His need for "love/ belonging" is driving him to return to school because, in his words, "I need money to make sure my kid finishes college." He believes that, though persistent, he "isn't very intelligent like other people."

Francis is a 25-year-old dropout from another training program. Her controlling need is "fun," to be laughing and enjoying herself no matter what. She is not clear on what she wants or where she is going, but she plans on "enjoying the ride anyway."

To receive the best competency-based performance from these students, the learning manager or supervisor would have to meet these challenges:

1. Perceive and remain aware of the individual needs of the learners

2. Create opportunities to encourage the learners to rise to their potential in a unique, need-fulfilling environment that places heavy responsibility for achievement on their shoulders

3. Ensure that the need-fulfilling environment is constantly changing

Our next example focuses on the business arena, specifically The Acme Pizza Company. Acme has a six-person team working rotating shifts at its downtown branch. The team has been working successfully as a unit for two years, and the company has been experiencing an annual growth rate of over 20%. Below is the profile of the team members.

Tom is a 28-year-old hardworking individual with energy and ambition. His most compelling need seems to be "power"—to have an impact on the organization. His need for "fun" is important as well, since he is eager to learn about anything that might help him do a better job.

Mary is a 23-year-old mother of one who has already exceeded her wildest expectations of employment by being appointed recently as the team leader. Mary's most prevailing need also is "power," but from the perspective of gaining status from rising within the company by doing a good job.

Paul is a 30-year-old newly married man with a child on the way. His controlling need is "love/belonging." He places a lot of importance on being part of the team and sharing the challenges of the job. However, he has recently been passed up for a promotion and is quite frustrated about it.

Jane is a 55-year-old woman who just entered the workforce for the first time. Her controlling need is "freedom," which she believes her job will offer by giving her a variety of choices to make on the job, and by giving her more options (via a paycheck) off the job.

Cliff is a thoughtful 38-year-old—the comic-philosopher of the group. His most important need is "fun." Cliff is eager to learn anything that will assist him in life, and he places a lot of emphasis on enjoying being at work and the time with his team. However, he has a hard time giving others direction, which has become part of his new role.

Bill is a 60-year-old longtime employee who is approaching retirement. Bill's most pressing need is also "love/belonging." He wants the team to work together smoothly to get the job done so their supervisor will be pleased. He looks forward to leaving the job to pursue his other interests and hobbies, especially fishing.

Here, the leader of the team, Mary, must learn to perceive the members' controlling needs, to maintain an awareness of those needs, and to understand members' behaviors in light of those needs. If she cannot do so, it will be difficult for her to assist the team and at the same time achieve the organization's goals. Both she and the first example's learning manager would find their challenges easier to meet if they became thoroughly familiar with the Choice Theory model and developed the skill of interpreting people's behaviors in terms of people's needs.

Clearly, in competency-based organizations of all kinds, leaders need a practical framework that supports their efforts to help learners and staff reach high levels of achievement in performance and personal growth. This requisite framework is no more crucial than during the change process. Fortunately, Holland College found such a framework in the Choice Theory model.

Moving From Old To New Paradigms at Holland College

As mentioned earlier, for years we at Holland College struggled with the dilemma of helping people deal with change as we watched students arrive, most with 12 or more years' experience in traditional learning environments behind them, and enter a competency-based environment. After a while it became evident that learners who displayed flexibility, self-confidence, and adaptability tended to make a quicker transition to the competency-based system; but until we discovered the Choice Theory model, we lacked a vehicle to help the rest overcome their difficulties with the change process.

Presently, a similar problem has confronted business organizations who have moved from traditional to performance-based management systems. The following account of how Holland College dealt with its problem, and found at least one effective model to assist both learning managers and learners in moving from old to new paradigms in organizational life, will, I hope, prove useful to those organizations. Information about the college's competency-based system is provided to augment the reader's knowledge of the background of these change process-related efforts.

Holland's Competency-Based Model: STEP

The institution of Holland College was conceptualized and developed by Dr. Donald Glendenning in the late 1960s as part of an expansion of post-secondary education in Prince Edward Island, Canada. In its first year, 1969, it served 102 students in four courses; it now annually serves over 10,000 students in over 90 full-time and part-time programs in a wide array of occupational areas.

In 1970, encouraged by an innovation-minded Board of Governors, Holland established a program-wide competency-based education model called "Self-Training and Evaluation Process" (STEP). The process takes a performance-based approach with the objective of helping students assume responsibility for their own learning as they acquire the skills needed to enter wage-earning employment.

The STEP program is characterized by these 12 principles:

1. Credit is given for previously acquired skills.

2. Learning is stressed rather than teaching.

3. Skills required in an occupational field are identified by persons working in it.

4. Learners are responsible for their own progress.

5. Instructors are responsible for students' progress.

6. Programs are individualized to the full extent that resources permit.

7. The instructor's role is to assess, diagnose, prescribe, tutor, and confirm information, not solely to purvey it.

8. Facilities, materials, and staff are scheduled rather than students.

9. Ratings on learning are based only on performance.

10. Students evaluate their own performance prior to confirmation by an instructor.

11. Students are able to enter or exit a program at any time.

12. Students are able to continue their learning in a systematic way after leaving the institution.

As faculty members in the Health Science Division responsible for over 30 full-time and 15 part-time students, as well as a campus child-care service facility, our 10-member staff team had many occasions to note the transition struggles made by learners in moving from the traditional learning and work environment to a performance-based one. We frequently lamented the need for a simple and effective model that learners could latch on to for help in moving to performance-based learning. At the same time, we also felt a need for something to help *us* in our challenges of meeting the demands of a constantly changing work environment.

Introduction of the Choice Theory Model

Fortunately, in 1986 a colleague, Frank Morrison, alerted me and another colleague, Joan McDonald, to William Glasser's work with Choice Theory psychology. We decided to explore its usefulness in a competency-based system.

Spending the next three years studying and practicing the model in our work with learners, we noted its effectiveness and were encouraged. Learning and using the model seemed to empower and energize learners, enabling them not only to make a smoother transition to performance-based learning environments, but also to rise closer to their potential. And as learning managers, we started to experience a greater sense of self-control in our own role, which enabled us to become both more effective and more satisfied as supervisors.

The Model Pilot Project

As we used the model with increasing success, we shared our learning within the institution on professional-development days and outside the organization in public workshops. The interest of colleagues was soon generated, and we received a small grant to do a pilot project in 1990. Its title was "Supporting the Adult Learner" and its stated purpose was (a) to offer the Choice Theory model to learning managers and staff in the Health Science Program's areas of Dental Assisting, Emergency Medical Care Attendant, Early Childhood Education Programs, and Administrative Support, and (b) to assess its impact on and value to the participants.

Over 150 hours of training was provided to six staff members over a 24-month period, employing a competency-based educational model. Five of the six participants achieved certification from The Institute for Control Theory, Reality Therapy, and Quality Management in Los Angeles. Near the end of the project, five of the participants completed a questionnaire on their experiences in using the model both professionally with learners and colleagues and personally outside the workplace. This involved applying a 5-point rating scale ranging from (1) "totally dissatisfied" to (3) "moderately satisfied" to (5) "totally satisfied."

The survey findings cannot, in light of the small sample size, be considered hard empirical data. But they do reflect the opinions of the participants in the project and lend some support to this model's value in assisting people in transitional situations.

All five survey respondents reported increased satisfaction with their performance in their relationships with students, colleagues, supervisors, and family members. They also reported greater effectiveness in dealing with learners' academic performance, work habits, personal interactions, and problems. There were reports of greater effectiveness in providing and managing learning environments, as well as increased satisfaction with their role.

Responses in the comment section of the questionnaire also testified to the value of the model. Comments included the following:

- *"I was able to clearly define my role. . . . I have developed communication skills that helped me to talk and listen more effectively. . . . I am now more competent and confident in acting as a representative of Holland College within our community. . . . My training has further developed my time management skills. . . . The Reality Therapy training has improved my performance and efficiency 100%."*

- *"Most of my answers are at a 4 level. . . . I feel my Reality Therapy training to this point has been a tremendous help in all areas of my work. I now feel comfortable facing unpleasant situations and feel confident handling them."*

- *"I can now separate my job from another person's job and do not have to take on their responsibilities. . . . This has enabled me to eliminate many sleepless nights. Also, through this process my level of stress is much lower than in the past."*

- *"The experience was a very positive one for me. . . . I feel the division is a much tighter group because of the experience, and we have all learned from and about each other. I, for one, will feel more comfortable in requesting help or resources from other members of the staff."*

- *"Reality Therapy has changed my way of thinking and doing in terms of my relationships with students, staff, and family."*

The Model Application Workshops

During this time period, 9 internal and 21 community workshops involving over 800 participants were conducted as well. Institute faculty were drawn from across the United States and Canada to conduct several of these sessions. These workshops involved applications of the Choice Theory model to such diverse groups as business supervisors, police supervisors, small-business operators, social workers, community groups, teachers, teacher assistants, foster parents, and guidance counselors.

Internally, other staff expressed an interest in learning about the model—and not just learning managers, but supervisors and secretarial, administrative, and maintenance staff as well. This resulted in over 54 Holland College staff taking workshops based on the model over the next three years.

Establishment of the Executive Training Department

At the same time, requests came forward from the business and corporate sectors for practical, efficient, and high-quality training to help individuals in organizations and government departments deal with emerging economic and organizational transformations. The result was the establishment of a new department—the Executive Training Department—at Holland College between 1992 and 1995, which offered organizational change training to the business community. The success of the endeavor will be described later in this chapter.

For the period ending December 1995, the department provided 44 training sessions, each from one to three days in length, to over 780 people from both small and large corporations in Atlantic Canada.

Acceptance for the Model

The Choice Theory model and its applications have in recent years received worldwide acceptance, with over 4,500 people certified in 23 countries. In

Canada alone there are over 800 people certified from a wide array of professional and occupational groups. In the United States there are over 3,000. To date, almost 30,000 people have taken some level of training in the certification process.

Results and Further Support for Choice Theory Training

The exposure to, and increasing use of, Choice Theory within Holland College has had many beneficial results, including:

- The establishment of The Holland College Center for Reality Therapy, in which an annual series of training events is offered internally to staff members and externally to the community

- The Sponsorship of Control Theory Certification workshops, offered between 1992 and 1995, involving 195 participants

- The ability of 86 Holland College staff members to access Choice Theory training opportunities in some form

- The establishment of the Executive Training Department from 1992 to 1995

Feedback from participants has consistently been positive and supportive of the value of this training.

The Facilitating Individual Adjustment Questionnaire

Recently Choice Theory training received further approval when 34 staff members who had participated in the training were asked to complete a new version of the 1991 questionnaire for the initial project, "Supporting the Adult Learner." Entitled "Facilitating Individual Adjustment to Change in a C.B.E. [competency-based education] Environment," the revised questionnaire also used a 5-point rating scale with 1 representing "Totally Dissatisfied" and 5 representing "Totally Satisfied"; participants were directed to assess the training's impact on their role as learning managers in building positive relationships with learners, colleagues, and supervisors (see this chapter's appendix for the complete questionnaire).

Of the 13 (38%) anonymous respondents, 11 (32%) had their responses tabulated for analysis. This tabulation and the percentages calculated were based on the number of respondents who rated their satisfaction level at 4 or 5, indicating high or total satisfaction. Selected questions and the level-4/5 response percentages are provided in Figure 1. Percentages on subcategories of questions are reported in brackets.

FIGURE 1: Selected Questions and Results

Selected Questions	Percentage: Level 4/5
How would you rate your degree of satisfaction . . .	
— in your relationships with students?	91%
— with your effectiveness in dealing with students in the following areas:	74%
(a) Academic Performance	[100%]
(b) Personal Health	[55%]
(c) Personal Interactions	[73%]
(d) Work Habits (punctuality, meeting deadlines, etc.)	[73%]
(e) Lifestyle (values, attitudes)	[67%]
— in managing your time as an instructor in the area of working with students (instructing, facilitating, counseling)	[91%]
— in relationships in the following meetings:	76%
(a) Between yourself and students	[82%]
(b) Between yourself and other instructors	[80%]
(c) Between yourself and your supervisor	[55%]
(d) Among personal relationships	[90%]
— with your job from the perspective of meeting your needs . . .?	80%
How would you rate your overall degree of satisfaction in your instructional role?	100%
Please indicate your level of satisfaction with the training you have received thus far in Control [Choice] Theory psychology.	100%

Some of the comments made at the end of the questionnaire reinforce the positive impact of Choice Theory psychology indicated in Figure 1. For example:

- *"CT/RT/QM [Choice Theory/Reality Therapy/Quality Management] has been a valuable instrument with learners, my family, and myself. I have had many opportunities within my family and the training/learning environment to apply the theory of CT/RT/QM."*

- *"I believe that one of the greatest contributions [Choice] Theory psychology brings to individuals is a much greater understanding of the relationship between themselves and 'their world' as they view it and journey through it."*

- *"Reality Therapy has helped me in two main areas. It has helped me find ways to get students to motivate themselves. Secondly, I have developed better working relationships with most of my students."*

- *"I am finding that [Choice] Theory/Reality Therapy is excellent in application to my entire life."*

- *"What is really neat is that my two girls who are in Holland College Child Development Center are using RT without realizing it! They actually ask questions that make each other evaluate their behavior. It's wonderful. It has taken me a few years, but I am 'relaxing' myself, [experiencing] less stress, enjoying life. I would like the opportunity to refresh myself."*

- *"One of the great things that RT does is to get people off the 'BLAME' wagon and on with making choices and taking responsibility."*

- *"From what I have learned so far, I feel my training in Reality Therapy has helped me in both my personal and professional life. I am better able to be a good listener and be supportive for students and guide them to make choices and problem-solve. The theory is great to get learners thinking about how they have the control in their lives. With only a few simple tips, learners can become more empowered. It makes my job easier."*

The Executive Training Department—Success and Later Developments

The Executive Training (ET) Department was quite a success. ET's four-member team clearly met their goal: to provide high-quality, customized training to business, community, and government in the areas of lead management, team building, planning, supervision, stress management, DACUM occupational analysis, competency-based education, and related areas, using the principles of Choice Theory. In its second year of operation, the department exceeded revenue projections by 60%; in its third year, it more than doubled them.

Over a three-year period, ET provided services and training to approximately 45 organizations and over 900 people, and worked with federal, provincial, and municipal governments. Staff members not only traveled the breadth of Canada, but journeyed to three other continents as well. They had the privilege of working with Malaysians, Jordanians, Chinese, Hungarians, East Indians, and others—a full array of people with diverse cultures and languages. They also continued work inside Holland College, with ET providing its range of services to at least ten programs or departments. Approximately 80 college staff members participated in team-building training alone.

Since 1995, ET has been renamed "Corporate Training and Consulting Services" and is being incorporated into the Information Technology in Education Center (I.T.E.C.). This new multi-party venture was set up by Holland College in partnership with The University of Prince Edward Island, the Provincial Government, and the private sector. Its mandate is to be an entrepreneurial service organization at the cutting edge of the learning revolution.

The Future

In Canada, there is an industry that boils large volumes of maple-tree sap down to its sweet essence, maple sugar. It has been said that when one boils down all the current trends in organizational development and education—such as total quality management, competency-based education, accelerated learning, and performance management—the essence is an individual who, as part of some kind of team, needs to learn better skills in communicating with both self and others. There are many people like "Snow White" who are not yet aware of their own needs, or how to get their needs met, in an organization facing ever increasing, fast-paced change.

Perhaps all organizational advances are really a reflection of advances in "relationship building." If this is true, then certainly the value of competency-based approaches is in their ability to create opportunities for learners to build more need-fulfilling relationships or partnerships inside a learning organization. Choice Theory offers managers at all levels a simple, effective model for facilitating this process so that learners or staff members may rise to their potential while the organization moves forward in a progressive, profitable manner.

APPENDIX

Facilitating an Individual's Adjustment to Change in a C.B.E. Environment

Based on your assessment of the effect of learning and using the "Control [Choice] Theory" psychology, please fill out the following questionnaire utilizing the satisfaction scale below. There is a space at the end of this form to add any additional comments you wish to make.

SATISFACTION SCALE

Totally Dissatisfied		Moderately Satisfied		Totally Satisfied
1	2	3	4	5

1. Overall, how would you rate your degree of satisfaction in your relationships with students? _____

2. How would you rate your degree of satisfaction with your effectiveness in dealing with students in the following areas:

    a. Academic performance _____

    b. Personal health _____

    c. Personal interactions _____

    d. Work habits (punctuality, meeting deadlines, etc.) _____

    e. Lifestyle (values, attitudes) _____

3. How would you rate your degree of satisfaction with the time that it takes to deal with your students in the following areas:

    a. Personal problems _____

    b. Learning problems _____

    c. Financial problems _____

4. How would you rate your degree of satisfaction in managing your time as an instructor in the following areas:

    a. Working with students (instructing, facilitating, counseling) _____

    b. Administrative duties _____

    c. Providing a learning environment _____

    d. Community work _____

5. **How would you rate your degree of satisfaction in providing a learning environment in the following areas:**

   a. Instruction methods _____

   b. Utilization of resources _____

   c. Organizing learning situations _____

6. **How would you rate your degree of satisfaction in relationships in the following meetings:**

   a. Between yourself and students _____

   b. Between yourself and other instructors _____

   c. Between yourself and your supervisor _____

   d. Among personal relationships _____

7. **How would you rate your degree of satisfaction with your job from the perspective of meeting your needs for:**

   Freedom (choices, decision-making opportunities) _____

   Belonging (feeling a part of, cared for) _____

   Fun (pleasure, enjoyment, laughter, learning) _____

   Power (importance, recognition, appreciation) _____

8. **How would you rate your overall degree of satisfaction in your instructional role?** _____

9. **Please indicate your level of satisfaction with the training you have received thus far in Control [Choice] Theory psychology.** _____

Comments: Any documents you might wish to make that could add information to this project would be greatly appreciated. As well, please feel free to include examples from past experiences.

Suggested Reading

Anderson, J. (1988). *Thinking changing rearranging.* Portland, OR: Metamorphous Press.

Butler, S. (1986). *Non-competitive games.* Minneapolis, MN: Bethany House Publishers.

Buzan, T., & Gelb, M. J. (1994). *Lessons from the art of juggling.* New York, NY: Crown Publishers.

Buzan, T., & Israel, R. (1995). *Brain sell.* Brookfield, VT: Gower Publishing Ltd.

Buzan, T., & Keene, R. (1994). *Buzan book of genius and how to unleash your own.* New York, NY: Random House.

Canfield, J., & Wells, H. C. (1976). *100 ways to enhance self-concept in the classroom.* Englewood Cliffs, NJ: Prentice-Hall, Inc.

Dryden, G., & Vos, J. (1994). *The learning revolution.* Philadelphia, PA: Jalmar Press.

Glasser, W. (1984). *Control Theory.* New York, NY: Harper and Row.*

Glasser, W. (1986). *Control Theory in the classroom.* New York, NY: Harper and Row.*

Glasser, W. (1990). *The quality school.* New York, NY: Harper Perennial.

Glasser, W. (1993). *The quality school teacher.* New York, NY: Harper Perennial.

Glasser, W., & Karrass, C. L. (1980). *Both win management.* Los Angeles, CA: William Glasser, Inc.

Good, E. P. (1988). *In pursuit of happiness.* Chapel Hill, NC: New View Publications.

Good, E. P. (1988). *It's O.K. to be boss.* Chapel Hill, NC: New View Publications.

Gossen, D. C. (1992). *Restitution.* Chapel Hill, NC: New View Publications.

Hermann, N. (1994). *The creative brain.* Lake Lure, NC: Brain Books Publishing.

Howard, P. J. (1994). *The owner's manual for the brain.* Austin, TX: Leorian Press.

Johnson, D. W., & Johnson, R. T. (1991). *Learning together and alone.* Englewood Cliffs, NJ: Prentice-Hall.

Kohn, A. (1986). *No contest: The case against competition.* Boston, MA: Houghton-Mifflin Co.

Kohn, A. (1993). *Punished by rewards.* Boston, MA: Houghton-Mifflin Co.

Leatherman, D. (1992). *Quality leadership through empowerment.* Amherst, MA: HRD Press.

Schniedewind, N., & Davidson, E. (1983). *Open minds to equality.* Englewood Cliffs, NJ: Prentice-Hall, Inc.

*William Glasser has recently renamed his model "Choice Theory," and some of his works are soon to be reprinted using the new name, rather than Control Theory.

Schuster, D. H., & Gritton, C. E. (1986). *Suggestive accelerative learning techniques.* New York, NY: Gordon & Breach Science Publishers.

Stilts, R. (1990). *Beliefs—Pathways to health and well-being.* Portland, OR: Meta Publications.

Tinsley, M., & Perdue, M. G. (1992). *The journey to quality.* Chapel Hill, NC: New View Publications.

Townsend, P. L., & Gebhardt, J. E. (1992). *Quality in action.* New York, NY: John Wiley & Sons, Inc.

Travis, J. W., & Ryan, R. S. (1980). *The wellness workbook.* Berkeley, CA: Ten Speed Press.

Wellins, R. S., Byham, W. C., & Wilson, J. M. (1991). *Empowered Teams.* San Francisco, CA: Jossey-Bass.

Wenger, W., & Poe, R. (1996). *The Einstein factor.* Rocklin, CA: Prima Publishing.

Wubbolding, R. (1988). *Managing people.* New York, NY: Harper and Row.

Wubbolding, R. (1990). *A set of directions for putting and keeping yourself together.* Cincinnati, OH: Real World Publications.

About the Contributor

Kenneth L. Pierce, M.A., R.T.C., has been with Holland College for over 19 years and is currently in Corporate Training and Consulting Services. He also holds a senior faculty position at the William Glasser Institute for Choice Theory, Reality Theory & Quality Management in Los Angeles. Mr. Pierce is a certified Master Practitioner and Trainer in Neuro-Linguistic Programming, as well as a registered psychologist. He has been a sessional lecturer in the psychology department at the University of Prince Edward Island, and has delivered keynote addresses and conducted workshops nationally and internationally on a variety of topics, including personal growth, management, wellness, and team building. Mr. Pierce has authored and co-authored chapters in educational texts on adult education, learning environments, and stress management. He maintains a private counseling and consulting practice and resides in Stratford, PE, with his partner Anna and his three daughters, Michele, Stephanie, and Leanna.

12.
MOVING COMPETENCIES "OFF THE PAGE" AND INTO PEOPLE

Karen Gorsline — Manager, Human Resources Strategy and Policy, Bank of Montreal
Tracy Hawthorne — Principal Consultant, Organizational Change, Price Waterhouse
Karen Ho — Compensation Analyst, Bank of Montreal

This chapter describes competency-related efforts within the Human Resources Department of the Bank of Montreal. It presents a competency model developed for the role of Human Resources Relationship Manager and explores the design and development of a workshop to reinforce the competency-model elements and to promote behaviors related to self-directed development.

Background

The Bank of Montreal, founded in 1817, is Canada's oldest banking service. Over the years it has grown into a highly diversified financial-services institution with a strong North American base, $151 billion in assets, and over 33,000 employees worldwide.

The institution offers a complete range of financial services in the three NAFTA countries (Canada, the United States, and Mexico), including personal and commercial banking in the U.S. Midwest and throughout Canada, and corporate, institutional, and investment banking in selected North American markets; in Mexico it has an ownership position with Bancomer, the country's second-largest bank holding group and largest retail bank.

On its global front, the Bank of Montreal maintains offices in 11 countries in Latin America, Europe, and the Asia-Pacific region and has a network of correspondent banks in 120 countries.

Key Issues and Events

In the early 1990s, major developments in the Bank of Montreal's business strategy took place, posing a challenge for those of us in the Human Resources (HR) Department. The new strategy for success was founded on three commitments:

1. To promote the well-being and respect the distinct culture of each community in which we do business

2. To excel as a disciplined, professional, financially secure institution with strong risk-management skills

3. To offer our clients not only financial products but also knowledge-based solutions to add value to their financial affairs

One of the strategy's main implications was that the contribution of Bank of Montreal employees would provide the business with a competitive advantage. Consequently, the HR function would have to support, effectively and efficiently, a new array of people-related business requirements. This meant reexamining our organization design, our understanding of employee roles, and our processes.

A vision for HR's alignment with the new business strategy was soon articulated, driving home the reality that the HR function of the future would be quite different from that of the past. We faced the need to change—and to change dramatically. The mapping of processes and the search for opportunities to streamline and to automate were begun, soon to be followed by the need to change mindsets and approaches.

Initiating the Competency Project

Realizing that these changes would have an impact on the competencies required of the HR staff, we initiated a project to articulate future competencies with more clarity than "I know it when I see it" or via a rehash of "hot" competencies based on who had read what book last. The new environment would demand well-defined competencies, new sets of decision rules, and innovative ways of thinking about jobs and work.

In our approach to the project, we also considered the business literature's growing focus on the need for "Me, Inc." and the "new employment contract," both of which simply mean that employees, even in large, stable organizations, should not get lulled into a sense of security or dependency. This caution, despite its negative tenor, is actually a positive motivator, suggesting the need for self-directed development.

The facts are:

- It is no longer possible for employees to rely on day-to-day workplace experience to ensure that the right competencies are in place.

- It is no longer possible for employees to attain a certain skill level and then expect that one-time education would suffice for a lifetime of work.

- Although organizations provide job-specific training, even the most committed employer, with the best skills inventory and the most dedicated curriculum and training staff, cannot cover all of the current and future work and employee-competency requirements of a large, complex organization.

Therefore, for employees to ensure that their skills are marketable both inside and outside the organization, they themselves must constantly monitor and maintain those skills, supplementing employer-provided job-specific training with their own understanding of future work requirements and their own personal development issues.

With these issues in mind, we focused our efforts on creating a competency model for the HR Relationship Manager role.

The HR Relationship Manager Competency Model

First Steps: The Role and Organizational Context

Inherent in the high-level redesign of the organization were three work roles: experts who provide specialized consulting advice and product development, individuals who provide support services and conduct transactions, and individuals who integrate HR activity and manage the relationship with the client. The latter role, the Relationship Manager generalist role, was seen as key in the transformation of Human Resources to meet its new mandate. It was through the evolution of the Relationship Manager role that traditional transactions would be streamlined, eliminated, automated, or redirected to a more cost-effective general service support area. The Relationship Manager role would require a gradual replacement of a transactions focus with more emphasis on strategic, higher-value activities that draw on broad professional HR expertise. However, the organizational-design concept was just that—a concept.

To provide a basis for communicating about the new organizational design, and to obtain feedback from those closest to the client, a role overview with areas of responsibility was developed. The role overview identified three components:

- Understand the client's business

- Translate the business needs into Human Resources strategies and initiatives that enable the business to move forward

- Bring value-added professional Human Resources advice and counsel to line management "partners" to enhance business unit competitive effectiveness

Also, major areas of responsibility were identified, and each area was illustrated by activities that might fall under its category. There were five major areas:

- Business Linkage

- Professional Integrity and Presence

The section "The HR Relationship Manager Competency Model" is adapted from "A Competency Profile for Human Resources: No More Shoemaker's Children" by Karen Gorsline, HUMAN RESOURCE MANAGEMENT, 35(1), pp. 53–66. Copyright © John Wiley & Sons, Inc. Adapted with permission.

- Support Change

- Generalist Human Resources Services Support and Problem Solving

- Role Relationship: Coordinations and Interactions (corporate/pillar or business unit, pillar/pillar, and intrapillar)

This preliminary planning and drafting of role-content illustrations was used to support communication about the change, to collect information about what might be unclear about the organizational design, and to identify at a preliminary stage some of the implementation barriers.

As a result of this communication phase, it became clear that there were many unanswered questions about the details of the role and how it would operate on a day-to-day level. There were also concerns about the extent of expertise it would require. Many job incumbents had a strength in either staffing or employee relations (or, in some cases, both), but overall, the move to a generalist concept with a broad HR overview would require individuals to broaden their competency base. Existing job incumbents identified a need to increase capability and training availability in the areas of consulting and managing change. Finally, there was the issue of capacity, especially in the transition period. So much time was occupied with transactions and direct service that concern was expressed about the feasibility of undertaking more strategic or proactive projects or initiatives.

While focus group meetings on the role provided jobholders with an information forum on the concept of the role, there were still many unanswered questions, both for employees and the organization. The focus group meetings stimulated dialogue on the need and nature of the change. However, the high-level role content did not address two questions: How is this role performed differently? And what is expected?

The Competency Model Methodology

Following the focus group meetings, the high-level output on the role content was used as a starting point for the competency model development. While there were clearly challenges ahead in the area of knowledge and skills, our most pressing concern was the "how-to" aspect of the job. What new decision rules would guide action on a daily basis? How would it be possible to shift the mindset from a transaction orientation to a more strategic orientation? We knew that a more strategic orientation would require basing choices on where energy should be placed to have the most effect. The service solutions focus of today would need to be balanced with the longer-range best interest of the client and an appreciation of how effective management of people can leverage the client's business. We also knew that the identification of knowledge and skills requirements was within the capability of incumbents given existing resources, and that the knowledge and skills issue would be with us on an ongoing basis as professional developments emerged and technology and processes developed.

We therefore focused the project on clarifying the personal competencies—the mindset, behaviors, and attitudes—needed for individuals to be successful in the new role. It was also clear from the outset that the first application of the competency model would be to support the training and development for the new role. The competency modeling project's output would also provide new criteria for staffing the role in the future.

The competency modeling project methodology was based on a Hay-McBer framework and included the steps in Figure 1. (For further detail on the methodology used in developing the competency model, see Gorsline, 1996.)

FIGURE 1: Project Steps

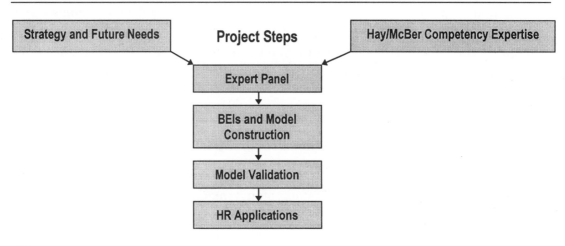

The competency model development process took place over a period of time and involved interaction with a large group of people. The process itself had the dual benefit of continuing the dialogue on the role change while also facilitating competency-related data collection from the managers and job holders themselves. This data illustrated both the current state of competencies and future competency requirements—information that would prove invaluable in the ongoing discussion on the nature of the change and the impact on development for jobholders.

The Competency Model

The competency model methodology used interviews that collected accounts of how incumbents were behaving and thinking in ways that enhanced effectiveness. The themes revealed by the interviews, and how the competencies were used to perform work, were captured in Figure 2; specific competencies identified as supporting these behaviors are shown in Figure 3.

FIGURE 2: HR Relationship Manager: What the Interviews Revealed

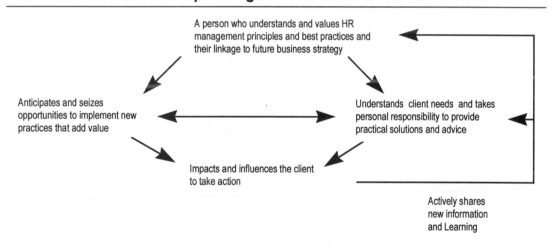

From "A Competency Profile for Human Resources: No More Shoemaker's Children" by Karen Gorsline, HUMAN RESOURCE MANAGEMENT, 35(1), pp. 53–66. Copyright © John Wiley & Sons, Inc. Reprinted by permission of John Wiley & Sons, Inc.

FIGURE 3: The Competency Model

Human Resources Relationship Manager

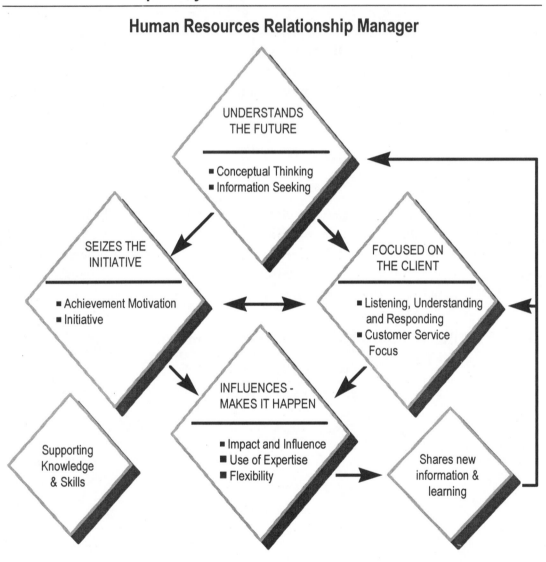

From "A Competency Profile for Human Resources: No More Shoemaker's Children" by Karen Gorsline, HUMAN RESOURCE MANAGEMENT, 35(1), pp. 53–66. Copyright © John Wiley & Sons, Inc. Reprinted by permission of John Wiley & Sons, Inc.

Affiliated with each competency were behavioral scales adapted from Hay-McBer to fit the Bank's needs. For each level of competency in the behavioral scales, examples extracted from interviews were available to illustrate the competency used in a work-related situation.

With this framework in place, it was time to move on to the real task at hand - that of developing a training and development initiative that would both support and drive the change embodied by the new role through the aligned change efforts of individual jobholders.

Communicating the Competencies Through Storytelling

One of the advantages of our approach was that it provided rich stories to support the communication of the competency model. The first task was to see if the model made sense to jobholders and others in the HR Department. Meetings were held with jobholders in affected areas to review the research methodology and the resulting competency model. The competency model represented a significant shift in how people would see their jobs, but there were aspects of that change already in place. Those authorities advocating continuous improvement and those speaking on shifting paradigms have indicated that it is important to find someone "doing something right" and then build on it. Although the new role would still be difficult for some to visualize, it was important to acknowledge that the seeds of the future were already evident. Consequently, actual behavioral stories were used to illustrate the competency cluster and the individual competencies. Examples of such stories appear in Figure 4.

In addition to the behaviors for the competency clusters "Focused on the Client" and "Seizes the Initiative," the stories revealed an interplay—a dynamic—between the two clusters. After experiencing several situations in transactions that could be characterized as "firefighting," or situations where managers—clients—could and should be able to respond more effectively, jobholders would develop an initiative to deal with the need that they had identified in the course of providing service to the client. Furthermore, those working in initiatives arising

FIGURE 4: Sample Behavioral Illustrations for Competency Clusters

Behavioral Illustrations for Competency Clusters

Understanding the Future

✓ Individuals who kept up to date with what was happening in their profession, in the economy, and in the world outside and used the information to project and understand the implications for the Bank and their client.

✓ Individuals who made efforts to keep up to date on Corporate and Business unit initiatives and projected impacts and anticipated identified opportunities.

Focused on the Client

✓ Customer service stories where service is provided on client-generated transactions

✓ Individuals taking the time and effort to add value beyond the specific scope of the request of the client and the transaction

Seizes the Initiative

✓ Individuals acting outside a transaction context to add value. The initiatives were based on projections and understandings beyond the scope of any client request. Often these stories involved linking Corporate initiatives to business-unit strategies and bringing new thinking to the client on issues such as workplace equality or performance management. These initiatives were clearly beyond the request or expectation of the client, but were in both the Bank's and client's best interest.

Influences to Make It Happen

✓ Influence is familiar turf for many HR practitioners. Stories of interest with respect to influence showed jobholders using more complex influence strategies and tailoring a number of influence approaches to the specific interest of the audience. Another learning from the stories is how some were using expertise. It was not the expertise itself that provided interest in the stories, but how it was being used. Rather than simply answering a question, some stories showed how a jobholder would explain the background reason for the answer. Some cases involved teaching clients improved interview techniques so they could be more self-sufficient and successful.

✓ Stories about Flexibility illustrated an understanding that the client's view was valid and deserved consideration while not simply "caving in." This respect for the client's perspective in the context of the other competencies in the model resulted in efforts to find practical solutions that took into consideration the client perspective, and incorporated the professional input, as well.

Sharing Information and Learning

✓ This sharing might be with colleagues, with clients, or with corporate functional areas or even the professionals outside the Bank.

from the cluster "Seize the Initiative" did not thrust their "wonderful" idea or initiative upon the client. Care was taken to position the idea or to develop client readiness. The initiative was linked to real client need evident in the transaction side of the model, consistent with the client's business strategy.

These stories, our internal "best practices," gave us a glimpse of the future and added significant clarity in response to the question, How will we practice our profession differently from today? More clarity about processes and workflows is required to satisfy some people, but for many this information served as a useful first step. It enhanced the awareness of the need and nature of change and facilitated an initial understanding of what is involved in changing behavior—an intellectual awareness.

In addition to meeting with jobholders in areas most affected by the role change, we conducted informal information sessions for other HR employees. We found they had a tremendous appetite for any information about the changes, the new roles, and the new expectations. In some cases, this interest arose out of personal development concerns; in others, it was linked to concerns about how the change would have an impact on their interactions with those in the role or even on their own role. Again, the process supported a broader need to communicate the change within the organization.

Designing the Training and Development Initiative

Design Considerations

First, we recognized from the outset the need for a change in "mindset." It would not be sufficient to develop a course or curriculum and "sheep dip" everyone through it. Training requirements would be very different from individual to individual. There could be no "one size fits all." Development of professional expertise was available through existing sources, university or college courses, or professional associations. Bank-specific expertise, policy, and practice could be supported by the respective functional disciplines (i.e., employee relations, staffing, etc.). Further, the Bank's Institute for Learning had developed and was continuing to develop programs to support general areas such as negotiating, influencing, consulting, managing change, strategy planning, development, and implementation and other advanced topics. With a focus on changing behavior and the way individuals perceive their role, it was clear that we needed a development approach that would help individuals select and possibly design their own experiential learning.

Second, individuals would have to take control of their own careers in order to make the kinds of shifts in expertise and mindset required by the new role. It would not be a passive journey where the Bank provided the curriculum; it would require individuals to actively engage in determining and directing the training and development most appropriate for them. Training options would include courses in knowledge areas and for applied skill acquisition. Development options would encompass the actual use of the training material in the workplace as well as much broader developmental-experience planning to adjust or hone behaviors. Development of this individual planning capability would be an ongoing asset that would help individuals adapt to the new role or make other career shifts.

Development Design

Subsequent meetings with managers validated the design issues above, and we agreed that our approach would be to support individuals in directing their own development toward the role. Because of work pressures and time constraints, only one day would be available for an off-site intervention. We therefore decided to design a one-day workshop that would introduce techniques for objective self-assessment, tools for self-assessment, planning approaches, and practical tips and techniques for self-directed development. During the workshop, participants would learn the techniques and get familiar with the tools through some practice use. However, they would complete the self-assessment and planning process after the workshop, depending on their own interest and need and its utility for them. In addition, participants would *not* be required to seek the input of managers as part of the self-assessment or to come to an "agreement" on their personal assessment.

The intervention would be a training intervention, but one focused on supporting development—specifically self-development, in the context of the new role of Relationship Manager.

The Workshop: Charting Your Own Course

Overview

The workshop's design comprised three major components:

1. Reinforcing self-confidence in the face of rapid change, and putting job changes into context

2. Introducing and practicing techniques for objective self-assessment and use of tools for self-assessment

3. Exploring self-management techniques to support personal change in the context of changing ways of thinking, behavior, or knowledge and skills.

To use the workshop's time most effectively, we relied on the previous communication about the role concept and the model design and simply recapped the information in the workshop; new information on the role was later added as needed. As originally intended, the workshop's emphasis was on introducing and understanding concepts and approaches, with practice in using the competency model framework for objective self-assessment, and becoming familiar with the "tool kit" for self-directed development provided as part of the workshop materials.

1. Reinforcing Self-Confidence and Putting Change Into Context

The first objective was to reinforce through group exercise that change is natural and not necessarily undesirable. We wanted to communicate that generations of humans—grandparents, parents, and workshop participants—

themselves have survived—*even thrived*—in the midst of enormous changes, including personal changes and responses to changes in the world around them; and that although the current organizational changes could seem overwhelming, individuals who have faced wars, major economic upheavals, or immigration to unknown lands not only have survived and adapted, but also have thrived. While change felt uncomfortable and risky, it also represented opportunities for growth, and given the resilience of people, the prognosis was good. A recap of some of the changes in the environment, the business, and the HR area and profession set the scene for examining the impact on the participants as individuals, as illustrated in Figure 5.

The second objective of this workshop component was to briefly review the previously communicated role content. This was done in the context of what the Bank was doing to provide direction and the tools available to support individuals as they consider the impact of the changes on them. The competency model's use as a framework or template in various human resource processes, such as behavioral interviewing, performance coaching, goal setting, and work analysis and planning, was discussed.

This early discussion of the use of a competency-model acts as a preamble for the balance of the day—using the HR Relationship Manager Competency Model to support self-assessment, goal setting, and training and development planning. The model is characterized as the map for a journey to a particular destination, with as many choices to make in reaching that destination as there are routes, detours, and modes of transportation. Also, it is important to determine where the starting point is for each individual; therefore objective self-assessment is a key element, because to get from "here" to "there," you have to know "where am I now," the point of departure.

2. Self-Assessment Techniques and Training

Not only is it important for individuals on a development journey to know the point of departure, but it is also important for them to stop from time to time to see if they are on course to the destination. The workshop introduces some basic

FIGURE 5: How Changes in the Environment "Trickle Down" to Me

The "Trickle-Down Effect"

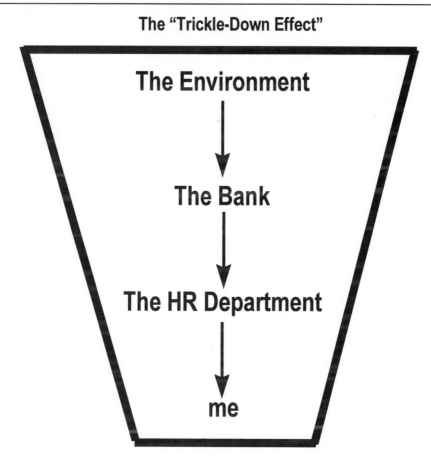

The Environment

↓

The Bank

↓

The HR Department

↓

me

concepts on specific, objective self-assessment—what an individual has done, said, and thought. While this sounds rather basic, many individuals do not take the time and effort for self-reflection, nor obtain objective feedback on behavior. Different individuals have different levels of self-awareness.

The idea that people are so busy "doing" that they are unaware of their behavior or of what they are actually "doing" is not new for HR practitioners. We see it every day in others—employees and managers. For example, a person may claim, in perfect honesty, never to behave in a certain way and then openly exhibit that behavior. Or someone may take action in a way that seems obvious to him- or herself, and believe it had a particular impact, when others aren't even aware that any behavior has occurred (e.g., a disciplinary action or a subtle request).

So the first challenge for objective assessment is to create an awareness and appreciation of the need for each individual to become much more specific about behavior and thinking, whether this is the individual's own behavior or that of others. Good managers instinctively know this is important. When something goes awry, they ask, "What did you do? What were you thinking?" This is their way of trying to get specific information about the behavior and what the individual intended by it.

The issue of increasing self-awareness is complicated by two other issues in organizations: the growing emphasis on teamwork and a tendency in large organizations to use "WE" and not "I." The emphasis of self-awareness is not directed at creating more individual contributors; it is critical for self-assessment to get to "I": *What did I say, do, think?* These questions may be posed easily in a team context. For example, the team objective was *x* and *We* all were committed to it. *I* wanted to help the team achieve the objectives, so *I* did such and such. The focus is on the specifics of the individual's behavioral contribution, whether it is in the context of an individual contribution, the contribution of a team member to a team effort, or a person's contribution as a leader/manager.

The workshop provides practice in thinking in specific terms about brief samples of text. Initially, participants practice identifying specific behavior in stand-alone statements. The competency model provides a specific framework and common language for differentiating between, and measuring, certain behaviors and approaches, such as information seeking, achievement, and customer service focus. Then participants practice using this framework in assessing behavior in the context of a "story" in which multiple behaviors are exhibited and espoused. Finally, participants privately assess their own behavior in actual past situations, both in and outside the workplace. This practice develops the techniques required to self-assess personal behaviors and provides a preliminary assessment of one or two of the personal competencies using the tool kit for self-assessment.

The Tool Kit

The tool kit was designed to help individuals assess themselves in relation to the HR Relationship Manager Competency Model. It also provides information and tools to help chart and maintain a personal development course. It includes the following:

- A role profile that contains an overview of the role, the major areas of responsibilities and valued results, and the personal competency model and a list of technical competencies

- A competency dictionary with behavioral scales

- A competency dictionary with behavioral examples for each competency level to illustrate the competency's use in a work context

- A competency assessment questionnaire

- A summary sheet consisting of a summary of the personal competency assessments in relation to long-range goals for the role, a knowledge and skills matrix, and tips and suggestions to assist individuals in prioritizing and focusing development plans for the immediate future

- An action planning worksheet to facilitate the systematic articulation of goals—an approach to planning actions to improve either the personal or technical competency level

- A resource guide that contains suggestions to assist individuals in selecting or customizing their own training and development interventions

The Role Profile. The Role Profile simply provides a ready reference for role overview, areas of responsibility, and illustration of activities and the personal and technical competencies.

The Competency Dictionary. A sample of the dictionary is shown on the following page, in Figure 6. For most participants, the various competencies and levels are fairly easy to use *after* getting over two hurdles: (1) being objective and specific about behavior, and (2) adapting to a common language as opposed to one's own definition of phrases like *customer service focus, achievement, flexibility,* and *use of expertise.* The hurdles faced are ones of different preconceptions and lack of specificity concerning language and behavior. Once these barriers are overcome, the participants quickly come to a fairly consistent application of the dictionary.

The Competency Dictionary with Behavioral Examples. The behavioral examples assist individuals in two ways: (1) by providing concrete work-related examples, and (2) by adding more specific content to help learners understand the differences between levels in the competency scales. Samples of behavioral scales with specific behavioral examples are shown in Figure 7.

The Competency Assessment Questionnaire. The questionnaire was designed to be used as a self-assessment tool. Space is provided to complete three illustrations of how the person being assessed demonstrates the competency. This information can then be compared to the behavioral scale to match the scale descriptions with the behavior being assessed. A sample questionnaire is provided in Figure 8.

All or part of the questionnaire can be used to collect information from peers, clients, managers, subordinates, or others. As part of their self-assessment, participants are encouraged to get feedback and validate their own ratings. The competency level is then determined, based on the highest level of the competency that is reliably and predictably demonstrated. Self-check questions in relation to the overall rating are provided as follows:

- Do you feel the level of competency in the particular situation is indicative of your/the person's behavior?

- Can you readily think of another example?

- Do you think others' perceptions would correspond with your own?

FIGURE 6: Sample Competency Definitions and Scales From Dictionary

Achievement Motivation

Achievement Motivation is a concern for working well or for competing against a standard of excellence.

1. **WANTS TO DO JOB WELL:**
   Tries to do the job well or right. May express frustration at waste or inefficiency.

2. **WORKS TO MEET STANDARDS:**
   Works to meet an established standard or expectation (e.g., Performance Planning and Review [PPR]).

3. **CREATES OWN MEASURES OF EXCELLENCE:**
   Uses own specific methods of measuring outcomes against a standard of excellence that exceeds established standards or expectations.

4. **IMPROVES PERFORMANCE/WORK PROCESSES:**
   Makes specific changes in own or related work methods to improve performance (e.g., does something better, faster, at lower cost, more efficiently; improves quality, customer satisfaction, morale, revenues).

5. **SETS AND PURSUES CHALLENGING GOALS:**
   "Challenging" means there is a definite stretch in order to achieve the goals, but they are not unrealistic or impossible (e.g., 50-50 chance).

Customer Service Focus

Customer Service Focus implies a desire to help or serve others, by discovering and meeting their needs.

1. **FOLLOWS UP:**
   Follows through on customer inquiries, requests, complaints. Keeps customer up to date about progress of projects. Gives friendly service.

2. **MAINTAINS CLEAR COMMUNICATION:**
   Maintains clear communication with customer regarding mutual expectations. Monitors customer satisfaction. Distributes helpful information to customers.

3. **TAKES PERSONAL RESPONSIBILITY:**
   Takes personal responsibility for meeting customer needs. Deals with their need promptly and non-defensively.

4. **MAKES SELF FULLY AVAILABLE:**
   Makes self fully available, especially when customer is going through a critical period (e.g., gives customer a means of easy access, or may spend extra time at the customer's location).

5. **ACTS TO ADD VALUE:**
   Makes concrete attempts to add value to the customer, to make things better for the customer in some way. Gives service beyond customers' expectations.

6. **ADDRESSES UNDERLYING NEEDS:**
   Goes beyond asking routine questions. Seeks information about the real, underlying needs of the customer, beyond those expressed initially, and matches these to available (or customized) products or services.

7. **USES A LONG-TERM PERSPECTIVE:**
   Works with a long-term relationship perspective in addressing customer's problems. May trade off immediate costs for the sake of the ongoing relationship. Looks for long-term benefits to the customer.

FIGURE 7: Samples of Competency Dictionary With Behavioral Examples

Achievement Motivation

Achievement Motivation is a concern for working well or for competing against a standard of excellence.

1. **WANTS TO DO JOB WELL:**
   Tries to do the job well or right. May express frustration at waste or inefficiency.

   (a) *I knew that she should be interviewed for the job. I was happy that he at least agreed to have her interviewed. I thought at least I've achieved that. But I was disappointed that he was not going to interview her personally.*

   (b) *I was asked to participate in a project and it also involved one of my clients. I knew there would be opportunities to talk and I thought, "This is great, this is exactly what I want to do in order to know the client better."*

2. **WORKS TO MEET STANDARDS:**
   Works to meet an established standard or expectation (e.g., Performance Planning and Review [PPR]).

   (a) *We are working under goals for hiring people with disabilities. I was able to find a candidate who was a really good fit for the job and would help us meet our goal. She was also well regarded in the community. I felt great; we managed to meet the objective of hiring people with disabilities and make a real contribution.*

   (b) *We had a vacancy and we had an obligation to consider a certain candidate. There were questions about the candidate's qualifications, but there was an obligation there. I found that resources were available for training and the candidate was approached. So, I felt that all the bases had been covered; we had done everything possible.*

Customer Service Focus

Customer Service Focus implies a desire to help or serve others, by discovering and meeting their needs.

1. **FOLLOWS UP:**
   Follows through on customer inquiries, requests, complaints. Keeps customer up to date about progress of projects. Gives friendly service.

   (a) *The manager and I discussed the situation and agreed that we needed to look at this employee's history. I agreed to pull together the information. I called and said, "I have the history. When do you want to get together to review it?"*

   (b) *I was asked to do staffing for a task force and was given the name of the task force leader to call. I called and introduced myself and asked if we could get together and have a meeting to discuss the job specs and the type of skills they would be looking for on the task force.*

2. **MAINTAINS CLEAR COMMUNICATION:**
   Maintains clear communication with customer regarding mutual expectations. Monitors customer satisfaction. Distributes helpful information to customers.

   (a) *At the conclusion of the meeting, I said, "I'll begin the candidate search right away. It will be a national search given the nature of the project and your staffing requirements. In addition, I'll research the names that you are going to fax to me tomorrow. I'll get back to you in two weeks and we can talk about the candidates and where to go from there."*

   (b) *When I sent out the HR Review proforma to the managers, I asked them to complete it prior to the meeting. I asked them to identify their high-potential people, their strengths, areas of development and where the next best move was for each person. I told them it would be important to have all of this information completed prior to the HR Review meeting date and gave them the relevant dates. Then I called them a week later to see if the information I provided was clear.*

FIGURE 8: Sample of Competency Assessment Questionnaire

Achievement Motivation

Achievement Motivation is a concern for working well or for competing against a standard of excellence.

0. IS NOT DISPLAYED

1. WANTS TO DO JOB WELL:
   Tries to do the job well or right. May express frustration at waste or inefficiency.

2. WORKS TO MEET STANDARDS:
   Works to meet an established standard or expectation (e.g., Performance Planning and Review [PPR]).

3. CREATES OWN MEASURES OF EXCELLENCE:
   Uses own specific methods of measuring outcomes against a standard of excellence that exceeds established standards or expectations.

4. IMPROVES PERFORMANCE/WORK PROCESSES:
   Makes specific changes in own or related work methods to improve performance (e.g., does something better, faster, at lower cost, more efficiently; improves quality, customer satisfaction, morale, revenues).

5. SETS AND PURSUES CHALLENGING GOALS:
   "Challenging" means there is a definite stretch in order to achieve the goals, but they are not unrealistic or impossible (e.g., 50-50 chance).

Behavioral Examples
(Note specific *Action, Dialogue, Thoughts* for each example)

1.

2.

3.

Think of the following questions before inserting the rating for this competency.
- Do you feel the level of competency you/the person being assessed in that particular situation is indicative of your/that person's behavior?
- Can you readily think of another example?
- Do you think other's perceptions would correspond with your own?

> Achievement Motivation
> Where Am I?

Several participants commented that they had completed some of the assessment materials the night before the workshop and had rated themselves high, but then after learning about the technique and identifying specific behavior, they had lowered their initial assessment. Others commented that the simple exercise on self-analysis of behavior in a concrete and specific situation gave them ideas of how they might have behaved differently, and that they could now try to behave differently when a situation warranted it.

While learning the technique can be a bit frustrating and tedious at times, it does seem to help participants think about their own behavior in objective, non-emotional terms, which aids the self-assessment process by minimizing a common problem: being too hard or too easy on oneself.

The Summary Sheet. As indicated earlier, the summary sheet consists of three parts. The first part is simply a place for individuals to transfer their individual competency assessments to a single chart. The chart contains all the competencies and levels. It also contains a "target" profile as illustrated in Figure 9, on the next page.

The "target" profile is provided to help focus development—no one person is expected to be a perfect fit. It serves as an example of a high level of professionalism for the top of this job family/role. In the terminology of tradespeople, it is the "Master" level. Participants are warned that this is a *picture*, not a *mold* where each level must be attained precisely. Human behavior is "bumpy" and people are able to compensate, often in quite acceptable ways.

The second portion of the summary sheet covers the technical competencies: that is, knowledge and skills identified for the role. This provides a type of skills inventory. However, given the transient nature of knowledge and skills (beyond a basic level), and given the volatility of demand for any particular knowledge and skill based on linkage to specific client interests and activity, the generalist is always in a position of not being able to know enough! Rather than a traditional skills-inventory approach with detailed knowledge and skills lists and proficiency levels, the approach was to provide a reference point so that individuals could make rough judgments about where they stood and which area was most relevant or pressing for development.

FIGURE 9: Personal Competency Summary Chart

Personal Competencies Chart

Instructions

❖ Transfer the results from the bottom right-hand boxes of your CAQ into the corresponding box on the summary chart below.

❖ Compare the results with the profile for the Human Resources Relationship Manager. Note any personal competencies where your self-assessment information is lower than the profile targeted for the HRRM. The purpose of the HRRM target profile is to help focus development. The profile is a model--no one person is likely to be a perfect fit.

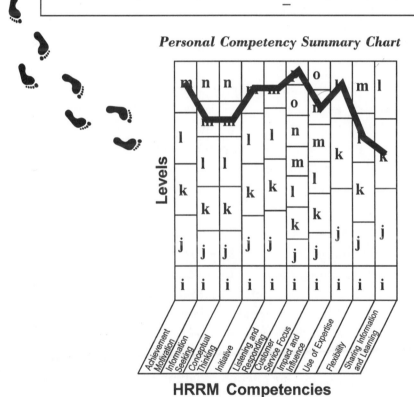

Personal Competency Summary Chart

HRRM Competencies

A simple process was outlined, which involved asking basic questions such as those shown below.

Determine which of the three categories best describes your situation:

- *Develop: You have little or no understanding in this area.*

- *Build: You have some understanding in this area and see a need to expand.*

- *Maintain: You have a good understanding in this area and display knowledge or skill where appropriate; you just need to keep current.*

Then make a determination with regard to urgency: Is this area important for this year's activities or important next year or beyond?

A matrix was provided to record assessments. Figure 10 (see following page) illustrates a completed matrix.

Even with this effort to categorize and prioritize, there is more to do than can be done. So the individual is guided through some ways of further determining priority and making choices given input from the manager, client, or considering other areas such as work activities, outside personal activities, long- and short-term "investment" strategy, and the present stage of his or her career. Individuals are encouraged to pick only two to four areas for development at a time.

Action Planning Worksheet. Action planning worksheets are provided to guide the development planning process. The sheet is designed to be completed for each area identified for development. The form contains a section to describe both the current situation and development goals in visual terms: what it looks like now and what it would look like if the goal had been achieved. Space is given to list activities or actions the individual will take to develop the personal competency, knowledge, or skill.

Self-management is a part of the action planning process. Self-check questions on anticipating obstacles, looking for support, and recognition of progress are used to encourage looking ahead and as support for maintaining

FIGURE 10: Sample of Completed Knowledge and Skill Matrix

Knowledge & Skills Development Matrix

	Develop	Build	Maintain
In this year's activities	Bank strategy Industry legislation BU strategy BU work processes Org. structure Org. culture Bus. strategy models Employee relations Workplace equality HR strategy Health & safety Operating procedures Legislation specific to BMO Services of functional area Corporate values Escalation	Staffing Compensation Benefits Training & development Performance management Labor economics Organizational behavior HR administration HR research & IS	Current HR issues
Next year or beyond	Cost/Benefit analysis Designing projects Working relationship	Problem solving Facilitation Time management Diagnostic tools Conflict management Coaching	Computer software Monitoring processes Communications Coaching

momentum. There is also a section—"Did You Reach Your Goal?"—in which an important distinction is made in how a person assesses success. The participant is asked: "Describe the extent to which you have completed your development actions. Did you reach your goal? How do you know? Record specific examples." *Both* the commitment to the plan *and* the effectiveness of the plan in achieving the goal are considered.

Resource Guide. To help participants identify available resources and design a training and development plan in their personal "intervention," a resource guide was developed for each area of personal and technical competency. This guide is not a set curriculum, but a reference for planning a course of action that best suits the individual's interest, needs, resources, and learning style. The nature of the suggestions for the personal competencies and technical competencies tend to be somewhat different, with personal competencies having a stronger experiential/development focus and the technical competencies having more of a traditional focus in training interventions, books, and so forth. Sample contents from each are provided in Figures 11 and 12.

3. *Exploration of Self-Management Techniques to Support Personal Change*

The final component of the workshop is a series of self-diagnostic techniques, tips, and facilitated experiences that support learning on how to maintain momentum on the development journey and how to stay on track with personal objectives. This is perhaps one of the simplest aspects of the workshop and could be characterized as "just common sense." It is proportionally brief, but has been very well received.

Practical advice on how to support success in accomplishing the goals includes:

- Techniques for coaching *yourself*—self-diagnostic, illustration of the importance of behavioral reinforcements and need to reward yourself; the need to anticipate the natural drop of excitement, energy, and motivation to stick to a plan and achieve the goal that occurs over time.

FIGURE 11: Sample Resource Guide Contents for a Personal Competency

Customer Service Focus

SELF-DIRECTED
ACTIVITIES

- Keep a client-service time log for one month. In your daily planning diary, make daily notes of how much time you actually spend providing services to your clients. At the end of the month, calculate the percentage of your time that is spent servicing clients versus administrative and other non-service activities. Set a goal for yourself to increase the amount of time you spend in service-related activity. Monitor your progress through your client-service time log the following month, and set a new goal the next month. Continue the process to help you focus more of your time in service to your clients.

OR

- Identify your three most important internal and external clients (those who depend on you for services or products). Set up a regular (quarterly) audit program with them. First, meet with them to review their present levels of satisfaction with your service. Ask them for specific examples of what you are doing well, for specific areas in which they would like to see improvement, and for areas where you are providing services that they no longer need.

OR

- A useful way to approach this conversation is to ask them to help you create three lists: Things you should START doing, things you should STOP doing, and things you should KEEP doing. Adjust your service levels to meet their newly defined requirements. Keep a written record of their suggestions and your plans. Follow up in the next service audit to get their feedback on the changes you have implemented. Evaluate your service levels to other clients and implement quality audits with them, as you feel appropriate.

READING

Desatnick, R. L. (1990). *Keep the Customer: Managing Your Employees to Achieve Maximum Customer Service.* ITM.

Hinton, T. (1990). *The Spirit of Service: How to Create a Customer-Focused Culture: A Customer Service Strategy for the New Decade and Beyond.* Kendall-Hunt.

Peters, T. (1987). *Thriving on Chaos.*

COURSES

Achieving Extraordinary Customer Relations (IFL)

OTHER IDEAS

_____

_____

FIGURE 12: Sample Resource Guide Contents for a Technical (Knowledge/Skill) Competency

Designing Projects, Contracting Specialists, Managing Projects, and Managing Accountabilities (e.g., Self, Client, Specialist, or Consultant)

SELF-DIRECTED
ACTIVITIES

• Identify someone who is good as a role model, and have them critique your approach in a project or arrange to work with them.

OR

• Get client and peer feedback during and after a project; identify improvements to be made.

OR

• Learn a project management software package.

OR

• Practice writing a consulting proposal and get it critiqued.

OR

• Practice brief documentation of role/accountabilities coming out of a meeting where a specialist is involved in work with you.

OR

• Collect a number of consultant proposals. What is common and different among these proposals? Identify what you would put into your own proposal.

READING

Block, P. (1981). *Flawless Consulting: A Guide to Getting Your Expertise Used*. San Diego, CA: University Associates, Inc.

Dinsmore, P. C. (1990). *Human Factors in Project Management*. New York: AMACOM.

Gilbreath, R. D. (1985). *Winning at Project Management: What Works, What Fails and Why*. New York: John Wiley & Sons, Inc.

COURSES

• Crafting Winning Proposals (IFL)
• Project Management Workshop (IFL)
• Internal Consulting Course (IFL)
• Selling on Your Feet (IFL)

OTHER IDEAS

_____

_____

_____

- Tips on giving feedback and eliciting and receiving feedback; experience in how it *feels* to be coached under various conditions and confronting discomfort with feedback; reinforcement of feedback's importance for objective self-assessment and to stimulate personal growth.

Key Learnings From the Workshop

The Workshop Pilot

The workshop was piloted in November 1995. Participants included HR practitioners at various stages in their careers. They were selected from human resource areas in a range of business client areas, and represented the geographic cross-section, across Canada, and from Harris Bank in the United States. The pilot was extremely useful in streamlining the day. Feedback from the participants indicated that some exercises needed to be refined. The flow, timing, and pace required adjustment, but overall the feedback was positive. The pilot confirmed our suspicion that what we were trying to accomplish was very aggressive, given the one-day time limit.

A major issue was expectation management. Although there had been significant communication regarding the HR Relationship Manager role prior to the workshop, participants' awareness of the role and of the strategy behind the role change was still uneven. In addition, some participants had expected to receive full details of the role in the workshop, with several expecting a level of detail equivalent to a full-blown detailed job description and documented work processes. This was clearly not possible, as some aspects of the organization would not be fleshed out for some time, and even then there would be an evolution of processes, technology, and workflows.

Although we recognized the need to develop procedures and processes, the workshop's competency-based approach was intended to create a mindset that would be adaptable to the ongoing evolution in how transactions are processed and new forms of client interface. The competency model called for the HR practitioner to be engaged in a leadership role within the HR team and with the client and to move from the present reality to a different way of doing business.

To address (at least in part) the issue of role evolution in subsequent workshops, we allotted more time for discussing the evolving role. The competency model clusters were used to identify where participants were currently spending most of their time at work and to illustrate how work might be different in the future. The reality was that the balance and emphasis in terms of percentage of time spent between transactional activities and strategic or proactive activities would be changing not only over time but in relation to each client's readiness, capacity issues, and the ability of the individual to exercise leadership with the client.

Although the workshop was designed as part of a larger change strategy, the experience in the pilot made it clear that this intervention, the workshop, was just one aspect of a broader cultural change effort that would need to encompass processes, continued clarification of organizational design and interconnections between roles, technology support, leadership support, and communication of the vision. It would be necessary to maintain communication between the learnings in the workshop and other aspects of the change process throughout the workshop delivery.

The Workshop Delivery

Participants

The workshop was conducted ten times for a total of nearly 100 HRD staff. Workshop attendance was not restricted to employees directly affected by the role change, and surprisingly, such employees showed a high level of interest. Functional consultant/specialists (e.g., compensation, staffing) attended, some believing that they were relationship managers because their roles were aligned by line of business client. This gave the group the opportunity to discuss the difference between "consultants/specialists" aligned by client and those responsible for the overall relationship and integration of various HR disciplines into a coherent HR strategy for the client. While the specific competency model did not directly relate to the functional roles, most of these individuals commented that the workshop was useful in terms of understanding themselves and their behavior better and that the use of self-directed planning tools could be adapted to suit their needs.

Other participants, including some in administrative support roles, were interested in the Relationship Manager role in terms of career planning. While the workshop materials did not provide these participants with a full curriculum guide, they did offer information on the range of baseline HR expertise that would be expected—information useful for selecting courses and training. Also, the personal competencies, or attributes, could help them identify whether this type of role would be compatible with their personal preferences and abilities.

In some cases, time pressures and conflicting priorities prevented individuals who could be characterized as "role models" from attending the workshop—some managers and some individuals leading the transformation efforts. When people undertake significant change, the press of daily work continues, and there is more work than hands to do the work. Still, in retrospect, it would have been desirable for more of these individuals to have attended for a number of reasons: role modeling, reinforcing the message that "we are all in this together," learning to use the common language of competencies for providing and receiving feedback, and supporting others on their journey.

New Ways of Thinking About Self and Work

The workshop not only encouraged self-awareness and self-analysis, but also dialogue on difficult subjects and sharing information. Although in a "transaction culture" these behaviors are often perceived as a waste of time, the competency model identified them as important. Moreover, these behaviors were very relevant to realizing the synergies and cultural shifts envisioned by the new strategies and organizational design.

The workshop encouraged personal learning and career ownership. Many participants found this exciting and helpful both in the context of the Bank's change and in terms of their overall career perspective. For some, this process seemed too complex and to take too much time; thus priority was given to the press and familiarity of transactions that constituted success in the past and that certainly would continue to be important in the near future.

Level of Detail on the Relationship Manager Role

As indicated above, some participants wanted a clearer understanding of the role and better direction from the organization. One question we asked ourselves was, "If we had it within our power to provide a step-by-step 'cookbook' approach, would we?" While a prescriptive (cookbook) approach was not really an option in this particular situation, there was a real question and concern as to whether that type of approach would reinforce some of the very things that we were attempting to change. Our competency model called for professionals who were able to understand broad future direction and take action based on this understanding. Our situation was, and would continue, evolving and refining itself. Accordingly, the workshop operated at the broad mandate level.

Pace of Change

While a slow evolutionary approach gives individuals time to understand and adapt, one danger of such an approach is that without a "burning platform," some get lulled into a sense of security and do not see the need to change. An evolutionary approach requires consistent and persistent reinforcement.

Related Roles

There were two roles that interrelate with the HR Relationship Manager role: the functional roles mentioned above, and a "call center" role designed to increase ability in the Relationship Management role and to efficiently and more cost-effectively handle transactions. Ideally, the work on these roles would parallel the Relationship Management role. The fact that there were many unknowns in these two areas made it difficult for individuals to compare and contrast them and to consider interrelationships and preferences.

Stimulating Thinking

One difficult aspect of a competency-based approach is that it requires individuals to actively utilize analytical and conceptual thinking skills. While most

HR individuals have well-honed analytical thinking skills as a result of focusing on problem solving, transactions/case management, or projects, conceptual thinking may not be in day-to-day use on the job. Understanding and utilizing the competency framework draws on both types of thinking skills, which for some participants seemed difficult or abstract. Others, without regard to age or rank, seemed to be very adept in this area and used the framework with minimal effort.

Support for Self-Analysis

The self-analysis component was quite natural for certain participants and easily attainable by most; but for a few it was very difficult. Most participants, with a little coaching, were able to recall specific situations from their recent past in considerable detail and to visualize behaviors easily. A challenge for any future workshop would be to find additional approaches that could give those individuals who found the recall and self-analysis/visualization difficult a way to get specific behavioral information on which to base their assessments. One obvious means is by incorporating an opportunity to process feedback from others. This activity would benefit all participants by offering practice in eliciting and receiving feedback and using the feedback to increase objectivity in self-assessment.

Positive Response from Participants

While the above description highlights some "traps" or issues to think about in terms of using this type of approach in future situations, overall the workshop was given very positive evaluations. Comments such as those in Figure 13 characterized the overall feedback on the workshop and the tool kit.

Potential as a Generic Framework

The workshop itself has the potential to be "stripped" of the specific competency model and developed into a generic workshop that could accommodate competency models for other roles. This type of workshop would

FIGURE 13: Sample Comments on the Workshop and Tool Kit

Typical Comments on the Workshop and Tool Kit

- *"Very in-depth, which helped me focus on the future."*
- *"Acquired better understanding of competencies; could apply tools learned from the workshop for other HR roles."*
- *"Workshop material and tool kit were informative; the competency dictionary with behavioral examples was particularly helpful; good development tool."*
- *"Provided good framework and sense of direction of what would be required for the future."*
- *"Expected more information on the Human Resources Relationship Manager role [comment made particularly in pilot]."*
- *"A lot of information to absorb in a day."*
- *"Would like more practice time on self-assessment and action planning."*
- *"Would be beneficial to have follow-up session after attending the workshop."*

---

be particularly relevant where there is a technical/professional skills component that is supported by external training and the emphasis is on how these skills will be deployed differently in the future.

Potential Modifications

Based on our experience, two design modifications warrant serious consideration.

1. Increase the workshop's length to two non-consecutive days, and possibly insert a time period between sessions to allow participants to complete more of the evaluation. This would be preferable to providing basic "hands-on" experience, with individuals left to complete the evaluation on their own. It would also give participants an opportunity to elicit feedback.

2. Spend more time on the action planning section of the workshop. Again, allow time for individuals to do more with the tool in the workshop.

Next Steps in Workshop Development and Follow-Up

Our needs for the future in the area of workshop development are presented below, along with follow-up issues that have merited our close attention.

- As part of the evaluation of the course, we asked for suggestions on what kind of support participants would like to see following the workshop. As with any specific initiative, when the immediate task of delivering the workshop is completed, there is a temptation to see it as a job done. But as part of an overall organizational development process, this is just one step in the journey; so the suggestions will be compiled and assessed to determine what ongoing support or dialogue might be helpful.

- As part of their work with the Resource Guide, participants "built" on a personal competency, "Sharing Information and Learning," by brainstorming ways they could increase their own competency in that area. This exercise illustrated how easily an individual can identify his or her own training and development initiatives and tailor them to meet personal needs and learning style; it also provided a means for the groups to share their ideas both within their groups and with all of the workshop participants. Suggestions related to this exercise will be compiled and added to the Resource Guide, and the entire Resource Guide will be available on the LAN for easy access by those involved in Human Resources. LAN access will also make it easier to incorporate additional suggestions into future planning.

- There is a need to do a post-workshop evaluation in terms of the impact of the learning and the utility/usability of the tools provided.

- During the workshop, some time was spent discussing connections between the individual's personal development plan and the development-planning portion of the ongoing performance management system. The connections could be strengthened and more discussion would be helpful.

- The competency model, as it now stands, is an implicit staffing template; but for us to reinforce the reality of the model and the change, we must ensure that staffing decisions are being made in the context of the evolving Relationship Manager role and the competency model. For this purpose, a simple generic staffing specification utilizing the language of the model has been prepared. We already utilize behavioral-focused interviewing in our staffing processes.

- Follow-up discussions with staff supporting the overall change will be needed to evaluate any future support actions required for individual development and the overall change of the role.

- The shift from operating at a "mandate" level to taking an evolving approach underscores the need to communicate clearly and to be as frank as possible about what is known and what is unknown and what will evolve with time and experience. Communication is also critical: The lack of detail and imprecise timelines do not indicate a lack of seriousness about the commitment to the change and the implications for individuals.

Closing Thoughts

We talk about change as a one-time event, and certainly dramatic change requires special efforts. We, and those before us, have survived change, and normally with great success! We, both as organizations and individuals, face a more rapid pace of change. Recognizing the changes around us and contemplating the implications for us as organizations and as individuals enable us to better take control of our destiny and have something to hold onto while we are between the old and new and realize that we may have to make this journey more than once.

Acknowledgments

We would like to acknowledge others involved in this project: Harriet Stairs, Executive Sponsor, along with the HR directors for the various lines of business; Kevin Scott and Chris Harcourt Vernon for help on role accountabilities; the

BMO Competency Team and Charles Bethel-Fox from Hay-McBer for assistance in model development; and the staff of HR who were interviewees and attended and provided advice on the workshop pilot and the subsequent workshops.

References

Block, P. (1993). *Stewardship: Choosing service over self-interest.* San Francisco, CA: Berrett-Koehler Publishers, Inc.

Bridges, W. (1994). *Job shift: How to prosper in a workplace without jobs.* New York, NY: Addison-Wesley Publishing Company.

Gorsline, K. (1996). A competency profile for Human Resources: No more shoemaker's children. *Human Resource Management, 35*(1), 53–66.

Maister, D. H. (1993). *Managing the Professional Service Firm.* New York, NY: The Free Press.

Spencer, L. M., & Spencer, S. M. (1993). *Competence at work: Models for superior performance.* New York, NY: John Wiley & Sons, Inc.

Urich, D., & Eichinger, R. (1995). *The 1995 Sota Report.* The Human Resource Planning Society.

About the Contributors

Karen Gorsline is a Manager for Human Resources Strategy and Policy at the Bank of Montreal and was the project manager of the Human Resources Relationship Manager competency project. Prior to joining Bank of Montreal, she was Director of Personnel Support, University of Toronto. She is President of the Toronto chapter of the Strategic Leadership Forum and has been on the board and served as Vice President of the Conferences of the Human Resources Professional Association of Ontario. Subsequent to the submission of this chapter in *The Competency Casebook,* Ms. Gorsline opened her own consulting practice.

Tracy Hawthorne is a Principal Consultant in the Organizational Change group in Price Waterhouse's Toronto office, where her work involves helping clients adapt to and leverage the business benefits of large-scale technology-driven change. Prior to joining Price Waterhouse, she was a Principal Consultant in the Human Resources Planning and Development practice at Hay Management Consultants. She is an active guest speaker on HR Transformation and Organization Change, and has been a part-time professor at area colleges.

Karen Ho is a Compensation Analyst at the Bank of Montreal and assisted in developing and facilitating the workshop for the Human Resources Relationship Manager role. Prior to joining Bank of Montreal in 1995, Ms. Ho was an Employee Service Manager at Hong Kong Telecom CSL in Hong Kong. She holds a degree in Economics and Econometrics from the University of Manchester and a diploma in Training Management from the Chinese University of Hong Kong.